MW00852662

RADICALS IN EXILE

**IBERIAN ENCOUNTER
AND EXCHANGE
475–1755 | Vol. 4**

SERIES EDITORS
Erin Kathleen Rowe
Michael A. Ryan

ADVISORY BOARD
Paul H. Freedman
Richard Kagan
Marie Kelleher
Ricardo Padrón
Teofilo F. Ruiz
Marta V. Vicente

The Iberian Peninsula has historically been an area of the world that fostered encounters and exchanges among peoples from different societies. For centuries, Iberia acted as a nexus for the circulation of ideas, people, objects, and technology around the premodern western Mediterranean, Atlantic, and eventually the Pacific. Iberian Encounter and Exchange, 475–1755 combines a broad thematic scope with the territorial limits of the Iberian Peninsula and its global contacts. In doing so, works in this series will juxtapose previously disparate areas of study and challenge scholars to rethink the role of encounter and exchange in the formation of the modern world.

OTHER TITLES IN THIS SERIES
Thomas W. Barton, *Contested Treasure: Jews and Authority in the Crown of Aragon*

Mercedes García-Arenal and Gerard Wiegers, eds., *Polemical Encounters: Christians, Jews, and Muslims in Iberia and Beyond*

Nicholas R. Jones, *Staging* Habla de negros: *Radical Performances of the African Diaspora in Early Modern Spain*

RADICALS IN EXILE

ENGLISH CATHOLIC BOOKS
DURING THE REIGN OF PHILIP II

FREDDY CRISTÓBAL
DOMÍNGUEZ

THE PENNSYLVANIA STATE UNIVERSITY PRESS
UNIVERSITY PARK, PENNSYLVANIA

Library of Congress Cataloging-in-Publication Data

Names: Domínguez, Freddy Cristóbal, 1982– author.
Title: Radicals in exile : English Catholic books during the reign of Philip II / Freddy Cristóbal
    Domínguez
Other titles: Iberian encounter and exchange, 475–1755 ; vol. 4.
Description: University Park, Pennsylvania : The Pennsylvania State University Press, [2020]
    | Series: Iberian encounter and exchange, 475–1755 ; vol. 4. | Includes bibliographical
    references and index.
Summary: "Examines how English Catholic exiles in Spain used print and other written media
    to promote the conquest of England and the spiritual renewal of Christendom"—Provided
    by publisher.
Identifiers: LCCN 2019048251 | ISBN 9780271086019 (cloth)
Subjects: Religious refugees—Spain—History—16th century. | British—Spain—History—
    16th century. | Catholic literature—History and criticism. | Reformation—England. |
    Spain—History—Philip II, 1556–1598. | Spain—Foreign relations—Great Britain. | Great
    Britain—Foreign relations—Spain.
Classification: LCC DP179 .D64 2020 | DDC 305.6/820892104609031—dc23
LC record available at https://lccn.loc.gov/2019048251

Copyright © 2020 Freddy Cristóbal Domínguez
All rights reserved
Printed in the United States of America
Published by The Pennsylvania State University Press,
University Park, PA 16802-1003

The Pennsylvania State University Press is a member of the Association of University Presses.

It is the policy of The Pennsylvania State University Press to use acid-free paper. Publications
on uncoated stock satisfy the minimum requirements of American National Standard for
Information Sciences—Permanence of Paper for Printed Library Material, ANSI Z39.48-1992.

With love and gratitude for
My parents, Lourdes and Freddy
My wife, Mary Beth
My children, Rose, Vivian, Laura, Niccolò, and Santiago

Contents

CONTENTS

Acknowledgments

This book exists because of Peter Lake. I stumbled upon my interest in English Catholics under his mentorship, and I have learned the historian's craft from him above all. He has offered loyal support and friendship in coffee shops on both sides of the Atlantic.

Working with Peter means getting to know his brilliant wife, Sandy Solomon. She is a fine poet, a kind host, and a warm conversationalist. At a crucial point in my career, she encouraged me to carry on when I almost left it behind. This book would not exist without her either.

This monograph is the accumulation of lessons taught by many fine scholars. Philip Benedict patiently mentored me as an undergraduate well before I knew what I was doing. Liam Brockey inspired my interest in Iberian things and has been an unflinching ally along the way. Anthony Grafton has displayed extraordinary patience and courtesy when none was warranted.

This project would be much weaker without the attention of Antonio Feros and Michael Questier, both of whom know more about both sides of this book than I ever will. I have also bothered Victor Houliston over the years, often out of the blue. He has only been generous in return when he could have swatted me away. Deborah Forteza has been a kind colleague and I've benefitted immensely from her work and our fellow conferencing. Mark Rankin has been a constant supporter and enthusiast in all things English Catholic.

This book has depended on the librarians and staffs of many institutions. I owe a great deal to so many people at the archives listed in the endnotes, but I would like to make special mention of a few. Above all, Daisy Domínguez offered the kindness of a thousand little favors at the start of this project. Javier Burrieza Sánchez at the English College in Valladolid and Aaron Pratt at the Harry Ransom Center have been, at various points, lifesavers. Thomas McCoog, SJ, whom I met when he was archivist at the British Jesuit Archives, has always been kind. I will never forget listening to him speak about Robert Persons at the Venerable English College in Rome—I a disheveled heathen among proper seminarians.

I've happily traveled around Europe and the United States while researching this book. This has required the kindness of strangers. Aside from substantial institutional support from Princeton University, the University of Arkansas, and Vanderbilt University, I am grateful for funds provided by the Harry Ransom Center, the Renaissance Society of America, the Huntington Library, the Mellon Foundation, the National Endowment for the Humanities, and the Fundação Luso-Americana para o desenvolvimento.

The final stages of this book were made easier by folks at my home institution. Special thanks to department chairs who have helped create a work environment supportive of research: Kathy Sloan, Calvin White, and Jim Gigantino. Although she was chair before I came to Arkansas, Lynda Coon has also been a voice of special encouragement throughout.

Without the consideration and help of Ellie Goodman at Penn State University Press and the Iberian Encounter and Exchange series editors, Erin Rowe and Michael Ryan, this book would still be a figment of my imagination.

I hope I've written a "good" book to justify the time spent on it, time that has been stolen from my family.

First and foremost, this book would not have been finished without the love and support of my wife, Mary Beth. Not only has she lifted me up when I needed lifting; she never thought twice of taking planes, trains, and automobiles with our bunch of screaming children to wherever I needed to research—and making all accommodations and practical arrangements. In doing this, I recognize that she has sometimes had to sacrifice her own research time. There are words I wish I had to describe my thanks, but I'll settle for *I love you.*

There is no better reason to avoid work than children. My daughters—Rose, Vivian, and Laura—could not care less about my studies and that is as it should be. Still, I hope they know that even this unrelated activity is to their credit. Their proximity is essential.

I wish Niccolò had lived to see this. In his absence, however, he taught me a lot that I wouldn't have learned otherwise. I'm grateful he is at my left hand while I write.

Santiago was spared the brunt of this book, but his imminent arrival got me to finish it!

This project began an embarrassing number of years ago. From the start, I've been lucky to have the unstinting support of my parents, Freddy and Lourdes. I'm not sure they knew what I was getting into, but they never blinked. Their love has been all-encompassing. No amount of thanks will do, but I offer it to them anyway.

Dom Sebastião, king of Portugal, died in a Moroccan desert near Ksar el-Kebir in 1578. His dream of Christianizing the Maghreb ended in failure, and worse, his death exacerbated troubles within Christendom. Dom Henrique, Sebastião's uncle—an old, childless cardinal—succeeded him, and in Portugal and across Europe, statesmen waited anxiously for his death and its aftermath. To ward off the vultures, Dom Henrique requested papal permission to marry in the frail hope of producing an heir.[1] He never wed and would be nicknamed "o Casto," the chaste. In the end, the king found no better legacy than the creation of a council to select a monarch from a list of several expectant candidates. Apart from internal claimants, others outside Portugal readied their own arguments, no matter how unlikely: even in France, some promoted scarcely tenable genealogical claims for the queen mother, Catherine de Medici, whose serious quest was shrugged off in Spain and Portugal.[2] Others could not be taken lightly, and no aspirant caused more concern than Philip II, king of Spain, already the most powerful monarch in Europe. Those who formed part of a politically engaged public in Portugal recalled the tense relationship between their kingdom and neighboring Castile, considered the hard-fought independence of their proud nation, and pondered the possibility of Iberian unity under a Habsburg monarch.

Negotiations took place in daylight and in shadows. Outside Lisbon's walls, Cristóbal de Moura, Spanish ambassador to Portugal, walked through a late-summer garden with Lope Centil, a local *letrado*. There, amid forced courtesies and implied promises, Centil agreed to write a foolproof defense of Philip II's rights. The prospect excited Moura so much that he could barely sleep that night.[3] Despite high hopes, however, the years between 1578 and 1583 showed that dynasticism alone would solve nothing. The specter of Spanish rule and the ambiguity of the moment unleashed currents of discord within Portugal that resulted in a civil war among several competing forces, some of which fought under the banner of Philip II and others under that of the homegrown pretender to the throne: Antonio, prior of Crato.[4] Diplomacy, propaganda, and violence would ultimately establish six decades of precarious Habsburg dominion over Portugal and its overseas territories, starting with Philip's coronation in 1581 and, more assertively, the defeat of Dom Antonio in the Azores two years later.

Discontent lingered in Portugal, but victory allowed Philip's regime to develop a triumphant narrative. When the king arrived in Lisbon, festivities emphasized soaring expectations. As he stepped off his ship along the Tagus, the king stood before a triumphal castle-shaped arch. The temporary structure displayed a complex decorative scheme featuring an image of Philip dressed in military garb, standing victorious over Atlas with the world at his side and Neptune, trident in hand, with his upturned ship. Beneath the king's depiction, austere Roman capitals celebrate Philip for his defense of the Catholic Church, his efforts to spread the faith "by land and by sea," and those quintessential effects of good governance: the conservation of peace and justice. Beneath Atlas, a book lay open with an inscription describing his "broken body" and the weakness that led him to place the weight of the world on the king's shoulders. Another beneath Neptune describes his own submission: having governed the seas for so long, now Philip is to keep watch so that "from now on, corsairs will not travel through these seas without punishment, nor will they take hostages, nor steal."[5] Those who organized the day's celebration wanted to link the king to the mythical power of the gods and to suggest his global dominion. The regime later synthesized these sentiments in more durable form: a medal struck in 1583 advertised that for Philip II, *Non Sufficit Orbis*—"the world is not enough."[6]

Such bluster may have been aspirational, given competing views and mixed feelings in Portugal, but it nevertheless promoted a perception of Habsburg might. From the outside looking in, the king's victory against Portuguese competitors seemed like a coup. Across Europe, many were gobsmacked by the implications of Iberian unity and the newly extended Habsburg reach across the world. With his newly won Portuguese imperial holdings in Asia, Philip reigned over an empire upon which the sun never set.

From inside the regime, the thrill of victory inspired some to exploit the moment. The marquis of Santa Cruz, fresh off a successful armada campaign in the Azores (1583), wrote to Philip saying that if God had decided to make him "such a great king . . . it is only just that this victory be followed by the necessary provisions so that next year the English enterprise might be carried out."[7] The insistence on fighting England was not new, but in Santa Cruz's mind, now it was feasible and desirable as a first step to eradicate heresy and stabilize Habsburg influence across Europe and beyond.

Some believed that defeating England would stifle fundamental threats to Philip's authority. Bernardino de Escalante, a sailor (and later clergyman) with close ties to the Spanish court, reveals a typical pro-war stance. In 1586, he wrote a memorial to the crown epitomizing what had become a truism among many, contending that war against England was necessary to solve several intertwined threats. English corsairs had threatened transatlantic commerce, and England had openly supported rebels against the king. Escalante argued that defensive measures would be costly and ineffectual; it would be better to strike the problem at its source. Only the conquest of England would do. He advised the king to take note of Julius Caesar, who had realized that his efforts to keep Gaul could only be achieved by conquering England. By no other means "could he render them obedient, as he in fact did."[8] Should the king want to take control of his Burgundian territories (Belgium and Holland), parts of which had been in open rebellion since the 1560s, the time had come to destroy their abettors in England.

Escalante emphasized feasibility. He explained that the English were ambivalent subjects and expounded on the auspicious geopolitical situation. He asked Philip to consider geography as well: islands were more vulnerable than other places to unexpected attacks. He recalled the importance of surprise along open coasts during the initial conquest of Portugal and the Azores campaign.[9] The thrill of this success over the Portuguese continued to inspire the conquest of England.

Escalante wrote with freedom unburdened by power, but Philip II did not have that luxury. From the time of Elizabeth's coronation (1558), his interactions with the queen were treated with appropriate delicacy. Even when the king's personal feelings for the queen soured, even as Elizabeth's Protestantism proved unwavering, he (and some of his important advisers) had little interest in war. Philip could not commit to aggression, especially amid instability on the Continent. He had to deal with the Dutch Revolt and reports that French heresy influenced his rebellious subjects there. Moreover, sources informed him that French Calvinists were planning to enter Iberian territories.

French Catholics also posed a threat. Franco-Spanish rivalries of the first half of the sixteenth century remained beyond the Peace of Cateau-Cambrésis (1559), which had tried to allay them. The king's hesitance about England was of a piece with his antipathy for the fleur-de-lis. Should Philip interfere against Elizabeth, he would help the Scottish queen, Mary Stuart, who while imprisoned in England promoted her pretensions to the English throne. Mary was supported by her uncle, the duke of Guise, head of an influential clan in France with pan-European interests.[10] Philip could applaud Guise efforts to defend French Catholicism but could not endorse their imperial designs.

Further, due to the multifront effort necessary to make an English expedition feasible, financing posed problems. While money came in shiploads from across the Atlantic, it was quickly spent. The second half of Philip's reign was plagued by cash shortages and several defaults.

Religious considerations and forms of political prudence made decision-making tense. At times, Philip's decisions resulted from messianic impulses, as described by Geoffrey Parker;[11] at others, more earthly calculations dominated. However, as M. J. Rodríguez-Salgado has suggested, secular considerations and piety were not antithetical. Many took for granted that the good Christian king should first protect his own subjects.[12]

When the English Jesuit Robert Persons left France for Portugal, he understood geopolitical realities but tried to overcome them. Persons emigrated from England in the 1570s, when English Catholic exiles had started to set roots in Belgium, France, and Italy. He quickly rose in the ranks after becoming a Jesuit and helped lead the first full-fledged Catholic mission back to England in 1580, along with the latterly sainted Edmund Campion. Campion was executed for his efforts, but Persons managed to escape to France where—despite deep emotional turmoil—he worked fervently toward fulfilling England's salvation. To this end, he became embroiled in plots led by the Guise along with Scottish clergymen to lead a campaign against Protestants in Scotland and then to overthrow the Elizabethan regime in favor of Mary Stuart and her son, James. Persons tried to ensure the support of both the papacy and Philip—easier said than done.

In 1582, Persons approached Philip in Lisbon. He came prepared with a series of arguments in favor of immediate action. The proposed course was necessary for "the liberation of the Catholics who are distressed and persecuted for their faith in England and elsewhere, and . . . the restoration of God's church in those regions, and the tranquility in other neighboring countries which have been troubled now for so many years by the malice of these heretics."[13] This appeal to Christian duty and this pitch for peace in Christendom came with a positive feasibility assessment. The moment was ripe given Catholic discontent in England and Scotland: Catholics were tired of oppression and fed up with perceived misgovernance. They were ready to fight against the "tyranny of heresy."[14]

Persons had to wait; Philip had fallen ill. Plans for a face-to-face meeting would be postponed, although communications with the regime began in earnest between Persons and Philip's principal secretary, Juan de Idiáquez. Through this intermediary, Persons would learn of the king's sympathy for English Catholics. However, cautious optimism soon faded. Philip could not offer full assistance until he resolved turmoil in Portugal—an armada was about to set sail against Dom Antonio in the Azores.[15] Moreover, he needed more assurances that the papacy would contribute its fair share of money. Persons would not be the first nor the last Englishman to receive little more than encouragement from Philip. On his return to France, he became seriously ill in Spain but would live to fight on for English Catholicism. He would be back.

Monarchia

In England, many had greeted Philip's success with dread. After the Portuguese conquest, Elizabeth's counselors thought they saw the writing on the wall. William Cecil, Elizabeth's chief minister, did not know "what limits any man of judgment can set unto his greatness" and warned of Philip's "insatiable malice, which is most terrible to be thought of, but most miserable to suffer."[16] Philip seemed to be creeping toward the British Isles. He battled against French Protestants, and his regime explored ever more violent expedients against Dutch rebels. Should Philip succeed on both fronts, England would be next. The king's efforts to establish universal monarchy posed an existential threat to church and state.

Elizabeth's counselors seethed, but the queen was circumspect. In the 1560s, she had few qualms about supporting profiteering ventures in the New World, where Spain claimed exclusive trading rights. Adding to growing tensions, she stood by while an important shipment of gold to fund Philip's war against Dutch rebels was held hostage in Dover in 1569. However, more direct engagements were avoided, largely because the regime feared Habsburg power and because the queen was unwilling to jump into perilous war. As her reign progressed—and in retrospect—many in and around court would become critical of her hedging. The explorer Sir Walter Raleigh would quip that the queen "did all by halves," and the earl of Essex, her sometime favorite, would say that English governance was hampered by "delay and inconstancy, which proceeded chiefly from the sex of the queen."[17]

Calculations about foreign engagements were always embedded within domestic troubles. Because the Wars of the Roses left deep wounds, because Elizabeth was a woman, and because she was the last Tudor, she faced inordinate pressure to find the right husband.[18] This created tensions between the queen, who considered the issue her prerogative, and subjects who advised, exhorted, and even tried to direct her. Without an heir, succession became a topic of overwhelming concern and a driving force of political culture throughout Elizabeth's reign. Until 1587, many hopes and fears were pinned upon Mary Stuart.[19] Elizabeth's counselors convinced Elizabeth to allow Mary's execution, but even then, the succession crisis did not flag, as the childless queen refused to consider her successor or allow others to discuss the matter despite the emergent possibility of Spanish dominion by dynastic arrangement or conquest.[20]

Succession debates became part of a cosmic contest between Protestantism and Catholicism. Mary Stuart sought help from Catholic forces on the Continent, and as her confinement continued, she became more cavalier in those foreign entanglements. The regime linked her to murderous plots against Elizabeth and uncovered efforts to bring England under the dominion of the Guise and, even more troubling, Philip. The long period of Marian subterfuge solidified a feeling within the regime that the threat of foreign conquest was part of a massive Catholic conspiracy promoted by English exiles, "unnatural subjects" who had betrayed Elizabeth and welcomed the dominion of Rome and Madrid. Within this context, the idea of England as defender of pan-European Protestantism gained currency.

As Catholicism and foreignness became more intertwined, the place of English Catholics changed within England. From Elizabeth's perspective, the challenges posed by religious dissidents to the regime were multifaceted and included a range of treasonous Catholics and no less treasonous Puritans. Many of her advisors would try to persuade her against what they saw as a false equivalence, and their case proved harder to ignore as time went on. A rebellion by Catholics in the north (1569) and the pope's decision to excommunicate and thus encourage Catholics to reject the queen (1570) were early turning points. A major threshold was breached in the late 1570s and early 1580s, when important English Catholics formed part of a rebellion against the queen in Ireland while others led the first comprehensive mission from Rome to England. This was, according to the Elizabethan regime, a two-pronged rebellion. By the early 1580s, many became convinced that English exiles along with the pope and the king of Spain would one day awaken a fifth column within the queen's realms.[21]

The regime sometimes overstated the threat, but they did not invent it. The relationship between English Catholics and the Elizabethan government was varied and capacious enough to include several kinds of loyalties and disloyalties, but the exile community abroad posed specific challenges.[22] From the early days of Elizabeth's reign, some wealthy Catholics attached to the court and a trickle of academics and priests felt forced to leave England as a result of resurgent Protestantism. They went to Catholic lands and became embedded in their new homes, often with the support of England's enemies. Some, especially in their early years of exile, did not become politically active, but others did in hopes of using foreign pressure to remove the queen and reestablish Catholicism.

Persons's appeals to Philip II epitomize the threat to Elizabethan stability. He went to see the king in Lisbon with England's salvation in mind but was ready to engage in hard-nosed politics. Not only did he hope Philip would be part of a pan-European invasion of England and Scotland, but he was willing, as John Bossy has argued, to consider the gravest of tactics: Elizabeth's murder.[23] If the Elizabethan regime would characterize such scheming as treason, Persons saw it differently. His entrée into dirty politics was a requisite of unfortunate times. Catholics were killed and exiled while the insidious powers of Protestantism destroyed the true Church and, consequently, the commonwealth. Rejection of heresy, even by the most extreme measures, was justified in defense of the true faith. If Catholicism needed to be reinstituted by Spanish forces, so be it.

English Catholic exiles found themselves between the proverbial rock and hard place. Not welcome at home, they had to hustle on the Continent for subsistence and for a greater cause: to save their homeland.

Spanish Elizabethans

Sir Francis Englefield had no choice but to leave England. Those who had been Mary Tudor's loyal servants did not expect generosity from their new queen, and Englefield knew that any courtesy from Elizabeth would only be at the expense of his conscience. While he pledged continued loyalty from afar, he refused to go back despite her demands. He claimed to be "rather an unwilling offender than a malicious one."[24] Englefield's departure was final unless the Elizabethan regime allowed Catholics to practice their faith freely. Until then, he took refuge in Philip II's realms, first for more than a decade in Flanders (with brief Roman forays) and from 1579 until his death in 1596 in Castile. Seeking the king's help seemed natural, since he had been one of Philip's counselors during his reign as king consort to Mary Tudor (1554–58). Even had such a relationship not been forged, there was no wealthier, no stronger, no more Catholic monarch than Philip—and thus no more obvious source of charity and support. Englefield felt no compunction about enjoying royal grace and, during his three decades on the Continent, worked to bring his countrymen within the king's orbit.

Englefield was one of many whom Albert Loomie in the twentieth century dubbed "Spanish Elizabethans."[25] Loomie's phrase recast language traditionally used by enemies of English Catholics who believed, as Oliver Cromwell put it in the seventeenth century, that papists "have been accounted, ever since I was born, Spaniolized."[26] Instead of emphasizing the monstrous Anglo-Spanish hybridity of Protestant nightmares, instead of taking up the cudgel against "unnatural" English subjects treasonously devoted to a foreign regime, Loomie neutralized the term.[27] For him, it simply described "refugees" embedded within Spanish Habsburg lands. Though he was no apologist for English Catholics, he tried to scrape away centuries of accreted vituperations to describe English Catholic exile activities.

I will employ a more specific definition for Spanish Elizabethans. For Loomie, a man like Englefield is not defined as such primarily because of his close relationship to the Spanish regime but because he became a "bursar" for his fellow exiles and coordinated the distribution of Habsburg charity. I, on the other hand, consider him a Spanish Elizabethan because he played a role in Spanish political culture, believed that Spain and England would have an entwined future, and became an abettor and promoter of the Habsburg regime. My definition has something in common with that of Protestant critics, minus the confessional animus. The men and women who will appear in this book plotted to save England from the blight of heresy and the evils of the Elizabethan regime. They undoubtedly planned to do so with Spanish help (though they were happy to get it from whoever offered it). While their motivations were spiritual and their piety often profound, their activities were necessarily political. This story focuses on a group of Spanish Elizabethans, mostly priests, allied with William Allen and Robert Persons: the so-called Allen-Persons party.[28]

Allen was born in Lancashire in 1532 and, after early academic success, left the Elizabethan scene haltingly at first and for good in 1565.[29] He then became the leader of the exile community, the founder of several English colleges on the Continent, and a polemicist. In 1587, he became a cardinal (at Philip II's behest) in time for the Armada. He generally led the exile community in the spirit of comity and compromise but was capable of steely calculation and forward political action.

Persons, unlike Allen, has always been controversial, partly because of his prickly personality.[30] Born in Somerset, his intellectual prowess was noted early on and through his time at Balliol College, Oxford. His university life was, however, cut short because of petty squabbles with colleagues. Later, upon crossing the Channel (1575), he joined the Society of Jesus. Persons quickly established close ties with Allen, who could pay no better compliment than sending him on the English mission mentioned above as a co-leader. After returning to France in 1581, Persons never went back to England. His name was raised for the cardinalate, though unlike in Allen's case, nothing came of those talks. Still, if he never reached the same ecclesiastical heights as Allen, his career had similar contours. He became a founder of colleges, a writer of polemical and spiritual books, and an aggressive politico.

Allen and Persons first became collaborators in proximity in France and Italy, and then at a distance while Allen tended to a Roman sphere of influence and Persons gained access to circles in and around Madrid. Both men had a direct line to Philip. Indeed, they arguably had easier access to the king than his "natural" subjects did.

Even among the most well-connected English Catholics, however, attachment to Spanish Habsburg authority did not mean security. Englefield, for example, skirted exile's most bitter consequences, but he understood his situation's fragility. Having lost his properties in England, he was lucky that Philip II thought financial support was as much a duty as it was pragmatic. Englefield's maintenance would be emblematic of the regime's charity and an important sign of goodwill toward English Catholics who might become useful allies. And yet despite principles of royal kindness, support in hard cash came slowly. Englefield learned this from his own experience and his efforts to help fellow exiles. To help his countrymen, he worked against a clunky bureaucracy and diminishing coffers that impeded expedient dispersal of royal largesse.[31]

As Englefield sought tranquility and solvency in Habsburg lands, he found himself in the strange situation of having to depend on "foreign" rulers and politicians to plot and execute England's Catholic future. The results were uneven and often frustrating. Despite the immense privilege of having the king's ear, men like him fretted about how much influence they had on matters of state and war. At times, it seemed he was part of an elite group helping drive and formulate foreign policy; at others, it felt like no one was listening. Englefield and many like him struggled to stay relevant.

But if English Catholics occasionally despaired, some exiles persevered through their belief in the cause and their faith in the perceived powers of words. As Englefield put it, because exiles did not have access to "the sword, which we cannot obtain, we must fight with paper and pens, which cannot be taken from us."[32]

Allen and Persons agreed. Here we will see either or both men writing books or facilitating their publication. These books were collaborative efforts among many authors, editors, and translators, some of whom have left few traces. There were die-hard allies among them, while others joined Allen and/ or Persons for the sake of a specific project only to fall away or follow a different path thereafter. Both men were the binding agents of an otherwise diffuse enterprise that reached beyond modern national boundaries. Collaborators generally lived in and around English colleges across Europe (Spain, Italy, France, and Flanders), and their books were printed on many European presses (in Madrid, Cologne, Rome, Rheims, Lyon, Antwerp, and others).

This book argues that English Catholics most effectively participated in and molded their circumstances through textual interventions. Books (in manuscript and print) amplified their voices on the Continent and in England, and the written word facilitated English Catholic attachment to the political and cultural landscapes they inhabited. This happened even as they formed an English identity based on the assumption that they had at their disposal the solutions to England's religious and political troubles. Indeed, they were better Englishmen for their principled displacement. Many Catholics in England disagreed and criticized their decision to flee as betrayal.[33] Ultimately, exiles had to balance attachments to their ancestral homes with those to their new, temporary ones.

Exile

The English Catholic authors discussed here have been labeled "refugees" in the past. When I first started this book, I planned to follow suit for aesthetic reasons justified by precedent. However, present realities intruded. When it came time to settle on a title, news reports had begun to cover (fleetingly but with real fifteen-minute zeal) the horrors of displaced peoples from the humanitarian crisis in Syria. Barbed wire, drowning masses on makeshift boats, hopeless faces, and desperate yelling filled airwaves and print. Then at the U.S.-Mexico border and in privately owned detention facilities around the country, news of crying children and wailing parents amid inhumane separation filled another page with contemporary atrocities. These men and women, many of whom fled their home countries for fear of violence and seeking asylum, also fit the bill of refugees and further clarified a dissonance between current experiences and sixteenth-century ones. The people I study left their homes in fear of religious persecution by the Elizabethan regime and as such could not, in the words of the Geneva Convention, "avail themselves of the protection of their home-countries." But they were, by and large, men of some means and had extraordinary institutional connections. They rubbed elbows with kings and popes. They tended to be among a privileged class of the displaced whose suffering, while no less real than others less fortunate, avoided the kinds of inhumanities that have formed a large part of the modern refugee experience.

Given these disparities, I have chosen to use the term *exile*. It seemed a natural choice both because it was a term used by the historical figures encountered here and because it allows for typological flexibility while still referring to a state of involuntary estrangement from "home" (as opposed to other possible terms like *expatriate* or *émigré*).

Exile as a trope and as a condition is as old as sand. The early modern Italian historian and political theorist Paolo Paruta once rightly asserted, "Infinite are the examples in every age of those driven by exile from city or state."[34] For people living in medieval and early modern Europe, the examples were mythical, biblical, and present. They could read about exile in classical poetry and in Scripture, but they also understood it as a modern phenomenon because it had become a tool of coercion and punishment used by consolidating medieval polities against deviants.[35] Early modern upheavals reoriented the notion of exile somewhat by underlining its religious significance. Nicholas Terpstra has suggested that the period of Reformation(s) was "Europe's first grand project in social purification."[36] Religious exiles became a central feature of the era's culture, at once hated by religious enemies and lauded by confessional allies.

Terpstra's rich synthesis of European history through the lens of forced emigration, *Religious Refugees in the Early Modern World*, signals the flourishing of exile studies, a topic that has not been central to early modern historiography.[37] Moreover, his work reminds us that early modern exile should be observed through a broad lens that considers the experiences of refugees across confessions, including various forms of Christianity, Judaism, and Islam.

Strangely, however, the Catholic side has received relatively modest treatment. Early modern Christian exile has largely been thought of as a Protestant phenomenon. If many have taken for granted, as Hugh Trevor-Roper did, that "the dispersal of European talent in the century after the Reformation is surely one of the greatest fertilizing displacements of European history," within the context of Christianity that talent has been described mostly as Huguenot (French Calvinist) during the sixteenth and seventeenth centuries or English Protestant during the early to mid-Tudor period.[38] In recent years, however, monographs have begun to describe the experiences of Dutch, French, and English Catholic exiles of various stripes.[39]

The study of English Catholic exiles has been limited by stubborn dynamics of national and confessional historiography. It is harder than it once was to write mainstream English history without taking "papists" into account, but only recently have scholars started to investigate the role of English Catholicism from an international perspective. Of course, anyone who has studied English exiles seriously understands their international contexts: the pages of countless articles in *Recusant History* (today, *British Catholic History*) prove this. But the orientation of such scholarship has been specifically *English Catholic*. This is true even of the most thorough, cosmopolitan project on British Catholicism, a three-volume narrative about British Jesuits by Thomas McCoog, SJ.[40] Of late, however, scholars have tried to integrate narratives of English Catholicism into broader frameworks. Work along these lines was started long ago by Loomie on Spanish Elizabethans and by John Bossy on English Catholic links with France. However, their most comprehensive works on the topic remain unpublished, and only in the last few decades have their leads been followed and expanded on to appreciate the significance of exiles in their host countries.[41] Katy Gibbons's groundbreaking book on English Catholics in Paris at the end of the sixteenth century remains the gold standard, and a volume on the links between English Catholicism and early modern Polish history points to a fertile field.[42] Most recently, Liesbeth Corens has written a volume on "confessional mobility" that focuses on cross-channel exchange.[43]

This book focuses on Spanish Elizabethan liminality. Because they were, to an extent, stateless and because their exile required the rejection of geographical fixity in favor of mobility, their activities were transnational. This lens offers two advantages. The first is accuracy. We will see that English

Catholic bookish activities were not linked to any one program but had to "fit" into various discursive contexts. Because of this, we can observe the plasticity of Spanish Elizabethan projects and identify the resulting ambiguities.

Second, a transnational approach tells different politico-religious stories about Europe during the sixteenth century. Because the authors and books discussed here did not obey modern or early modern political boundaries, we can see the interconnections of a broader European discourse, a European war of words that Spanish Elizabethans belonged to and helped constitute.

This book builds on recent scholarship showing that studying exiles allows us to tell important stories about early modern cultural interactions. As Diego Pirillo has argued in an innovative book on Protestant "diplomats" to England from Italy, exiles (in his words, "refugees") were intermediary figures central to early modern cultural exchange.[44] Similarly, Peter Burke has suggested that the exilic experience provides views into the process of "transculturation," a process by which both hosts and visitors are transformed.[45]

While Burke curtly dismissed the ability of English Catholics to assimilate abroad, here I will suggest that Spanish Elizabethans became formidable players on the Continental scene. To this end, the following chapters revolve around an Anglo-Iberian axis. By examining this relationship, we will see how English Catholics—through their books—became part of an Iberian landscape. We will also see how Iberian attitudes, assumptions, and ideas shaped English Catholic polemics and were transmitted outside of Iberia.

Spanish Elizabethans also speak to something greater than England and Spain; they were part of a Counter-Reformation project to defeat heresy. While the authors studied here do not define this phenomenon, they exemplify an important and understudied strand of Catholic combativeness that focused on political interventions and institutional change.

While this book is about the products of exile within specific contexts, the story also conforms to certain transcultural and transhistorical patterns. It resonates with many other accounts of exodus caused by intolerance and violence. Indeed, the experiences that produced the books under discussion here parallel elements in Edward Said's discussion of "modern" exile. In "Reflections on Exile," he explains that despite or because of the tragedies of displacement, the modern exile is often at pains to create "a new world to rule." It is not surprising, he says, "that so many exiles seem to be novelists, chess players, political activists, and intellectuals." Occupations of these kinds, he continues, require "a minimal investment in objects and [place] a great premium on mobility and skill." These men and women are aware of their difference, their estrangement, which "translates into an intransigence not easily ignored."[46] Regardless of how this exilic stance manifests, Said argues that their experiences are "contrapuntal," that the "habits of life, expression or activity in the new environment inevitably occur against the memory of these things in other environments."[47]

Spanish Elizabethans believed their survival depended on movement and their wits, sometimes shown off stridently as a function of their non-belonging. The exiles studied here were not "naturalized" members of the places they lived, and their attachments, though real, remained linked to their foreignness. Their polemical efforts are remnants of their intransigence and artifacts of their contrapuntal existence: various versions of their Continental selves were refracted through memories of their pasts and hopes for their futures in England.

Said points out the tension between the experience of exile and exile as a quintessential modern metaphor. He notes exile's bitter effects have often been transformed into "a potent, even enriching motif of modern culture." Heroic narratives of victories over estrangement and loss are typical. It is tempting to focus, as Peter Burke does in a recent study, on the "silver lining" of exile as a realm of *fruitful* exchange benefitting culture and the mind. Indeed, one might think about Spanish Elizabethans belonging to a "republic of letters," which is often evoked wistfully as an intellectual space or network with "no borders, no government, no capital."[48] This book, however, does not claim to describe its subject in such a benevolent light. Instead, this is a sordid story about a group of men and women clawing at what tools they had to promote warfare, political sabotage, and deepening confessional divide, albeit for a cause they believed godly.

Public Sphere

English Catholics were not the first to understand the power of print. Indeed, historiographical tradition once claimed that Catholics were slow to use printed material effectively. This is not true, but there is no doubt that the printed word's strength was unleashed by the Reformation; as Andrew Pettegree has described, Martin Luther ranks among the most sophisticated (and successful) users of the medium.[49] Print did not produce the Reformation, but its leaders and their opponents learned to use it quickly and effectively. As a result, the sixteenth century saw profound changes in the ways "paper wars" proceeded, increasingly shifting ideas about who should have access to information and the propriety of "publicity."

Historians have suggested that the period covered by this book witnessed an expansion of the *public sphere*. Jürgen Habermas's crucial thoughts on the topic have made it hard to resist his construal of the Enlightenment phenomenon, with its combination of participatory politics and the emergence of public spaces like coffeehouses. But recent scholarship has sought to broaden the term and push back its viability to the sixteenth century. Within English historiography, Peter Lake and Steven Pincus have argued that the late Elizabethan period saw the emergence of "spaces for or modes of communication or pitch making in which appeals to a general audience were made through a variety of media, appealing to a notion of the public good." These activities, justified by the authority of the communicator and the message itself, "necessarily called into being an adjudicating public."[50] In Spanish historiography, Fernando Bouza and others have enlarged our understanding of public discourse and its various audiences within Iberia.[51] Michele Olivari, in a pioneering study of Habsburg political culture, has soundly reminded us that the trepidation about speaking of the existence of a "public sphere" in pre-Enlightenment cultures has relatively late origins and that prior to Habermas, many took for granted that pre-Enlightenment actors partook in public activities aimed at shaping public opinion.[52] Based on years of work on (Spanish) political culture, J. H. Elliott has concluded that "there can be no doubting the existence of at least an embryonic public opinion in the societies of early modern Europe."[53]

Historical conjunctures provided the basis for a nascent public sphere. In England, the challenges posed by female rulership during the second half of the sixteenth century together with consternation about the Elizabethan succession and confessional strife all created a "need" to speak to different political publics. As Lake and Questier have shown, this dynamic is observable in the way that Catholics tried to engage the Elizabethan regime and the apparent need felt by the regime to respond in kind.[54] In Spain, fears about Protestants and Philip II's weakened position amid war and economic troubles encouraged the regime to show greater sensitivity about its public image in response to highly publicized attacks. Those who resisted Habsburg authority used a range of media to combat the regime, and the regime responded accordingly. The 1591 revolt in Aragon, for example, witnessed the explosion of pent-up anger in public forums. There, Philip II met violence with violence, but he also met words with words.[55]

This book is a case study of a group in action within a framework of public politicking. As such, it is indebted to a strand of early modern scholarship that seeks to describe the period's public sphere and its concomitant practices—performance, print, manuscript circulation, networking, and so on—to rewrite narratives of the period. Peter Lake, Michael Questier, Alastair Bellany, and Thomas Cogswell, among others, have at various points revealed the realm of pitch-making as a central thread of "new" political narratives.[56] The story told here is about how English Catholic exiles tried to achieve a certain goal—the (spiritual) reconquest of England—by speaking to and, to an extent, forging different publics. By focusing on transnational figures, we will see how the game was played on a broader European level, impinging upon Spain, England, and Counter-Reformation Europe as a whole.

Although scholars have questioned the unvarnished supremacy of the written word in this period, this book traces textual manipulations as a primary means of discursive intervention among Spanish Elizabethans.[57] I will show how English Catholic authors used editorial means to speak to a variety of audiences, sometimes simultaneously. I will often compare various editions of books to better understand how a series of strategies—rhetorical, paratextual, mediatic, and linguistic—tells us something about authorial intentions. I want to show what authors were doing when they said what they chose to say. To achieve this, I will also place texts in a series of discursive contexts with an emphasis on borrowings and rejections that, again, provide clues about significance. Together with what was said and what was assimilated (or rejected), this book will explore what English Catholics gave their (friendly and hostile) readers. I will show how they managed to influence various conversations outside of the English community by providing a language to deal with broad concerns about Christendom. By showing how their projects worked or failed and the ways they coincided or pushed against the Habsburg regime's efforts, this book will also bring into focus forms of Iberian publicity.

The Cauldron

Each of the following three sections will examine the textual tools used by English Catholics and their allies at critical moments between 1585 (the starting point of Armada preparations) and 1598 (Philip II's death), a time when the most radical efforts to re-Catholicize England seemed to match Habsburg willingness to do so. This period also marks the third decade of the wars in Holland and France, both of which impinged on Habsburg interests. The Dutch Revolt challenged Habsburg authority itself, while the potential victory of French heresy meant its possible extension and the diminishment of Spanish power. While Dutch troubles continued apace during the period studied here, the French situation experienced a forceful jolt. Partly with Spanish support, the French Catholic League rose to challenge the French king, Henry III, and his successor, Henry IV. The Armada's failure in England, possibilities in and worries about France, and tensions in Iberia all made the period tumultuous and allowed for the amplification of Spanish Elizabethan voices.

The Plan

Part 1 of this book is a close reading of the first history of the English Reformation from a Catholic perspective: Nicholas Sander's *De origine ac progressu schismatis Anglicani* (On the origin and progress of the English schism). I will show how the book tried to promote war against Elizabeth and how the project became increasingly "Hispaniolized," first through a second Latin edition aimed specifically at Philip II and then through a Spanish adaptation written by the Spanish Jesuit Pedro de Ribadeneyra. Part 2 reveals how some English Catholics became key propagandists for Philip II in the aftermath of the Armada and how the regime appropriated an English voice at a delicate moment of Iberian unrest. Part 3 explores books by Persons meant to facilitate a longed-for second Armada. First, I examine *A Conference About the Next Succession to the Crowne of Ingland*, which tried to establish the premises of a future Spanish succession to the English crown. Second, I discuss *A Memorial for the Reformation of England*, which provided a road map for England's spiritual renewal by drawing on theocratic tendencies promoted by Spanish Jesuits at the end of Philip's reign.

PART I

HISTORY IN ACTION
England's Heretical Past on the Eve of the Grand Armada

Almost forty years after Henry VIII rejected papal authority (1534), Nicholas Sander, an English priest, wrote the first full Catholic history of the English "schism": *De origine ac progressu schismatis Anglicani.* The book argues that Henry's decision to break with Rome resulted from his misguided will to divorce Catherine of Aragon and satisfy his lust for Anne Boleyn, who, Sander claimed, was Henry's own daughter. The book reveals how the king, having overturned proper ecclesiastical authority, pilfered Church lands, strayed from good theological precepts, and murdered Catholics. The narrative then describes England's further descent into heresy during the short and tumultuous reign of Edward VI, largely as a result of evil counselors and heretical theologians. His reign was followed by a brief return to Catholicism during Mary Tudor's five years on the throne. The book ends with a dire assessment of the current situation under a ruthless, violent, illegitimate queen bent on destroying Catholicism: Elizabeth I. Sander's history recounts Protestant horrors, interspersed with the deeds of good Catholics who spoke truth to power and often paid the ultimate price.

Since its first printing in 1585, *De schismate Anglicano,* as Sander's book was called in early modern times, has inspired both respect and derision. Protestants have considered it nothing but a mishmash of falsehoods. In the 1660s, cleric and controversialist Peter Heylin dubbed it a "pestilent and seditious" book worthy of its author, whom he called "Dr. S*l*anders."[1] In the 1670s, Gilbert Burnet, a respected historian and bishop of Salisbury, thought much the same and found it troubling that a peddler of lies had achieved respectability. He marveled at how Catholics still relied on Sander's book and considered it "as a good authority."[2] Burnet would have been disappointed but unsurprised to know that centuries later, Sander still had plenty of (Catholic) readers. David Lewis's 1877 English translation judged *De schismate Anglicano* "the earliest and the most trustworthy account which we possess of the great changes in Church and State that were wrought in the reign of Henry VIII."[3] Catholic efforts to prove Sander's accuracy and integrity continued in the twentieth century, pursued by such respected scholars as J. H. Pollen. Despite criticisms, he insisted, "we shall always find him [Sander] a witness on the Catholic side who is well worthy of attention."[4]

De schismate Anglicano survived for centuries not as an oddity but as a powerful historical statement with polemical force. Burnet found Sander's history disturbing nearly a century after it had been penned because it continued to deepen prejudices against the English. In the wake of a recent French translation, he reckoned that those who once spoke modestly about the English Reformation now saw it "as one of the foulest things that ever was."[5]

Three hundred years later, Sander's book could still sting. A nineteenth-century English translation printed in Ireland by Irish patriots became a weapon against English oppressors.[6] Meanwhile, in Spain, a more conservative reader of a Spanish version identified in Henry VIII's reign "the modern origin of the revolutionary idea, developed later in France to such horrible effects!"[7] Such writers and readers did not invent the book's polemical tone or potential; they accurately identified what had been a signature from the start.

Today, *De schismate Anglicano* does not arouse the passions it once did. Even as English Catholic scholarship has flourished over the past twenty years, the book has received meagre attention disproportionate to its past popularity.[8] Perhaps the stench of crude partisanship has led to its marginalization among scholars eager to remove English Catholic history from its confessional precincts. Only in the past decade have some tried to understand the polemical tack employed by Sander.[9] But even its most sophisticated readers have not done much to place the book in its broader contexts. Peter Lake is rightly unapologetic about using *De schismate Anglicano* to tell an English story about confessional polemics in public arenas, but he also says that such an English story has Continental ties because Sander's book was a response to geopolitical situations in Europe and because the author wrote it for audiences there.[10]

This section will discuss three early editions of *De schismate Anglicano* produced for European consumption within specific circumstances between 1585 and 1588, the most important of which involved entangled English Catholic and Spanish interests leading up to the Armada. During these years, the book underwent forms of "Hispaniolization," culminating in an adaptation/translation by Spanish Jesuit Pedro de Ribadeneyra: the *Historia ecclesiastica del scisma de Inglaterra* (The ecclesiastical history of the English schism). This English Catholic text—which, as we shall see, was originally meant to promote war against England—quickly became a tool to promote the 1588 Armada campaign. Moreover, the following pages will show how an English Catholic narrative gave some in Spain a way to talk about hopes and fears at home. The transferability of an English Catholic history in Spain resulted from a political moment, a shared fear of heresy, and something that has been ignored by modern scholarship on *De schismate Anglicano*: a mutual understanding of *Catholic* failures.

The authors and editors discussed here shared assumptions about the potential of English history as an antidote for widespread lethargy, but the absorption of English history on the Continent was not osmotic. English Catholic exiles promoted Sander and his message to establish relevance for their community during a pressure point in European history. These chapters reveal the extent to which they succeeded by providing an important discursive tool in a Spanish context. The books discussed here tried to mold minds and manipulate perceptions, as would any propaganda worth its salt, but they had a loftier goal as well: to inspire a change of heart that would lead to *active* resistance against heresy.

I

THE RADICALIZATION OF EXILE POLEMIC

Nicholas Sander died well for having lived hard in defense of the Church.[1] As he had long wished, he gave his heart and his life for its maintenance,[2] but exactly how he died in the fall of 1581 is a matter of speculation. The more popular narrative has him alone in the Irish wilds—a sign of his sacrifice in the eyes of his supporters, a sign of his punishment to his enemies. William Cecil, Elizabeth's chancellor, fantasized about his nemesis in a destitute frenzy.[3] Another version has Sander in the middle of nowhere, surrounded by a few intimates, calling on the most important of them, Cornelius, bishop of Killaloe, to perform the last rites, and ultimately being buried in hallowed ground.[4] Either way, death would not erase his memory; Sander had done too much to become ephemeral. After leaving England in the 1560s, he became a respected theologian, an admired writer, and a vocal advocate for anti-Elizabethan aggression. Largely because of his written work, he would remain, depending on the reader, a positive or negative exemplum.

Sander had not planned to stay in Ireland. He dreamed of seeing the gentle ripple of a brook near his childhood home in Charlwood, the jutting spires of Oxford where he'd once studied, even the salty life on the Thames that he had last seen when he left England for good. And yet knowing that life itself was exile from God's embrace made his earthly travels more bearable. Wonder and satisfaction colored memories of backroom wrangling with theologians and politicos at Trent, of long walks in green pastures with important churchmen in Poland, of holy sites he had once visited in Rome, of silent hours writing learned books in Louvain, of the penetrating gaze of Philip II as he stood before the king in Madrid.[5] He moved so easily from one place to another because he did not feel the need to re-create himself with each displacement. Through many changing backdrops, he embraced a singular Christian mission. His name would not be spoken with those of the martyrs, but he lived life mostly uncompromised by the earthly concerns that had forced others to waver or temporize. Such zeal, of course, came with dangers. It led him down the path of imprudence that could make enemies out of necessary allies. When he left Lisbon for Ireland in 1578 to help promote and lead a papally endorsed rebellion against Elizabeth, Sander was confident of ultimate success, and when the tide turned, he did not give up. Even amid financial ruin, he risked death by a hundred angry unpaid soldiers rather than abandon what increasingly looked like a hopeless cause—but for God's will.[6]

Sander's intransigence, his forward critiques of the Elizabethan regime, often created more problems than it solved. His involvement in the Irish rebellion and the anti-Elizabethan polemics he wrote in Ireland cast a long shadow that would come back to haunt the English Catholic mission.[7] His words and actions would provide a pretext for the murder of his equally zealous brethren. News of Sander's Irish efforts allowed the regime to link his treachery to a contemporary mission to England led by the Jesuits Edmund Campion and Robert Persons in 1580–81, despite the missionaries' apolitical stance. Cecil defended Elizabethan efforts to prosecute Catholic priests by showing that the accused "would not disallow the Pope's hostile proceedings in open wars against Her Majesty in her realm of Ireland, where one of their company, Dr. Sanders, a lewd scholar and subject of England, a fugitive and principal companion and conspirator with traitors and rebels at Rome, was . . . commander . . . and sometime a bursar of that war."[8] During interrogations and even as condemned Catholics stood on the scaffold, the regime threw scraps of Sander at their faces. Quoting from *De visibili monarchia libri octo* (Eight books on the visible monarchy)—considered by Catholics Sander's most respected theological work—interrogators asked prisoners if they agreed that the queen was a heretic and that her subjects were freed from obedience: Did they agree with Sander's defense of Pius V's excommunication of the queen and call for rebellion, or when Sander condemned Elizabeth's prosecution of Catholic traitors? Or would they reject his wicked words?

Sander backed his allies into a corner. As an avid promoter of regime change in England, he attacked viciously when his cause appeared to gain traction and even when it seemed stalled. This made things difficult for those who, while sympathetic to the cause and the author, urged patience and preached pragmatism. Thus Sander's muscular defense of papal powers, especially of Pius V's excommunication of Elizabeth in 1570, upset some English Catholics. In the aftermath of the failed Northern Rebellion of 1569 and enhanced Elizabethan retribution thereafter, William Allen insisted that Sander take a book on the topic out of circulation.

The fears that led to this censorship also played a role in the decision not to publish a version of *De schismate Anglicano* Sander had completed in Spain around 1573.[9] The book complicated Catholic efforts to compromise with the queen, as exemplified by the *Treatise of Treasons* (1572), an anonymous tract that tried to pin treason on the queen's closest advisors.[10] Its author had hoped to displace blame from Catholics involved in recent anti-Elizabeth activities while posturing as a true defender of the regime. Contrary to such efforts, *De schismate Anglicano* did not minimize its anti-Elizabethan, pro-papal message. Instead of squirming after a recently failed Catholic rebellion, Sander justified it. He also praised men like the duke of Norfolk, who had been plotting against Elizabeth with Mary Stuart, and insisted he had been wrongfully punished for following his conscience.[11] In private correspondence with Philip II, Sander felt no shame in emphasizing *De schismate Anglicano*'s central goal to render Elizabeth illegitimate.[12] Few would have missed the point.

English Catholic hesitance over Sander's polemics must have been deepened by Spanish qualms. Philip II and his regime knew that Elizabeth and her counselors were aware of polemics against the queen and her ancestors. Around 1569, the republication of Juan de Illescas's book on papal history, the *Historia pontifical* (first edition, 1564), caused diplomatic unease.[13] The queen disliked its attacks on her father, so Philip II had his ambassador to England perform damage control. The ambassador assured her that Philip did not know about the offensive text.[14] Such was the concern that when a new edition of the book came under scrutiny in 1573, some inquisitors were more worried about the offensive language against Henry than the positive kind used to describe him before he broke with Rome.[15] In this context, Habsburg authorities also tried to suppress Sander's work. After Sander's *De visibili monarchia* was first published in Antwerp (1569), the regime tried to distance itself from the project. To placate Elizabeth, Philip's representatives insisted that censors had tried to delete offensive sections of the book written against Henry and the queen. Questions remain about how rigorous those efforts were, but clearly the regime was not willing to support Sander fully while trying to keep diplomatic channels alive with England. If Sander had hoped that *De schismate Anglicano* would receive support in Madrid when he first wrote it, he had misread the situation.

After Sander died, fellow exiles had to deal with his legacy. In his official defense of recently executed Catholics, Allen had kind words for his fallen comrade even as he tried to make him out to be an outlier. He described how Sander acted and wrote out of great zeal and had his own "special reasons" for doing so.[16] In *Leicester's Commonwealth* (1584)—a libelous attack against the queen's favorite, the earl of Leicester, likely written in part by Persons and supported by Allen—a moderate Catholic interlocutor invokes Sander, listing him among those who had partaken in what the author refers to as second-degree treason of the sort that "containeth some actual attempt or treaty against the prince or state, by rebellion or otherwise."[17] Though they loved him, even his closest friends did not want to be seen as his closest allies.

Sander's aggression seemed perilous in 1584, but just a year later, Catholic exile leaders decided that things had changed. The most public statement in favor of his rehabilitation appears as paratextual material in a posthumous 1585 edition of Sander's *De iustificatione contra colloquium Altenburgense* (On the justification against the Altenburg colloquy).[18] A prefatory letter originally written by Sander to students at the English colleges in Rome and Douai helped reinforce his view that intellectual prowess, deep reading, and learned theological disquisitions should be employed as tools and armature in the service of God and nation against heresy. Such activities should enhance scriptural understanding to better instruct and console heretics and true Christians alike. While their efforts should not be in the name of worldly glory, they should not stray far from the real world. They were encouraged to become good missionaries: they should risk their lives to restore those who had strayed back to the right path.[19] The letter presented Sander's own words to establish a link between scholarship and worldly sacrifice—a resonant message in 1585, given Sander's own demise a few years earlier.

After this letter, the anonymous editor provided a short biography, defending Sander's character against recent attacks by the Elizabethan regime and praising Sander's charity, modesty, erudition, and eloquence.[20] Sander certainly supported the true Church, but this was a far cry from the treason of the Calvinists, who undermined Elizabeth's own authority and embraced rebellion. Still, Sander's biographer leaves no doubt that his subject embodied unstinting Catholic zeal of the sort willing to suffer and die to uphold the true Church and papal supremacy.

Defending Sander's honor signaled an important shift. The time for prudential hedging seemed to be ending. Embracing Sander meant embracing his brand of defiance. That he would be chosen to tell the truth about England's heresy through *De schismate Anglicano*—that his voice was summoned to speak openly of a past that England was still paying for—makes plain the move toward intransigence. To better understand the importance and the extremity of this polemical tack, let us consider in more detail the type of polemic produced on the eve of a renewed Sanderian turn.

Calm Before the Storm

During the summer of 1584, Allen and Persons tried to rekindle anti-Elizabethan conspiracies. More than two years had passed since the first stirrings of a joint Hispano-papal-Guise enterprise on behalf of the Scottish prince, James, and his mother, Mary. But these promising gestures came to nothing. The duke of Guise (a linchpin of the proposed British intervention) refocused on French affairs in light of his mounting estrangement from the crown and the growing Protestant threat. Philip II and Pope Gregory XIII were unperturbed by the anticlimactic end of recent machinations; they had been ambivalent from the start. English and Scottish exiles, on the other hand, awaiting action with bated breath, were left disgruntled and disappointed. Nevertheless, they kept faith in the written word's ability to move efforts against Elizabeth forward. By the end of 1584, two books were printed in France that, according to Persons, left enemies at the English court "wonderfully disturbed."[21] The books were Allen's *True, Sincere, and Modest Defense of English Catholics* and *Leicester's Commonwealth*.[22] If hopes of Elizabeth's removal were at a lull, on the printed page, the shift from compromise to resistance was just getting started.[23]

Persons described *Leicester's Commonwealth* as a book "against this Earl relating all his wicked life."[24] The authors showed how Leicester duped the queen, usurped her power, and planned to take the crown for himself. Salacious in tone, the book exposed the earl's immorality and, as Peter Lake has suggested, depicted him as a "sex monster or addict"; it was an "immediate and racy account of the interiority of tyranny."[25] Along with this spicy world of the evil counselor, Persons echoed the genealogical arguments recently promoted by John Leslie, bishop of Ross, on behalf of Mary Stuart, the would-be English queen.[26]

Despite its flammable content, *Leicester's Commonwealth* maintained a veneer of moderation. Fixated as it was on the earl, criticism was deflected from Elizabeth herself. The authors could claim they wrote "nothing repugnant to charity or to our bounden duty toward our most gracious Princess."[27] They bore no contempt toward the queen and lamented "the grief of her most excellent Majesty, whom we see daily molested."[28] The book also avoided attacking Protestant foes, seeking instead a "middle way" that would, in theory, allow for dialogue between moderates of conflicting confessions. The text was framed as a conversation among three men, one of whom "was inclined to be a papist," a fact that did not preclude his loyalty to England and the crown. Indeed, the Catholic interlocutor was said to have "many friends and kinfolk of contrary religion to himself, so did he love them never the less for their different conscience," and the three speakers were sensitive to the perceived need to punish Catholic troublemakers, "especially in such suspicious times as these."[29] Still, they suggested such instincts be tempered. England should try to "live in peace and unity of the state, as they do in Germany notwithstanding their differences of religion."[30] Moderates on either side of the religious divide could live in relative harmony were it not for those atheistic Machiavels (like Leicester) who used religious divisions to cement their power.

As Lake has suggested, Allen's *Defense* plays bad cop to *Leicester's Commonwealth*'s good cop. The book responds directly to Cecil's *Execution of Justice in England* (1583), a short pamphlet arguing that English Catholic missionaries were treasonous and deserved to be executed. Allen showed that, contrary to the Elizabethan regime's claim, the persecution of missionaries was not a matter of sedition but an effort to punish individual consciences. He insisted that there was no proof missionaries were involved in rebellion and that the "bloody questions" used by the regime to elicit confessions intended only to interrogate the defendant's religious convictions. Allen also questioned the legal basis on which Catholics were sentenced. Priests were condemned for violating a treason law imposed during Edward III's reign, but he argued that "in the time of the said King Edward," they "should not, nor could not have been convicted of treason, treasonable assertion, or evil affection to prince or country": England had not yet been tainted by heresy, and Edward's contemporaries would not have killed a Catholic priest.[31]

As with *Leicester's Commonwealth*, Allen's *Defense* tries to maintain some distance between its critique of the Elizabethan regime and the queen herself. Allen, instead of attacking Elizabeth, went after that "Sir Libeler" (Cecil) and, by extension, those "few powerable persons abusing Her Majesty's clemency and credulity."[32] Nevertheless, if the queen is not the object of Allen's ire, she is verbally bruised along the way. Allen suggested that she was limited by her sex: Elizabeth was "otherwise truly of most excellent gifts," but as a woman, she was "easily seduced and not hardly led and drawn by those whom she either trusteth or feareth." Worse, gentility made her more susceptible to "the tyranny of such as occupy . . . principal authority."[33]

Allen cut closer to the bone in his discussion of ecclesiastical authority. First, he flatly denied the queen's powers over the English church and claimed that "as before it was deemed in her father a layman, and in her brother, a child, very ridiculous, so now in herself, being a woman, is it accounted a thing most monstrous and unnatural."[34] Worse still, from an Elizabethan perspective, Allen offered a long argument in favor of papal rights to depose errant monarchs. The *Defense* insists on the superiority of the spiritual sword to the temporal one and that the pope has a duty to punish monarchs who put the soul of the commonwealth in danger. To make his point, Allen used a range of biblical and other historical examples, many of which raised direct parallels to contemporary English situations. Unwilling to dissolve superficial friendship, however, he made these claims behind a thin exculpatory veil. Anything said in favor of Rome "neither hath been nor shall be by us anywise spoken, meant, or applied against our natural princess or country."[35] He insisted that the complicated issue of papal supremacy could be broached without danger of sedition because affirming that the queen *might* be deposed by the pope as a heretic "doth not at all avouch her to be one; no more than the like assertion of the King of Spain would imply him to be such an one."[36]

To use more violent language against Elizabeth would have been imprudent. Both *Leicester's Commonwealth* and the *Defense* were meant mostly for a broad English audience (though the *Defense* also had a Latin edition) that would have disapproved of any full-throttled attack. Too forward an approach would only inspire royal rage, which would then be taken out on recusants. Furthermore, without certainty of actual military action against England by Catholic forces, the time was not ripe for a true verbal hazing—at least not in English.

The Editors and the Shift in 1585

Unlike Sander, Edward Rishton was not a superstar.[37] Rishton had gone back to England from the Continent knowing that if he was arrested by the Elizabethan regime, he could have been martyred. But he was "saved" when in 1585, after five years' imprisonment, he and several fellow prisoners were exiled and narrowly escaped the noose. After having been spared a supreme sacrifice, he settled on disappointment. He was angry and resentful of Elizabeth's construal of her own cruelty. She disingenuously offered exile out of "gracious clemency," a gift to men who, as she put it, might have been killed "as by our laws we might do."[38] Worse, the queen and her minions lied, saying that the prisoners had confessed treason.

Safely in France by the spring of 1585, Rishton wanted to give a true account of his forced departure—not only for honor's sake but as part of a larger project to counter false Elizabethan claims of moderation. Aside from his own experiences, he brought news of martyrs' valor and heretics' savageries, including the execution of Edmund Campion. We can imagine priests huddled around as Rishton solemnly recounted things lived and seen (and heard); we can imagine him in private conferences with Allen, alternating between rage and melancholy.

Rishton also helped write a version of the recent past. Sometime in 1585, he caught up with an old friend, Jodocus Skarnhert, who, in talking about ecclesiastical histories, suggested printing Sander's *De schismate Anglicano*. Rishton had his doubts. It would be hard to get a copy, and he worried about printing the book while its protagonists still lived.[39] Skarnhert insisted. Who was better for the job than someone who had been in the thick of recent troubles? Most importantly, the project would benefit the public good. There were important lessons to be learned from "the deeds of heretics and schismatics."[40] Rishton bent to his friend's logic, got a copy, corrected certain passages, and rewrote Sander's account of Elizabeth's reign. He then sent it to a printer in Cologne, asking only that the job be taken seriously and carried out carefully.

This is the story told in Rishton's prefatory note. From it, we also learn that Sander's posthumous editor knew he stood on shaky ground.

Rishton's purposefully vague and/or misleading statements are as telling as any initial hesitations. There was no Skarnhert. While once thought to be a pseudonym for Persons, it is just as likely a cover for long-suffering Allen, who fit the name perfectly: Skarnhert means "brokenhearted" in Dutch. And who was the printer in Cologne? He was not mentioned by name in the preface, nor on the title page. And was Rishton really the sole editor? Because *De schismate Anglicano* deals with events that occurred in August and September of 1585 and because we know that Rishton died in June, there must have been others who went unmentioned.[41] In the 1586 edition—more on this below—the evasions continue, as the title page advertises new, anonymous emendations.

Such studied ambiguities are reminders that the polemical pivot described here was not taken lightly. While on the one hand, printing *De schismate Anglicano* suggested a turn toward radicalism, the fingerprints of the living remained hidden. The editors strategically pinned all controversial arguments on the dead.

While Sander and Rishton were on the title page, *De schismate Anglicano* was an Allen-Persons production. A contemporary summary of the book that circulated in Spain describes it as Allen's own, and evidence of his and Persons's editorial hands survives in an early manuscript at the English college in Rome.[42] As men who were neck-deep in recent spiritual, political, and polemical activities, it is hard to imagine such a momentous project could evolve without their input.[43]

Knowing the dangers involved, why did they dust off a manuscript that had remained (more or less) hidden for more than a decade?

The Moment

Allen and Persons acted on equal parts desire and necessity. Among the arguments to convince Rishton to finish editing *De schismate Anglicano*, "Skarnhert" mentioned the troubling possibility that a non-English editor would soon do it. Were this to happen, he warned, its execution might be faulty.[44] To some, this nationalist line might read as boilerplate, but the concern seems too concrete to ignore. Was there any real risk of the book escaping English Catholic control? Concerns about "foreigners" suggest Allen and Persons understood that there were others who had come to understand the utility of Sander's book.

Consideration of the book's European potential begins with a mystery: Where was the book printed? The title page claims Cologne, but this is most likely a false imprint. While bibliographic tradition suggests it was produced at Jean de Foigny's print shop in Rheims, more work needs to be done to certify this claim against other possible contenders.[45] Based on bibliographic evidence—paper stock and signature markings—it seems likely that the book was a product of a press in northern France, but currently there is no reason to rule out other printing centers such as Paris or Rouen.[46]

Though false, the Cologne attribution is instructive. Its verisimilitude—Catholic sources at the time assumed its accuracy—depended on its likelihood. There was nothing strange about publishing a Catholic book in a city that was reasserting itself as a site of international Catholicism and a hub for communications among various sorts of (Catholic) exiles.[47] Moreover, Catholic strongholds within the Holy Roman Empire, in line with a general European trend, provided an active market for English Catholic texts.[48] Just a year before *De schismate Anglicano*, bits of Sander's writings were stitched together in an unattributed short pamphlet published in Ingolstadt: *De iustitia Britanica, sive Anglica* (On British or English justice).[49] Indeed, English authors were adamant about cultivating German readers. In prefatory material for a polemical book by the Jesuit John Gibbons printed in Trier, author and printer underline the connected histories of England and Germany in matters both "sacred and profane."[50] In general, Catholic publishers in Germany believed English Catholic books were valuable for their exemplarity—the tales of the martyrs could nourish German Catholicism in the way that so many English missionaries had done in antiquity.[51]

The gesture toward Cologne may have been related to *De schismate Anglicano*'s pertinence in Germany specifically at the time of printing. It was not the only Sanderian revival in the Holy Roman Empire in 1585. Sander's commentary on the Altenburg conferences, mentioned above, was published in Trier that same year. The contemporaneity of these books does not seem to be coincidental, especially because they were published at a moment when religious conflicts in and around Cologne seemed to be at a turning point. Cologne had been mired in a war set off by Gebhard Truchsess von Waldburg—archbishop of Cologne and one of three ecclesiastical electors of the empire—when he decided to convert to Lutheranism and marry a local noblewoman, Agnes von Mansfeld. For his rash and unexpected decision, Emperor Rudolph II deposed him and the pope excommunicated him. The conflict garnered international attention and provoked several forms of Catholic and Protestant intervention. The Catholic side more or less won, or managed to move the conflict elsewhere, in 1585.[52] Sander's books thus entered the public sphere at a moment of great sensitivity, when Catholic forces contended with threats from heretics inside and out, together with ongoing reforms within the Church. Papal nuncios in the region played particularly important roles as coordinators within the imperial politico-ecclesiastical mosaic. Among them, the recently appointed Cardinal Giovanni Bonomi, a man with whom Allen corresponded at the time, stands out as someone who could have encouraged English Catholic publications.[53] He or someone like him could not have missed the potential force of Sander's criticisms against failed Protestant efforts at theological cohesion during the Altenburg colloquy. *De schismate Anglicano* would have also seemed uniquely relevant, as it showed the horrors that ensued after a once good Christian prince gave way to his lusts and abandoned the Church.

While *De schismate Anglicano* might have worked in German territories, Allen and his colleagues would not have undermined their own goals for the sake of others'. They must have decided that independent of any external pressures, Sander's history met English Catholic polemical needs.

To get a better sense of the context in which Sander's editors promoted *De schismate Anglicano*, we should look to another book, perhaps by Persons, likely published in Cologne in 1585: *Crudelitatis Calvinianae exempla duo recentissima ex Anglia* (Two very recent examples of Calvinist cruelties).[54] The pamphlet is a bundle of short texts offering an update on Elizabethan atrocities. It contains the transcript of a recent anti-Catholic Elizabethan statute that criminalized the Catholic priesthood and its supporters. The editors surround the document with damning marginal annotations and a brief commentary linking it to similar efforts by ancient schismatics and tyrants. The second text tells of the earl of Northumberland's recent, dubious death. The regime called it suicide, but the author cried foul play by the regime itself. Finally, a short letter reveals an assortment of English activities detrimental to the international community: Francis Drake plagued Spanish waters, the regime cut deals with Dutch rebels, Elizabeth helped antimonarchical forces in France.

The book was clearly an assault on the Elizabethan regime, but its author also promoted fear. England had been a bastion of Catholicism that quickly went asunder after heretical infection. The results were horrific for the kingdom's spiritual health and the well-being of the commonwealth more generally. For example, Northumberland's murder—the murder of a great noble—exemplified Calvinistic disregard for hierarchy and served as a lesson for potentates in other kingdoms: heresy overturns proper social order. England was now run by inferiors who killed their superiors. Left unchecked, so went the domino theory, heresy would inevitably spread. The mechanisms were in place for that eventuality. Elsewhere in the pamphlet, readers saw evidence of how, by means of treachery and piracy, the English spread their filth.

As a long prefatory note makes clear, the book intended to rally Catholics on the Continent.[55] Flattery could not hurt; the author lingered on recent Catholic triumphs. If English kings and queens were complicit in heresy's rise, other lands, by God's grace, were spared such royal deficiencies. In France, the Valois had long been staunch defenders of the Church. Despite foibles—concessions ill-advisedly made to heretics—the author praised recent back-stiffening. He congratulated the French king, Henry III, for revoking an extant pacification edict that had ensured limited toleration for Calvinists. Henry had happily stayed true to his kingdom's faithful past. The book also cheered Philip II's incessant efforts against heretics, particularly in the Netherlands. Moreover, the faithful could not help but rejoice in Sixtus V's recent election. The pope was pious but warlike, and a visionary nun in Lisbon predicted that his reign would bring honor to the Church.

Although things were better, the author believed a prayer was still in order to instill the pope and Catholic princes with "keen and vigilant" spirits to defend God's vineyard. That such an exhortation was necessary suggests that the author knew good Christian behavior was not certain—far from it.

Such wariness is consonant with an implicit warning in *De schismate Anglicano*. In a brief preface, Sander explained how Christianity had first been taken to England by Joseph of Arimathea around the year 50 C.E. and how, about 130 years later, Eleutherius sent Fugatius and Damian to King Lucius to baptize him and his subjects. After a pagan relapse, Gregory the Great sent Augustine and Mellitus, among others, to convert pagans and baptize Ethelbert, king of Kent. Since that time England had remained faithful to Rome. Indeed, just before Henry, Christendom seemed on strong footing. The history's proper narrative begins with a description of tranquility across Europe at the start of the sixteenth century and, by contrast, schism among the dreaded "Mahometans." In England, Henry VII had overcome all challenges at home and proved himself a most prudent and strong king.[56] With a proper succession secured in Henry VIII and a good match for the young prince in Catherine of Aragon, things should have gone well. But Henry was given to luxury and libidinous excess. He quickly strayed from his place as a supporter of the Church—indeed, its defender.[57] If centuries-old success could easily crumble, more recent successes were even frailer.

Aside from a general sense of human debility, the recent past warned English Catholics against optimism. Inaction seemed ascendant against Elizabethan cruelties. After Pius V, who had excommunicated Elizabeth, subsequent popes swung between pious bellicosity and resignation. No one seemed sure how to deal with the English question, and according to Allen, no one seemed to understand the severity of the problem. A weak response to Allen's fundraising for English colleges on the Continent suggested diminished support. Gregory XIII's election (r. 1572–85) had not helped. Papal funding for English seminaries plummeted. Worse, excitement for

missionary efforts in England seemed muted, even among erstwhile supporters like the Jesuit general, Claudio Acquaviva.[58] Allen alternated between
stunned incomprehension and bitterness. In August 1584, he wrote to Jesuit
Alfonso Agazzari (rector of the English college in Rome) bemoaning the fact
that they who lived in "most tranquil peace" could not know how to act where
the Church was wracked by war. A year later, Allen complained about Rome's
ignorance again. Apart from the Society of Jesus, he wrote, "which is immediately engaged in . . . spiritual hunting," no one seemed to care, and worse,
there were "many who scorn such far-off matters."[59] He was at a loss: "From
so many books written about the persecution, the martyrs, the institution
of the colleges and the sending of priests . . . from so much bloodshed before the whole world, from so many and such cruel writings and public laws
published against our and your efforts, these things could have been very
well known by leaders of the Church and I do not see what can be added."
Allen wished he were in Rome before the recently chosen pope, Sixtus V, to
describe Catholic miseries under heretical rule.[60]

Such frustration had a long pedigree in English Catholic circles. Sometime
in the early 1570s, an anonymous English exile—perhaps Sander—attacked
Catholic princes for their failure to participate in plots against Elizabeth. After
describing the "stench emanating from her [Elizabeth's] legs," the critic prod-
ded Christian potentates who seemed more interested in appeasement than
helping Catholics forced into exile. Elizabeth harassed supposed Catholic
allies, and the afflicted responded by "honoring her and offering her gifts."
She paid German soldiers to fight for heretics in France, and yet Catholics
continued to send ambassadors and accept English counterparts. Worse still,
princes did not come through with their promises. Help to the Northern rebels had not been forthcoming, and exiled students in Flanders were not given
pledged subsidies. These slights had dire consequences: otherwise faithful
Catholics, seeing that allies on the Continent "cared little about them, or
more to the point did not care about them at all," negotiated with Elizabeth.
The disaffected Catholic exiles were mystified "that such great princes [were]
so fearful of such a heretical and excommunicated woman."[61]

More often than not, Philip felt the lash of critical tongues. From the
days of Henry VIII's break with Rome, a certain type of forward Catholic
came to believe that English affairs could only be resolved with Habsburg
help. Even then, however, some complained about their would-be savior's
inconstancy.[62] Years later, little had changed. After Elizabeth's rise, Philip
seemed unwilling to stand up to her. Some said that English Catholics were
so tired of the king's inaction that they were willing to "appeal to the French,

or even to the Turks rather than put up with these heretics [in England]."[63] In 1577, Sander insisted Philip was no pacifist, as some claimed, just frightened: he was "as fearful of war as a child of fire."[64] With typical boldness, Sander warned that should he fail to act, Philip might be punished as the Israelites were for having failed to destroy the Canaanites. The king would have to pay for English heresy if he did not "destroy them when he might do so to the great glory of God."[65]

The year 1585 must have seemed like a pivotal one, because if past behaviors repeated themselves, all recent Catholic gains would be for naught. No one intuited this more than English Catholics, who had seen what had happened at home and knew the dangers of heresy could not be brushed off. It should come as no surprise that in the aftermath of Spanish victories in Flanders, an English exile, Thomas Stapleton, raised a voice of caution. In October of that year, he preached on the fragility of recent gains, arguing that once heresy takes root, it is hard to cure. He called for resolve and vigor to avoid future dangers.[66] Although Stapleton spoke of heretical recidivism in the absence of true, profound reforms that would ensure a change of heart, the point is not unlike that which undergirded Allen's and Persons's thinking: failure to seize the moment and embrace God's cause would lead to further ruin.

Desperation also played a role in "radicalizing" elements of the English Catholic exile community. The years between 1581 and 1585 witnessed frequent legal experimentation as the Elizabethan regime tried to deal with the threat of Catholic treason, which had been exposed with the Campion/Persons mission of 1580–81. Catholics had long been fined for nonattendance at sanctioned church services, but the first half of the 1580s must have seemed like a time of fierce aggression that ultimately passed the threshold of barbarity. Legislation in 1585 dictated that all priests trained abroad had to leave England within forty days, ruled it treasonous for priests to enter England, and made it a felony to receive missionaries. As Leslie Ward has pointed out, this was the "first comprehensive treason policy aimed at a distinct and identifiable group within society" and, as such, firmly entwined persecution with religious vocation.[67] Allen and Persons saw it this way. Now that Elizabeth could not cling to her former pretense of self-defense or nonreligious aggression, there seemed less hope for her clemency, less reason to talk to her.

How, then, did *De schismate Anglicano* fulfill its two central functions: facilitating anti-Elizabethan efforts and convincing European powers that the time was now?

A Secret History

Sander's book would become a respected source for Catholics interested in the origins of English strife. Its editors, however, saw it as a first step. Throughout the 1590s, Persons and his associates wanted to write a substantial ecclesiastical history of England that would incorporate elements of Sander's original work while expanding the chronological scope and paying close, critical attention to primary sources.[68] Such a project had to wait past the sixteenth century. The parties interested in spreading *De schismate Anglicano* sacrificed erudition for an immediate polemical punch.

And yet Sander's history was no trifle. Sander and his editors purported adherence to the norms of early modern historical scholarship, including the use of primary sources to the extent that they were available.[69] The book's survival as a reference work on English affairs among Catholics is evidence that it conformed to contemporary scholarly ideals. Learned readers believed that *De schismate Anglicano* fulfilled the basic requisites of an ecclesiastical history.[70] As such, it was, within the context of confessional enmity, inevitably polemical. Sander and his editors looked to find, in Donald Kelley's useful phrase, an "ideologically useful version of the past."[71]

Sander and his editors did not care about generic purity. Their history could be linked at once to a Eusebian tradition of ecclesiastical history and a more penumbral Tacitean one of "secret histories" that divulged all the corruptions at court. In fact, English Catholics sometimes pushed *De schismate Anglicano*'s shadier elements. The English exile Richard Verstegan insisted that it bulged with "curiosity and novelty in personal affairs." The polemical force of libelous and scandalous books constituted part of English Catholic arsenals as far back as the *Treatise of Treasons* (1572) and through to the more recent publication of *Leicester's Commonwealth*. By embracing Tacitean narrative elements and analytical modes, exiles took part in a multifaceted intellectual craze.[72] Though the presumed benefits of Tacitus's own histories and those written in a similar style varied depending on the reader, the writer, and the moment, people like Sander and his successors believed that by divulging *arcana imperii*—secrets of state—they provided insight into the kinds of nefarious activities that had led to England's destruction and, by inference, the types of behaviors that should be avoided.

But Sander and his editors could not have been innocent of the genre's baser potential. Unveiling "dirty" secrets allowed them to smear the enemy. Another book printed in 1585, the *Flores calvinistici* by an anonymous English Catholic author, proves the nasty spirit of Sanderian polemics.[73] Framed as a response to Oxford theologian Laurence Humphrey's anti-Jesuit rants of the 1580s, the book locates the origins of English Calvinist evils in Leicester and Anne Boleyn.[74] The author draws directly from the slimiest parts of *Leicester's Commonwealth* and *De schismate Anglicano*—there is plenty of incest and murder—to show the iniquity at the heart of Protestantism and its violence against Catholics. The book attempts to tarnish the image of the Elizabethan regime and appeals to foreign powers for intervention. As the dedication to the duke of Parma suggests, the book was intended to raise the temperature of anti-Elizabethan hatred and to inspire a great warrior (under Philip's pay) to take on the English enemy.[75] The author took parts of Sander's book because he understood its libelous force, but *De schismate Anglicano* went on to accomplish much more than the *Flores* because it had the aura of scholarship and consequent legitimacy.

Bad Queen Bess

There is no more secret place than under the covers, and so it is no surprise that important parts of Sander's book take place there. If we take him at his word, *De schismate Anglicano* was primarily about the queen's illegitimacy, which was proven by the outcomes of her father's sexual habits.[76] This is certainly how some Protestant critics of the book read it, and this is the way we must as well, particularly if we consider that the bulk of its longest section—the part devoted to Henry VIII—discussed the issue in all its salacious detail.[77] This section will describe the contours of these delegitimizing efforts to show the book's strategy of attack and how it justified efforts to remove Elizabeth from the throne.

Henry had good qualities and, early on, seemed to fulfill his potential, but his negatives ultimately prevailed: dissolution, lust, vindictiveness. Prone to sin, his marriage to Catherine of Aragon was doomed. Sander and his editors argue that his divorce from her was based solely on his desire for Anne Boleyn.

However, Elizabeth's was no run-of-the-mill bastardy. Drawing from preexisting rumors, *De schismate Anglicano* has astonishing things to say about Anne's parentage. Contrary to popular belief, she could not be Thomas Boleyn's daughter; she was conceived and born during the two years her putative father spent tending to Henry VIII's interests in France. Understandably, upon his return to England, Thomas wanted revenge for his double crossing . . . until he discovered the king was the other man. Thomas swallowed his pride.[78] Years later, hearing rumors that Henry planned to marry Anne, he tried to impede the match, but the king brushed him off and laughed at the predicament. Henry thus knowingly married his own daughter; incest was at the root of England's false church and its false queen. As horrible as this was—indeed, because it was so horrible—God's hand was clearly all over it. God himself had allowed this spectacle to reveal that "they were the children of darkness, nor could they be brought into existence except by the works of darkness."[79]

Elizabeth did not sit on the throne by any natural right but because of human error. *De schismate Anglicano* pinned the blame on Parliament. By supporting her, that once venerable body acted against its own statutes. Henry may have willed Elizabeth his heir, but neither she nor the marriage that produced her was declared legitimate.[80] Extant parliamentary law, instituted during Mary Tudor's reign (1553), explicitly rejected Henry's marriage to Anne and, in turn, their progeny.[81] By suggesting this together with the incest narrative, Sander and his editors gave as sharp a rebuke of the Elizabethan regime as had been ventured in over a decade. In the past, even those who supported Mary Stuart's claims to the crown did not question the rights of the queen regnant or those of her potential offspring.[82]

Sander and his colleagues went beyond Elizabeth's ancestry. More was at stake than the legality of her reign: Christendom's safety stood in the balance. If parentage did not impede the queen's de facto rule, the pope could. Many Catholics harbored this opinion privately but rarely aired it publicly, because the recent past had shown that open pronouncements against the queen fell on deaf ears: Pius V's excommunication bull against Elizabeth—*Regnans in excelsis* (1570)—might rank as one of the great papal missteps of the age.[83] As Arnold Meyer has suggested, "Whenever in later ages men's minds were stirred up against the Roman Church . . . the remembrance of 1570 was enough to justify their implacable hatred."[84] From an Elizabethan perspective, by releasing Catholics from their allegiance to the queen, the papal decree proved that executions of traitorous Catholics were "just and necessary actions, only for the defense of herself [Elizabeth], her crown, and people, against open invaders." Papal and royal imperatives were fundamentally incompatible. Elizabeth had no choice but to fight against the bishop of Rome, who claimed "by his bulls or excommunications . . . to depose any sovereign princes, being lawfully invested in their crowns by succession in blood or by lawful election, and then to arm subjects against their natural lords to make wars."[85]

Even those who believed in the pope's right to meddle in secular affairs knew the bull posed practical inconveniences. Famously, prior to initiating the first Jesuit mission to England in 1580, Persons and Campion wanted to know how *Regnans* should affect their activities. Ten years after its promulgation, was it still in force? If so, should obedience be rendered unto the queen? Responses were ambiguous. The missionaries were told they (and Catholics generally) need not challenge royal authority. The bull had been drafted when success seemed possible, but since then, political contexts had changed. It should not be enforced "unless everything has been arranged that hope of victory is certain and ready, in which case the bull binds those who would be able to take any action."[86] Gregory XIII echoed this sentiment in the faculties conceded unto the missionaries. The bull could be sidestepped—*rebus sic stantibus* (things being as they are)—until it could be enforced. This hesitance to embrace *Regnans* spilled onto the printed page.[87] Just a year before *De schismate Anglicano*, Allen tried to divorce the bull from "mainstream" English Catholicism. He insisted papal deposition powers were ignored within Continental seminaries because it was "incident to matters of state . . . and consequently might be interpreted by the suspicious to be meant to her [Elizabeth] whose case men liked least to deal in."[88]

Sander's editors did not hide their papalism. *De schismate Anglicano* recalled the pontificate of Pius V, another Phineas who diligently "pursued heretics, Turks, and other unbelievers with a zeal wholly beseeming the sovereign pontiff." The same spirit that led him to form a Holy League against the Turks led the pope to excommunicate and depose Elizabeth. In a true coup de grâce, the editors printed the full text of *Regnans*. The reader could revisit Pius's effort to "root up and destroy, to scatter and to waste, to plant and to build" in order to keep the faithful "in the unity of the spirit" (Jer. 1:10). The bull attacked Elizabeth for "monstrously" usurping the Church's authority and forcing all subjects to take an oath "against church liberty." Worse, she allowed heretical doctrines to spread through pulpit and print. *Regnans* concluded that "all who adhere to her . . . are cut off from the unity of the Body of Christ." Pius thundered, "We declare that nobles, subjects and peoples are free from any oath to her, and we interdict obedience to her motions, mandates and laws."[89] *De schismate Anglicano* held within its pages a document that had been dormant for over a decade and, in its new life, reminded readers that the queen was no queen at all.

Elizabeth's behavior confirmed the probity of excommunication and the truth of her illegitimacy. By assuming a woman could have religious power, Elizabeth turned all laws, human and divine, on their heads: "It has come to pass that . . . the highest place in government of the church is filled by one who not only is not in possession of it—this applies to Henry and Edward also—but by one who never can possess it."[90] Sander and his editors claimed, using the words of Church fathers and the apostles, "It never can come to pass that Christ should govern God, or any man govern Christ, so also it can never be that a woman may govern either man or the Church of Christ."[91] The misogynistic language was unrelenting. Evoking Eve, Sander assured readers that women were Satan's favored tools for teaching "man how to break the laws of God," leading to the destruction of the human race.[92] Sander's editors went further than their manuscript source, adding, "Experience shows that women, eager in pursuit of anything, especially if that thing be wrong, are more eager and more dangerous than men in that pursuit, and that men always are most easily and most fatally ensnared by them."[93] Elizabeth's usurpation of ecclesiastical authority surpassed the malevolence of history's most evil women: Jezebel, Herodias, and Selene paled in comparison.

De schismate Anglicano lacked traditional forms of condescension. Unlike polemics produced between the 1570s and mid-'80s, Sander and his editors did not suggest that the queen could help solve English problems if only she rid herself of evil counselors. The queen knew what she was doing. From the start, she had treated ecclesiastical matters as political tools. Elizabeth decided, upon the advice of certain counselors (particularly Cecil), to feign loyalty to the Catholic Church, but while her advisors played a key role in ensuring that the queen embraced heresy, she ushered it in with purposeful dissembling.[94] She took an oath to defend Catholicism and was duly anointed according to ancient customs even if she disliked them: she pointedly complained about the stench of the chrism.[95] By submitting to a traditional coronation, she nodded toward Catholics, but by showing her displeasure, she nodded at heretics, thereby coaxing both.

In time, she would not be so coy, and subsequent religious changes occurred at her will. She flattered and bribed lower and (especially) upper houses of Parliament to pass her new religious settlement.[96] Ecclesiastical and theological matters evolved at her whim: "She suspends her bishops when she pleases, she grants a license to preach, either to those who are ordained according to her rite or to simple laymen, and in the same way at her pleasure reduces whom she will to silence. To show her authority of these things she occasionally, from her throne, addresses her preacher, and interrupts him in the presence of a large congregation, in some such way as this: 'Mr. Doctor, you are wandering from the text, and talking nonsense, return to your subject.'"[97] These are not the words of a foolish gender-impaired victim. Sander and his editors showed that the queen ruled forcefully, that she went out of her way to manipulate her ecclesiastical servants.

Elizabeth's church was an intricately woven web of secular concerns and spiritual lies. Only pragmatism led Elizabeth to maintain aspects of Catholic ceremonial. The queen wanted to preserve the veneer of Catholic tradition to assert her authority. She wanted to ensure the "glory and splendor" of the new church and, more importantly, hoped to convince Catholics that the English church was not unorthodox: she held out the carrot of a possible return to the Church. Moreover, the queen knew that Protestant ministers would destroy "all order, good manners, policy, and civilization itself—yea and even their own religion—by their savage rudeness, if civil power did not put some check on them."[98] The queen created a religious mixture to keep both heretics and Catholics at bay. Like her father, she based none of her decisions on faith, but on power. In line with this strategy, Elizabeth allowed known Catholic clerics to stay in their parishes, preferring "at first, the more easily to deceive the people, the services of true priests to those of the false."[99]

Elizabeth posed a danger both to her realm and to Christendom as a whole. Heresy was contagious, and with the queen to incubate it, dangers intensified. She knew that promoting Protestantism would trouble many in England and across Europe. To prevent any backlash, she chose to disturb her neighbors so that "all the Catholic sovereigns being fully occupied with their own affairs might have no time to attend to those of others."[100] In Scotland, she facilitated rebellion against Mary; in France, she joined Huguenots against the monarchy; and in the Netherlands, she contrived against the king of Spain. This was all done "in order that through the misfortune of other sovereigns and other countries, they might themselves live in peace at home, and by the scattering far and wide of the poison of their heretical corruption secure themselves a longer continuance in their sect."[101]

By discussing this dynamic, Sander and his editors attacked Elizabeth to rally Catholic troops abroad. Emphasizing the threat posed to French and Spanish interests, *De schismate Anglicano* publicized what had long been key elements in their appeals to potential allies, especially Philip II, various French monarchs, and the Guise in France. But advocacy for anti-Elizabethan action required moving beyond the description of a problem. Authors and editors wanted to justify the queen's removal. As seen thus far, this was done by reminding readers of past iniquities, duplicity, and the threat Elizabeth posed to Christendom. All of this only reinforced, or helped reveal, an illegitimacy rooted in a nefarious birth. And yet Sander's history was more than a hatchet job. It insisted that Elizabeth's behavior—politic, Machiavellian, and self-serving—was not unique and that England's demise resulted from prevalent attitudes and habits reaching back to Henry's reign.

False Prudence

If the myriad theatrical productions inspired by Sander's book throughout the late sixteenth and seventeenth centuries are any indication, Sander's take on old king Hal sparked the imagination more than that of Elizabeth's reign.[102] Henry's fall was titillating because of its contemporary resonances. His reign was a cautionary tale worth heeding, especially among well-meaning Catholics. To ignore it would ensure future demise.[103]

Henry VIII became paradigmatic of lost potential and the dangers of heretical monarchs. His divorce from Catherine and marriage to Anne highlighted the full extent of his lust and tyranny. Henry had been willing to stay within the Church and under the pope's spiritual tutelage so long as he could get rid of his wife. When Rome failed to bend, the king decided to break away and execute his ecclesiastical takeover. Like Julian the Apostate, he went against Scriptures and the learned counsel of Church fathers. He was so far gone that he was deemed unworthy by other hardened heretical evildoers. Sander and his editors emphasized that Henry's church was a wholly new creation—he had succumbed not to old or new heresies but to his own strange desires.[104]

And yet despite errors, Henry never lost all sight of the true faith. He, for example, continued to defend the Eucharist, holding it "in the highest honor."[105] When once told that he might take Communion sitting down because of illness, the king boomed, "If I could throw myself down, not only on the ground, but under the ground, I should not then think that I gave honor enough to the most holy sacrament."[106] He even considered returning to the Church late in life, but worldly affairs intruded: the wealth amassed by destroying monasteries scarcely seemed worth sacrificing to the demands of his conscience. The king's story was that much more troubling because he had a sense of right and wrong but would not let moral imperatives overwhelm the allures of worldliness.

Henry would eventually have to pay. God gave the king up "to the service of his passions," and only in the end, as he died a larded death, did he realize the severity of what he had done.[107] When his final moments came, Sander and his editors say he called for a goblet of wine and screamed, "All is lost!"[108] Henry's legacy was forever tainted. His children would erect no monument to his memory, a stinging blow in an age of heightened historical consciousness preoccupied with long-lasting glory. Sander surmised that Henry's spiral into oblivion occurred by the judgment of God, describing the parallelism of how "a man who scattered to the winds the ashes of so many saints, and who plundered the shrines of so many martyrs, should lie himself unhonoured in his grave."[109]

Had Henry's punishment been a matter of one lost soul, no scathing history would have been necessary. Sander wrote his book because England went on to suffer for the king's errors. If the king stole, his heretical successors stole more. If the king killed, his heretical successors killed more. If vestiges of the true faith remained during Henry's reign, they were being obliterated under subsequent Protestant rule. England was sinking into a perverse Calvinistic state church under Edward and his beastly sister.

English schism resulted from a culture of duplicity, and nothing proved this better than the double-dealing that led to Henry's divorce. First, the king tried to present the issue publicly by means of a foreign ambassador. Henry had Cardinal Wolsey approach the bishop of Tarbes, who was then in England representing Francis I's interests. Wolsey was instructed to tell him that questions had emerged about the king's marriage to Catherine. Were the marriage dissolved, the king might marry Francis's sister. The cardinal encouraged the bishop to raise the question publicly because "an Englishman should not be the first to touch it or bring it forward."[110] The bishop did as bidden. Henry feigned displeasure and astonishment, but as it "touched his honor and his eternal salvation, he would take time to think of it."[111] At the same time, news came that Charles V had sacked Rome, which provided an opportunity to promote the divorce further and tighten relations with France. Wolsey encouraged the king to help the pope, thereby establishing credit as Defender of the Faith. By doing so, the king would also "lay him [the pope] under lasting obligation, would find him not only a favorable judge in the matter of the divorce, but also his earnest defender."[112] Moreover, he would secure bonds with Francis I, whose children were being held hostage by Charles V. The king played along. He sent Wolsey to France to provide money against Charles and to discuss a potential marriage between the two crowns. Henry soon dropped the French marriage initiative, having already fixed his sights on Anne, leaving a confused Wolsey in the lurch. Henry was a grand manipulator; once he decided on his future wife, he became a puppeteer among so many marionettes. Secret deals, dissimulations, and a series of political decisions motivated merely by Henry's desires revealed a policy of convenience and lies that served the king alone.

Henry represented a common way of proceeding. He was not the only one who embraced a self-serving logic, nor was he the only one to suffer punishment for it. *De schismate Anglicano* is largely a story about inadequate counsel and the corruptions at court. Royal errors were enhanced by servants who placed their personal needs over those of the common good and God. This is true of Anne Boleyn, who led Henry into devilish fires, but is perhaps most exemplified by Wolsey, who, according to Sander, had once wielded complete control at court and had his eyes on the Church as well: he wanted to be pope.[113] Surprisingly, not Henry but Charles V took advantage of the situation. The emperor "began to flatter the man," thereby making him "minister to his own designs." He dangled the papal tiara before the cardinal's eyes in hopes of cementing an Anglo-Spanish alliance, but it was all a ruse. Charles eventually promoted the election of Adrian VI. Wolsey hid his disappointment momentarily but grew impatient and eventually shifted his alliance to Charles's enemies: the French. Worse, noticing Henry's estrangement from Catherine, he supported the divorce because it "would be advantageous to himself, not unpleasing to the King, hateful to Catherine, and most disagreeable to the emperor."[114] The results were dire, and Henry sank further. Wolsey, in turn, received nothing for all his troubles. After being arrested for high treason (amid a courtly plot against him), he lamented, "Oh that I had been guiltless of treason against His Divine majesty! Now indeed, while intent on serving only the king, I have offended God and have not pleased the king."[115]

As Wolsey's story shows, forces outside England were complicit in England's decline. Charles—known then and now as a defender of Catholicism—tried to use Wolsey for his own ends, thus unwittingly facilitating the latter's French policy and partial (if feigned) embrace of Anne Boleyn. Rome also bore some of the weight of England's heretical origins. Even the pope had been, on the advice of self-serving clerics, slow to react. While some noted the corrosive effects of leniency, others, "fashioning ecclesiastical affairs for political ends, and complaining loudly of the heresies that had lately grown up in Germany, and the tepidity of other princes in defense of the faith, were of the opinion that Henry, most zealous defender of the faith, should be gently dealt with." They insinuated that a compromise could be reached, especially since, according to rumors, Catherine might contemplate monastic seclusion. Those who argued thus also wanted to accommodate the king's request for legatine adjudication of the divorce under the assumption that royal resolve might be softened with time.[116] Such arguments initially swayed the pope, in part because he believed false claims about Catherine's monastic inclinations but also because he wanted to please the king.[117] Sander's history, aside from revealing Henry's own evil behavior, evoked a whole political culture—a world of half measures and compromises—that caused England's fall. Blame could just as easily be pinned on Catholics as it could on heretics.

A critique of Catholics was an important component of Sander's narrative beyond the Henrician period. Despite the lessons of long and fruitless negotiations between Henry and the pope over the divorce, Rome still favored diplomacy with Elizabeth. Paul IV tried to mend relations with the queen and instructed his nuncio that "if on account of her doubtful birth she was afraid that her title to the throne might be questioned, the matter could be easily settled, for the Apostolic See is indulgent."[118] The queen flatly refused papal overtures. Insistent, however, the pope sent yet another nuncio, this time asking her to send representatives to the Council of Trent. The queen's bishops were promised protection of body and freedom of speech. She curtly refused. Emperor Ferdinand, a Catholic stalwart, also failed to learn from the past and tried to placate the queen by offering his son in marriage. To avoid jeopardizing these efforts, he prevented the fathers at Trent from making open declarations against Elizabeth. If the proposed union were to come through, he insisted, England might yet see better days. But of course, the queen only led her suitor on and grew "day by day more obstinate and to the Catholics more cruel."[119]

Sander and his editors also suggested that Continental powers had left English Catholics unsupported at critical moments. They had hoped a Christian prince would rescue them but waited in vain for the emperor or anyone else. When the pope finally excommunicated the queen and released Catholic subjects from obedience, his pronouncements fell flat. Though there were many reasons for this, uncertainty about where Continental princes stood undoubtedly diminished enthusiasm among Catholics. They were aware that habitual commerce with England continued, which suggested there would be little support for homegrown revolt. *De schismate Anglicano* catalogued a series of failed opportunities and misguided diplomatic stratagems often motivated by financial and political incentives, beholden to a logic divergent from truth and justice.[120]

These were key lessons for the intended Continental audience of 1585 that stood, as described above, at a hinge moment in its battle against heresy: somewhere between militancy and stupor, between potential victory and continued malaise. The moment required renewed efforts, guided by the spirit of Pius V's excommunication and without the hesitancy and failures of a political class that had left English Catholics, who Sander insisted made up most of the population, unsupported.[121]

Conclusion

In 1585, Sander's editors wrote defiantly. Toward the end, they emphasized the gift of fortitude given by God and reasserted their apostolic mission, as opposed to the political one imputed by the Elizabethan regime. Though there was little hope for heretics, telling the enemy about recent events was still worthwhile: at least they had tried to bring them to their senses. More importantly, Sander's editors wanted to inspire constancy among the faithful. In time, God would punish, as he always did, those who usurped his authority. Though the end of the story was known—heresy would ultimately lose—the exact path toward salvation remained hidden. And so the book closed with a promise: so long as Elizabethan monstrosities continued, English Catholics would not keep quiet.[122]

By airing these matters publicly, Sander's editors were signaling not only animosity toward their Protestant oppressors but also a new kind of engagement with Catholic allies. As discussed earlier, Allen and Persons had to be careful. While they might have privately fumed about the slothful responses to their pleas by Philip II and others, they tempered *public* utterances depending on prevailing circumstances. By publishing Sander's history, they not only rejected previous efforts to avoid overt denouncements of the Elizabethan regime but also made dissatisfaction with Catholic failures known far and wide.

Sander's history and its implications would interest a broad reading audience during religious discord and amid perceived threats of heresy. Allen and Persons were doubtless counting on a positive response among established English Catholic supporters across Europe, from Cologne to Rome, Madrid to Rouen, Louvain to Cracow. But for the book to succeed, it would also need to move beyond networks already established by English Catholics. Supportive gestures by some communities in Europe and kind words by individual rulers had led to little action against the Elizabethan regime. Private memorandums, backroom meetings, and occasional sermons had not sufficed. Allen, Persons, and their colleagues considered the printed book a medium of choice to publicize recent English history and thereby strengthen the feelings of many in Europe against the Elizabethan regime. They believed a more thorough understanding of English heretical rule would create a general opinion that action was necessary.

2

CALLING THE ARMADA

Soon after its first printing, *De schismate Anglicano* required revision. Despite William Allen's and Robert Persons's lingering concerns, by the summer of 1585, they had pursued hints that Spain would finally act. Allen wrote a letter to Alessandro Farnese, duke of Parma, supporting any future efforts against England. The letter was linked to news that Hugh Owen (another Catholic exile) had just been sent by Philip II to help the duke with English affairs.[1] Allen and Persons relished the good news coming from Antwerp, where Parma had savagely starved the citizens and notched an important victory against Protestant rebels in August. The two men may have been caught under the spell of this new Alexander, who some contemporaries fawningly described as far better than that of antiquity: he struck like thunder, not against pagans, but heretics.[2] The brilliance of one warrior aside, some English Catholics found hope in the broader geopolitical shifts that his victory enabled. Rattled by events across the Channel, on August 20, Elizabeth signed the Treaty of Nonsuch, by which she allied with Dutch rebels against Spain. The cold Anglo-Spanish war eventually became hot.[3] Word of an Anglo-Dutch union must have reached Allen and Persons by September when they set off on a previously planned trip to Rome. During their travels from France to Italy, they must have discussed Philip II's next moves. The king would surely have to fight back. Once in Rome, their hopes soared: by October, gossip in and around the curia probably spread that Philip had decided to go to war. Allen and Persons knew that in this new context of imminent conflict, *De schismate Anglicano* could play an important role, but they also thought that the new situation required an augmented, tailored version of English history to meet the demands of the moment. Previous efforts to elicit anti-Elizabethan action had tried to coax a range of Catholic powers, sometimes in tandem, but now Philip had become a prime target.[4] The resulting text sharpened key arguments in the 1585 edition and aligned more closely with Spanish interests.[5]

Polemicists for the King

Although the 1586 edition would be the one everyone read, the editors had one particular reader in mind: Philip II. Allen and Persons, cognizant of Philip's past indecisiveness, insisted Spanish efforts move at a quicker pace. In May 1586, Persons sent a message to the Spanish court through a priest, Miguel Hernández, who was instructed to convey "all that we feel and desire for the service of God and His Majesty and for the salvation of so many souls that depend on our negotiations." This messenger should insist that past dithering had caused serious problems for English Catholics and left them subject to ongoing danger. He should underscore, Persons wrote, that "we are truly, completely lost unless His Majesty helps us in some way." Amid this groveling, Hernández was to deliver a copy of the freshly printed Roman *De schismate Anglicano*. In it "can be seen," Persons told Philip's secretary Juan de Idiáquez, "what has been said in defense of His Majesty's interests." The mix of epistolary pleading, Hernández's viva voce report, and Nicholas Sander's history itself would undoubtedly persuade Philip: the messenger must tell the king to "not let those men be entirely lost to you, who are serving you so faithfully."[6]

The most important addition to the 1586 edition—the defense of Spanish interests that Persons pitched to Idiáquez—came at the end, in a response to William Cecil's broadly disseminated pamphlet justifying Elizabethan pro-Dutch efforts: *A Declaration of the Causes Moving England to Give Aid to the Defense of the People Afflicted and Oppressed in the Low Countries* (1585).[7] Cecil argued that England felt forced to support Dutch rebellion both because of Spain's missteps and because of ancient, "natural" diplomatic and trade alliances.[8] The king's advisors—the pamphlet did not attack Philip directly—had blatantly abused their power and caused horrific bloodshed. They convinced him to "appoint Spaniards, foreigners and strangers of strange blood, men

more exercised in wars than in peaceable government, & some of them notably delighted in blood."[9] While the king lived in the Netherlands, he relied on
the help of locals, but when he left, the duke of Alba and others established
tyrannical rule shrouded under a false veil of religion. At first, Spain justified
violence "for the maintenance of the Romish religion, yet they spared not to
deprive very many Catholics and ecclesiastical persons of their franchises
and privileges."[10] Despite these trespasses, England had used peaceful means
to help their oppressed neighbors. They first offered frank advice to the
king. When this failed, they offered rebels money. Now Elizabeth had to use
force, a decision required by Spanish threats. Despite England's many warm
overtures, Spanish hostility increased. In recent years, men like Bernardino
de Mendoza, the king's ambassador, had plotted rebellion against the queen,
and worse, they had fomented actual rebellion in Ireland. Were the Spanish
to take control of neighboring territories, then considering the "precedent
arguments of many troublesome attempts against [their] realm," England
would be open to invasion.[11]

Allen and Persons wanted to debunk claims of Elizabethan pacifism.
They argued that the queen only feigned friendship with various monarchs
and was especially bent on harassing Philip, whom she "hated and feared
more than the others."[12] Swelling international ill will against Spain simply
provided an opening for Elizabeth to drop all pretenses. She attacked the king
in Portugal, the Indies, and elsewhere. In Flanders, she employed the help
of homegrown rebels and the duke of Anjou (the king of France's brother),
who had recently allied with William of Orange, leader of the Dutch Revolt.
To pay for intervention across the Channel, Elizabeth imposed forced tributes on all English subjects, especially Catholics, to whom the queen promised freedom of conscience and impunity. With false hope in heart, some of
them quickly complied, only to face betrayal. Dutch rebels would also pay for
their errors. Divine providence ensured punishment in Leicesterian form:
Elizabeth chose the same earl of Leicester who had already ruined his own
country to lead the Dutch expedition. He would soon tyrannize and pillage
across the Channel, and his terror would make purported Spanish oppression seem absurd.[13]

Allen and Persons rejected the queen's logic for intervention. They
characterized Elizabeth's concern for Dutch liberties (against their *legitimate*
ruler) as strange, since she was simultaneously stripping English Catholics
of their ancient rights of free worship and placing them under Egyptian ser-
vitude. Criticizing Philip for violating ancient liberties when he only tried
to punish long-condemned religious sects seemed ludicrous. Although

Elizabeth (supposedly) wanted to revive commerce in and provide general stability to the Netherlands, her intervention only enlivened a war that had been coming to an end. While she claimed to crusade against Spanish cruelty, Philip and the duke of Parma showed nothing but clemency over the vanquished. They had, for example, lessened taxes in many cities and had ensured the temperance of successful troops otherwise prone to pillaging.[14]

Sander's editors employed the simple rhetorical strategy of inverting Cecil's arguments. While Elizabeth's affronts never ceased, the king nevertheless responded with "mildness and benefits." The queen was thoroughly unfamiliar with the king's brand of clemency, as shown by her betrayal of faithful allies and mistreatment of her own subjects. Even though Catholic rebellion had been easily quashed in England and Ireland, the queen harshly and unflinchingly punished rebels. Abroad, while the king's ambassadors stood accused of inciting war in other kingdoms, it was in fact English representatives who were instigating it—not only in the Netherlands but also in Scotland and France.[15] In light of these realities, prudent readers would see through Cecil's feeble defense of Elizabethan atrocities and would judge that specious justifications could not "excuse her conduct, but revealed it, did not defend, but seemed to add injury to injury."[16]

Allen and Persons argued that Cecil's book was a desperate ploy to defend Elizabeth from widespread criticisms.[17] They suggested that some of her counselors voiced concerns about breaking an ancient alliance with Spain and that many more abroad censured the queen's temerity for attacking a king who, while given to patience, always emerged victorious once he decided to fight. Not only did Cecil rationalize a political strategy, but by contradicting foes in Elizabeth's court, his book tried to keep that strategy afloat. By arguing this, Allen and Persons seem to confirm a line of modern scholarship that has shown the ways that print was used by the queen's counselors to solidify their position at critical moments of policy disagreement.[18]

For our purposes, this interpretation of Elizabethan propaganda is interesting because it reflects what Allen and Persons were themselves doing. Their defense of Philip II took place at a hinge moment in Spanish foreign policy, during which the outcome was not certain. *De schismate Anglicano* was a tool to ensure that efforts against the Elizabethan regime persisted.

By rejecting the *Declaration*, Sander's editors provided a firm justification for Spanish self-defense against illicit Elizabethan assaults while removing themselves (and English exiles generally) from the narrative of imminent war. Whereas in the 1585 *De schismate Anglicano*, the fight against Elizabeth was undertaken (verbally at least) by the author(s) against the queen and her regime, in 1586, Spain shared the burden. Selling the Catholic king's case to a European audience made the looming battle an affair between two warring kingdoms trying to settle disputes, not (only) between exiles and their monarch. Moreover, by framing the battle between Philip and Elizabeth, the editors publicly backed Spain into a corner. The justice of their cause required decisive action, something that in 1586 seemed likely but as ever uncertain with Philip at the helm. The explicit defense of Spanish interests reinforced (or perhaps established) an alliance or at least a motivational commonality between English exiles and Philip.

There is also an element of seduction in Allen and Persons's efforts, wherein Spanish Elizabethans displayed their polemical mettle to the crown and showed off their value as propagandists for the king—a role that they would take on more and more during the last decade of Philip's reign.

Still, Sander's book was not simply Spanish propaganda, even if it was framed by Spanish interests. A stronger bond with Spain did not lessen the need to appeal to the sensibilities of Catholics in general. The authors promoted anti-Elizabethan sentiments in other political spheres by, for example, revealing how Elizabeth manipulated political figures in France and elsewhere. Without losing sight of the specific and purposeful Spanish resonances throughout the text, the following pages discuss these key "universal" messages in Sander's history that were meant to stiffen Catholic resolve.

On Saints and Sinners

Sander's editors once again focused on Henry VIII's reign, this time describing it in darker hues. While echoes of the king's virtue remained, the Roman version downplayed these by insisting his actions were inexcusable. The editors admitted the king's late efforts to atone for possible errors but determined that such efforts were thwarted by his immoral core.

Allen and Persons also rejected what in 1585 could be construed as the king's laudable qualities. If he seemed to lessen the rigor of reform through ecclesiastical directives (known as the Six Articles), the fact that sacramental matters were taken up by secular authorities confirmed the king's evil intent. The editors reminded readers that "human industry is vain, where there is no divine protection."[19] While the 1585 *De schismate Anglicano* mentioned the king's continued veneration of the Eucharist, subsequent editors would insist that his acceptance was predicated on the destruction of the Mass and sacred laws: Henry would allow the sacrament—but only in a church where the king's name replaced the pope's and where prayers for the pontiff were prohibited. If he still believed penitence a necessary precondition for the Eucharist, he nevertheless denied that Christ instituted the sacrament and eliminated the notion of satisfaction.[20]

These and other editorial emphases offer a damning portrait of a heretical regime that could not be trusted in the past nor, by implication, the present. But more than this, the book's image of the king clarifies the impossibility of being a "sort of" bad king or a "less bad" schismatic. A heretic is a heretic is a heretic. Half measures were tantamount to inaction, and kings would be wise to steer clear of any behaviors that would grease that slippery slope toward damnation. The seeds of heresy planted by Henry could not be accepted. Christian warriors—Philip—had to go all in against any heretical behavior.

If Henry was a villain, *De schismate Anglicano* also had its heroes, some of whom were puffed up specifically to inflate Spanish egos. Spanish monarchs received special attention as perennial defenders of the faith. Whereas the 1585 *De schismate Anglicano* seemed to take some swipes at Charles V for failing to respond to the English plight, such references were more muted in the 1586 edition.[21] Barely a word was uttered against Philip's father; instead, the editors were careful to evoke many of the emperor's victories against Muslims and heretics. Catherine of Aragon also received effusive praise. She had previously been noted for her sanctity, but the inclusion of (spurious) letters exchanged with her confessor, John Forest, increased her saintly aura. In these she revealed a longing for martyrdom and a belief that earthly punishment should be rewarded by eternal salvation;[22] she exemplified Spain's deeply rooted Catholicism. From another point of view, of course, both Charles and Catherine may have stood less for what the Spanish intrinsically were and more for what they could be.

Apart from nods at Spanish goodness, Persons and Allen said much more about English suffering. As Anne Dillon has suggested, this was partly because men like Persons "understood the book-buying market on the continent."[23] Through key additions, including secular priest John Hart's description of imprisonment in the Tower of London (1580–86), the editors sated a Catholic audience hungry for heroic saintly acts. But Persons and his colleagues also worked to mold reader perceptions and sympathies. Martyrologies had been used for multiple interrelated purposes—to inspire, to scare, to prod—and no doubt these intentions remained. Within the presumed context of England's reconversion to Catholicism, however, it is worth noting certain unexpected emphases that were placed on recent spiritual warriors and their significance.

Allen and (especially) Persons wanted to link recent heroics to the Jesuit mission. In recounting the execution of Richard Whiting, abbot of Glastonbury during Henry's reign, the editors noted the coincidence of this bloody event and the foundation of the Society of Jesus as a purifying force among floundering monastic institutions.[24] Not surprisingly, some of the most emotive additions to the Elizabethan narrative involved Jesuit suffering, especially the description of Edmund Campion's demise: Campion fulfilled a providential plan not just for himself but for the society to which he belonged, a society that would continue to be on the frontlines against Elizabeth. Granted, this is plain cheerleading, but it also forecasts the important role of Jesuits in the mission ahead: namely, the Armada campaign.

Amid the predictably hagiographical, there are also unpredictable nuances. Since the early days of anti-Henry polemics, the deaths of Thomas More and John Fisher offered key evidence that the king had followed a devilish path.[25] The 1585 version of Sander's history followed suit but chose to emphasize More's story; however, in 1586, Fisher regained some lost prominence. In one of the book's most fawning moments, editors give readers an ample list of the bishop's virtues: there was never a "more learned, saintlier, more vigilant pastor" than him.[26] Under his watch, two new colleges were built at Cambridge (where he eventually became chancellor), and he established new lectures on theology there and at Oxford. He attracted prominent scholars from the Continent, and by his labors, many in England had reached a high level of theological achievement. Moreover, "in his writings, as in his preaching," he defended the Church against Protestant attacks. Fisher fulfilled his episcopal duties to near perfection. He visited prisons and hospitals, and every Friday, he would make house calls to the sick, offering counsel, consolation, and last rites. He followed an honest, godly life, devoid of riches or overindulgences. Henry could not understand him. The king, thinking he would be able to make money from the bishop's demise, had his henchmen search Fisher's quarters for valuables. All they found were objects of self-mortification and penance: a hair shirt and a whip.[27]

Reginald Pole also exemplified a righteous way of living. If anyone had reason to abet Henry, it was he who had claims to royal lineage and had developed strong bonds with the king. Henry tried to lure him, but the soon-to-be cardinal and future almost-pope would not give in. The two finally reached the point of irreversible hatred over a book: Henry hoped Pole would defend his claims to spiritual governance, but instead of supporting the king, Pole wrote *De unitate ecclesiastica* (On ecclesiastical unity), in which he attacked secular claims to ecclesiastical rule. More than this, Pole showed his mettle when he returned triumphant to England as papal legate and helped achieve the momentary revival of the true Church there. During Mary's reign, he worked hard to restore Cambridge and Oxford to its ancient laws, censure heretics, and promote Catholic professors. He brought to England such foreign talents as the Spanish Dominican Pedro de Soto and, perhaps most importantly, promoted curricular reforms reestablishing scholasticism.[28]

Despite the positive emphasis on Fisher and Pole, the book's depiction complicated what could have been pure adulation. Both men faced serious trials, and both nearly failed. Under constant pressure from Henry, Fisher momentarily recognized the king's pretended ecclesiastical authority and, worse, convinced others to do so. He thought it best to compromise until Henry could be set straight. Meanwhile, the bishop quieted his conscience by swearing allegiance to the king only in those things allowed according to God's word. Such excuses did not diminish his error. To his credit, however, Fisher soon recognized this and expressed deep remorse for not having met his duties as a good pastor. Pole also struggled. Fearing the repercussions his family might face were he to reject the king's desires, he almost gave in to them: falling victim to "human prudence," he planned to meet Henry to compromise on the divorce. When in the king's chamber, however, his tongue was miraculously tied. Once he regained his powers of speech, he, by the grace of God, spoke his mind.[29]

Fisher and Pole were not made of stone, and their frailties were as much a part of their stories as their heroism. Their momentary debilities showed the real struggles that English Catholics had to face—struggles that Allen and Persons knew well, since both were in England during Elizabeth's regime and had momentarily acquiesced to the queen's demands. Past mistakes, of course, did not preclude reform. In his unpublished life of Campion, Persons made the same point: he did not omit the martyr's attachments to worldly things, the "hopes for speedy and great preferments," but despite momentary Protestant overtures, Campion's turn toward the right path ensured that his sin "was now fully forgiven, so that he should trouble himself no more with the memory of it."[30] Sander's editors did not want to excuse past mistakes but sought to highlight the fortitude Fisher and More eventually showed and the spiritual benefits that accompanied their sacrifices. Such turmoil conformed to generic norms that emphasized victory over worldly temptations as a mark of sanctity. But there was a more general lesson as well. The great tension between man's earthly concerns and his Christian duties is normalized here to emphasize the possibility of repentance and the gifts attained by good works. The editors called for spiritual resolution and spine-stiffening that should mark the good Christian life.

Valiant men stood in contrast to the many other Catholics who, as Sander's previous editors also recognized, were part of the problem. In a revealing episode added in 1586, Allen and Persons contemplated the actions of several Catholic bishops during Edward's reign. While various important clerics—Stephen Gardiner, Cuthbert Mayne, and Nicholas Heath—resisted heretical impositions by the king's protector, the duke of Somerset and his clique, they were still weakened by having ascended during the initial throes of schism and because they had been instituted by Henry, not the pope. Fearing the loss of their bishoprics and contingent honors, they indulged the boy-king and his advisors, allowing novelties that did not appear to contain "open heresy." To their credit, they did not give in on other matters impinging more directly on true faith. Because they would not preach the government's line fully, initial attempts at accommodation came to nothing. These priests faced rigorous punishment by Edward's regime and, later, by Elizabeth's.[31] Though their suffering revealed heretical cruelty, there was another lesson to be learned. God willed such miseries because of Catholics' (regrettably) acquiescent instincts.

The theme is further explored during Mary's reign. Allen and Persons, unlike Sander and his 1585 editors, ruminated on this period of hope and disappointment, its virtues and its failures. They dutifully replicated the image of a saintly Mary in the 1585 edition: how she stayed true to her faith, even amid various efforts to make her stray. Although Somerset had duped most people at court, Mary would not budge. She would not close the oratory in her quarters or celebrate a Calvinist service.[32] Fervent adherence to the Catholic Church, however, should not be mistaken for fanaticism. Far from the ogre of the Elizabethan imagination (as perpetuated by John Foxe's *Book of Martyrs*), Mary was clement and often shuddered at the idea of executing confessional enemies, especially those who had been part of the Edwardian hierarchy. Even bishops made under schismatic regimes seemed off limits to her simply because they bore that sacred title. Since they were priests, she thought it wholly inappropriate to adjudicate their cases. And yet she did oversee important executions—none more important than that of the archbishop of Canterbury, Thomas Cranmer. He was convicted of treason by secular courts, stripped of his archbishopric, and burned.

Still, the queen's greatest achievement was not bloodshed but abrogating heretical laws against free Catholic worship and the reinstitution of the Catholic Mass. The Church seemed on track to a swift restoration.

But it was not. In 1585, *De schismate Anglicano* had no real answer for why Catholicism's revival was so brief, save for providential platitudes. In 1586, the book's editors offered a more penetrating analysis. Failure was at least partly due to errors of governance. From the beginning, Mary knew that the renewal of Catholicism depended on assistance from Rome, so she immediately requested Cardinal Pole be sent as legate. At first, he hesitated. He wanted to gather information to be sure that the ground had been readied for his effective services. After an initial pause, a letter from Pole to Mary (newly printed in 1586) suggested that he was ready to go and assume his charge. Politics, however, got in the way. Charles V, who was in the middle of finalizing his son's marriage to Mary, held Pole back until the deal was concluded, much to the latter's chagrin. Although *De schismate Anglicano* does not elaborate, in later works, Persons underlined the detrimental effects of Pole's delay and the political machinations that caused it.[33]

Despite good intentions, reform was incomplete. Whereas clemency should be lauded in a prince, overindulgence posed dangers. Mary rid England of noted heretics, but she was too forgiving of clerics who had fallen victim to the wiles of Protestantism during previous reigns. Allen and Persons lamented that neither queen nor cardinal had created mechanisms to assess the priests by whom they had been instituted. There was no practical means to ensure quality control. As a result, even well-intentioned priests carried out their duties rashly and inadequately. This was all of a piece with a papal policy that tried to cope with the challenge of reestablishing England's clergy after years of spiritual desiccation, where illicit clerical marriages would be dispensed, illegitimate children would be legitimized, and bishops instituted under heretical regimes would be reconciled. Such leniency bred corruption. Allen and Persons insisted that the disruption of Church discipline could only lead to further errors.[34]

Marian and papal forces also conceded on Church property. Initially Mary and Pole wanted to reappropriate all the rents and lands stolen from the Church. The history of Westminster is emblematic of their efforts. The abbey had once belonged to the Benedictines, but Henry VIII had turned it into a collegiate church. When Pole tried to restore the property to its "original use," the secular priests who then held possession did not want to forfeit their rights. Mary and Pole, however, persevered and chased them away through a combination of force and bribery. This event frightened others who had reaped the benefits of Henry's treachery, and Marian authorities feared malcontents might soon start trouble. To avoid imminent danger, the pope offered absolution and allowed the secular retainment of ecclesiastical lands. Allen and Persons claimed those who kept Church property would suffer divine punishment, even if ecclesiastical authorities did not pursue their "canonical rights."[35]

These brief comments on Marian inefficiencies seem important, considering hoped-for Spanish efforts against Elizabeth. Though Allen and Persons barely mention it, Mary's reign as queen coincided with Philip's own time as an English monarch. Spain (as embodied by its monarch) was thus complicit in past failures. Sander's new editors wanted to make sure that history did not repeat itself. To ensure success, the future king of England had to be unflinching. Like a *basso ostinato*, a message of rigor was sounded in equal measure throughout Sander's history. By highlighting Marian faults, the editors reinforced notions of fortitude propounded time and again in stories of the damned and the saved. Mary's story provided a barely coded set of messages for the Spanish monarchy about its duties as they stood on the brink of England's salvation.

How the Heretics Do It

Marian failures occurred within a specific context. Although thorough reform had not been achieved, the Marian regime could not be blamed for promoting heresy, much less creating it. Allen and Persons spent a lot more time examining the death knell of English Catholicism in their narrative of Edward's brief reign, during which England had turned to Protestantism. They claimed that only two people, Mary and Pole, remained unspoiled in its wake. How did heretics destroy true faith and long-observed traditions?

In short, Somerset, the king's protector, destroyed English Catholicism through educational reforms. Allen and Persons argued that heretics most desired, "after having poisoned their young king, to destroy and corrupt universities so that the source and fountain of religion and education having been infected, the pestilence [heresy] might more easily remain in the commonwealth."[36] Thus began university visitations that led to the destruction of their ancient decrees, which were replaced with new ones conforming to heretical precepts. Learned scholars were quickly traded for young men with "petulant tongues and blasphemous mouths" who did little more than corrupt students. The reforms hijacked the universities' solid scholastic curricula, which were heavy on the works of Aquinas and Lombard: their books were ripped out of libraries and their names mocked and defamed, thus preventing access to learned works that would have easily uncovered heresy's fallacies. As a result, universities and then cities were increasingly stuffed with "new preachers, stupid adolescents, poets, and grammarians."[37]

During Edward's first years, homegrown teachers proved scarce, so the regime sought talent elsewhere, in the likes of Martin Bucer, Peter Martyr, and Bernardino Ochino, "men who were better exercised in fraud."[38] They and lesser heretics taught not the brightest and most tried English minds but essentially anyone who knew some Latin. Such mediocrities imbibed errors from evil books and lectures containing false interpretations of doctrine and history. Students were encouraged to interpret matters as they would, not as they should.[39]

Though Sander's editors had no doubt that Catholic truth would always win over heretical lies, they suggested that heretical regimes were effectively crafty. Much like the 1585 *De schismate Anglicano*, the 1586 edition showed that when both sides of the confessional divide confronted each other, Catholics easily won—and yet the word never got out. For example, when Richard Smith, a Catholic priest, called for an open debate with Peter Martyr about the Mass, the Catholic side won, but Martyr colluded with a corrupt judge to make it seem that they had lost. After the event, a print campaign completed the deception: authorities published a partial and wholly inaccurate transcript of the confrontation.[40]

The debased level of discourse during Edward's time did not improve under Elizabeth. At the outset, the queen decided to put religion up for debate, but the wizened Catholic bishops who survived Mary Tudor's reign were suspicious. They saw no point in discussing things that had been settled in past centuries by many Church fathers, popes, and learned councils. Nevertheless, a dispute took place. It was, of course, a farce arbitrated by Elizabeth's minister, Nicholas Bacon, "a layman, a heretic unlearned in divine matters." The archbishop of York was named his assistant but only for show. As was customary, the organizers established evil and unjust conditions for disputation, leading to nothing but disorder. The whole time was spent in useless declamations—Bacon was an awful moderator—and in the end, it all came to nothing.[41]

Edward and Elizabeth's regime managed to take control of the narrative. Heretical regimes used formal disputations, show trials, and other public spectacles to manipulate the truth and thereby owned the political and religious message. To Sander and his editors, the notion of talking with the enemy seemed dubious and of little profit because of the incommensurability between Catholics and heretics and because there were no avenues for real, free, open discourse. On the other hand, of course, English Catholics also knew how powerful and effective (mendacious) printed propaganda could be. Indeed, Allen and Persons played the dangerous game of showing the manipulative potential of the media they themselves employed; the success of their finger-pointing depended on a sympathetic reader already attuned to Elizabeth's evils and ready to believe that Catholics would generally come bearing truths.

Perhaps there were some lessons to be learned from heretics. If there was no doubt that all heretical subterfuge should be avoided and that specific policies (such as their spurious educational reforms) should be rejected, Sander's editors wanted to insist on the need to capture men's minds. Just as heretics had done this by taking control of universities, under a Catholic regime, proper schooling was the key to long-lasting change. Heretical machinations on this front were—in terms of content, not strategy—the flip side of positive efforts by such models as Fisher and Pole and their exemplary reforms in Oxford and Cambridge. The emphasis on education points to a powerful reformist impulse among English Catholics on the Continent, nearly all of whom had close ties to the English seminaries there. Allen, who had established the first English college in Douai (1568), thought of himself as a successor to Pole and would have been aware of his predecessor's legacy.[42] He surely would have agreed with Persons, who, as we shall see, would argue in a text meant to be read by Philip that a policy of free debate, seminaries, and a revamped university curriculum would lead to Catholic renewal.

Talk of educational reform would have resonated with certain English Catholics who continued to observe the decay of the true faith—even among their own ranks. The 1586 *De schismate Anglicano*, unlike its 1585 template, described a much gloomier picture of English Catholicism than its predecessor. While in 1585, the book suggested most people remained in one way or another Catholic, the 1586 version concluded that very few were immune to Elizabethan heresy. As Lake and Questier have recently discussed, the 1580s witnessed deepening rifts between Catholics who had fundamentally different opinions about how to interact with the Elizabethan regime.[43] Tensions were not contained within England, either. Beginning in the 1570s and throughout the period covered by this book, enmities, sometimes based on burgeoning nationalism (between English and Welsh priests, for example), plagued the English colleges. Given these problems, Persons and Allen's rejection of accommodation and their emphasis on the virtues of the English colleges were both aspirational and implicitly critical. Sander's history allowed Persons and Allen to cut their eyes at misbehaving Catholics within their community.

Conclusion

Texts might be unstable and interpretations ultimately unpredictable, but authors play an important role in that faulty circuit. A perfectly serviceable version of Sander's history was already printed in 1585, and subsequent print runs might have helped it reach more hands and eyes. Clearly, Allen and Persons did not think that would do. This may have been a result of dissatisfaction with the first printed edition, but as suggested here, it probably had as much to do with changed circumstances. Allen and Persons believed not only that Sander's book was essential amid recent political events but that their editorial decisions were necessary to achieve their goals. This, in turn, signals the extent to which they believed their books could inform and enhance the animus against Elizabeth.

De schismate Anglicano was not meant to be a neutral academic exercise, but it was not meant to be taken as crass propaganda either. Allen and Persons's changes deepened the narrative, offered more details. The inclusion of several more "primary sources"—several letters and a diary written by a Catholic reader as an appendix—made it read like a more serious enterprise. The legitimacy of the genre mattered to the editors. They might have favored a more obviously exhortatory or condemnatory rhetorical stance, but instead, they chose to enhance previous efforts to produce a "truthful" narrative.

The legitimacy provided by history must have been important, as was the generosity of the form. Not only could different types of texts—chronicle, polemic, martyrology, and so on—be combined into one narrative, but it allowed spaces for interpretive freedom. The lessons must have seemed clear enough to the authors, but they did not have to resort to sharp language against the *Catholic* readers that the book wanted to criticize.

A fundamental ambiguity—perhaps a duality—abides. If, as suggested here, the book encourages fortitude, such encouragement can be perceived in several ways. On the one hand, authors might have wanted to build on the reader's virtue; on the other, they might have wanted to compensate for the reader's sins. This thin boundary between compliment and critique was crucial, especially for men who needed to advocate for the English Catholic cause without alienating potential allies. Allen and Persons needed to accomplish the unenviable task of standing their ground against English heresy, appealing to a general Catholic audience, and ensuring that action was taken by those who had failed in the past.

Unfortunately, we do not know how Philip II or his advisers reacted to Sander's book or how its didactic possibilities influenced the king. However, there is no doubt that readers at court thought Sander's history worthwhile; otherwise Philip would not have supported the book's translation to Spanish on the eve of the Armada. By examining the Spanish version in detail, we will get a sense of the polemical potential intuited by a prominent contemporary in Spain and observe the value of Sander's double-edged message of encouragement and reprimand there.

3

ENGLISH HISTORY MADE SPANISH

While the Armada readied on Lisbon docks, Pedro de Ribadeneyra fell victim to anxieties born of past disappointments. He had gone to London nearly thirty years before on a double mission: to help restore Queen Mary's health and introduce the Society of Jesus to Britain. Neither goal was achieved. He would eventually recall only one positive outcome of his time there: he managed to get out alive. London's chill must have worsened a "chest ailment" he overcame only by God's grace.[1] Toward the end of his thankless visit—after Elizabeth's coronation, after the dismantling of Mary's short-lived settlement had begun—Ribadeneyra started to feel, as he put it at the time, the winds of a tempest that lay in England's future.[2] He might have stayed longer, but it would have been useless.[3] It was God's will, he wrote years after the fact, that Mary should die shortly after his arrival "and that Elizabeth . . . should succeed her, and that matters concerning our holy faith should alter and change as punishment for that kingdom that today still feels and mourns its affliction."[4]

Despite a mounting feeling of impotence, Ribadeneyra's interest in those afflictions did not waver. He developed close friendships with English men and women on the Continent and stayed current on English sufferings.[5] More importantly, he supported their cause and was among the hawks looking to attack Elizabeth, especially after his return to Spain from Rome in the 1570s. At that point—amid a very active retirement—he chose to fight against heresy and Christian lassitude in the manner of his closest exiled friends: with pen and paper, ink and press.

As soon as he could, he got hold of *De schismate Anglicano* (the Roman edition).[6] He immediately knew it was "a book worthy to be read by all" and wanted to make sure they did. Ribadeneyra considered translating it, but instead, he did something more complicated—he made Nicholas Sander's book his own.[7] The *Historia ecclesiastica del scisma de Inglaterra* (The ecclesiastical history of the English schism) is mostly a faithful translation of *De schismate Anglicano*'s take on Henry VIII and Edward VI, but it has updated and expanded sections on Mary Tudor and Elizabeth, including an extensive discussion of Mary Stuart's fall. The care taken to build on Sander's template suggests Ribadeneyra's deep investment in the project.[8]

In the summer of 1587, with news of Francis Drake's attack off the coast of Cádiz swirling, he rushed to finish his manuscript; Ribadeneyra wanted to intervene at a moment of great political and spiritual disquiet.[9] More than a decade after its first print run, an English Catholic narrative (with its implicit messages and modes of analysis) became Spanish. In the process, Ribadeneyra's history may have overtaken its source in popularity.[10] This was certainly the case in Spanish-speaking lands, largely because it became the centerpiece of Philip II's promotional efforts for the Armada.

Changes in tongue, context, and readership all affected the book's meanings. Aside from the slippages inherent to translation, Ribadeneyra's book reveals strategic authorial decisions that reflect specific aims. And yet there are elements of continuity amid this transformation from a "Hispaniolized" Sanderian book to a Spanish history proper. Both texts reveal a similar understanding of English history and its value under contemporary circumstances. Indeed, it is worth thinking about Ribadeneyra's book as an interpretation and explanation of Sander's original work. Much like Sander and his editors, Ribadeneyra sought a balance between support for Philip II and support for a greater cause. This dynamic implies a shared assessment of the problems afflicting Catholic Christendom and the necessary solutions.

Hard Times in Spain

For many, the prospect of an Armada bent on destroying the Elizabethan regime and dealing a hard blow to heresy seemed like a good and necessary thing. But even those who thought the end of English heresy would benefit Christendom had doubts about Spain's ability to save the day. The unease was such that it disturbed the sleep of a young woman named Lucrecia de León. Prophetic dreams had turned her into an important player in and around court circles as her nighttime visions—transcribed by priestly superiors—infiltrated contemporary political conversations. One such dream in November 1587 contained warnings that must have resonated with many contemporaries. One of Lucrecia's oneiric guides took her to see Francis Drake, Elizabethan privateer extraordinaire, and the marquis of Santa Cruz, admiral of the Armada. The latter looked ill and diminished, the former in full bloom. The sad-looking marquis had with him a golden eagle that she had once seen in Drake's possession, minus the sword that had been in its beak. Lucrecia asked why the sword was missing, and her guide responded with requisite gloom, "Drake has had more power than the marquis will have in his life." He continued sarcastically, "Do you think that England has been won?" Clearly not. "England is more to be won than won, and the powerful man will not see it won."[11]

Even the potential of victory at the hands of another commander, as implied in this dream, would be erased in future ones, where Lucrecia envisioned the Armada's defeat. That such an awful fate awaited Philip's fleet was indelibly linked to what many in Lucrecia's circle considered the king's failings. Her visions offered a stark view of contemporary Spain during a period of discontent and trouble resulting largely from (perceived) monarchical inadequacies. In one morbid instance, she saw Philip's corpse in mud. It rose slowly, and an imagined chorus asked, "Do you remember the harm and injustice you have done?" Those injustices, as revealed to (or by) Lucrecia, concerned the king's oppression of the poor, his mismanagement of ecclesiastical matters, his greed, negligence, and lack of faith.[12]

Lucrecia's premonitions and criticisms were not unique. Before her, there was, for example, the cranky street prophet Miguel de Piedrola Beamonte.[13] He too had been a dreamer and had been eager to spread his prophetic misgivings to anyone who would listen—most importantly, to the king himself. He sent memorials advising Philip on how to conserve his kingdoms, adding ominous warnings that if his advice were ignored, Spain's *infantes* would die. Piedrola described the awful fate of many Spaniards "who suffered unjustly with no remedy for their pain save their cries to the heavens." He spoke ominously of the "great events of the year 1588" and the "imminent destruction of Spain."[14] At more or less the same time in Lisbon, a nun—Maria da Visitação—had achieved pan-European fame for her ecstatic communions with Christ, miracles performed, and marks of the stigmata. Much to the king's dismay, she also became a political figure. She predicted the Armada's failure and, like Piedrola and Lucrecia, mixed foreboding with critiques of Philip's regime.[15] In Rome, home of Philip's most powerful and most grudging ally, Sixtus V, dread abounded. English Jesuit Joseph Creswell recalled talking to a saintly man who "had such communications with our Lord that he could know something of his intentions." He had warned that the Armada would soon "go up in smoke." God would punish Philip's regime for persecuting the Society of Jesus.[16]

Such prophecies reflect a pervasive discourse shared by both the king's Protestant enemies abroad and many of his "natural" allies at home, for whom a sense of *desengaño* (disillusion) had set in.

Ribadeneyra must be counted among the naysayers. He was skeptical of modern-day prophets, but he belonged to circles that did not share his skepticism. He was a confidante of English Catholic exile Lady Jane Dormer, duchess of Feria, who had been a supporter of Piedrola and later Lucrecia (to whom she was also a landlady). Ribadeneyra was privy to what these shady figures said and was present at certain salons hosted by Dormer to discuss them. He would have had no problem agreeing with their criticisms or their grim visions of the future.

Ribadeneyra wrote one of his most direct critiques of the regime in 1580, during the prelude to Philip's conquest of Portugal. In a letter to the archbishop of Toledo, Gaspar de Quiroga, he did not reject Philip's rights to the Portuguese throne but warned against acting on them. He thought the king's efforts against another Christian kingdom would endanger "that part of Christendom that alone seems to have and conserve peace, justice, and pure religion, and maintains religion in the provinces outside it" and predicted that aggression would only lead to disasters and punishments "that God sends to kingdoms to afflict them and destroy them."[17] Although it seemed that Portugal was weak, it being a small territory and Castile having more resources, he doubted that Spanish troops could do the job. He said the campaign would fail because of a general lack of enthusiasm. Philip's subjects had become embittered and showed "little interest in seeing His Majesty's power grow." They were oppressed by taxes, grandees felt ignored, knights received few benefits, clerics were upset by the subsidies required of them and prelates by the selling of Church lands, and monks were put off by attempts to reform their orders. All this led to a situation in which Philip, while still powerful, was not "as well loved" as he had been.[18] War against Portugal would only lead to further excruciating demands of already disturbed subjects. Squeezing Castilians for the purpose of imperial glory, apart from further alienating them, would prod the Portuguese into (successful) resistance against Philip to avoid a similar Castilian fate. Ribadeneyra thus argued that the king's efforts would fail because of divine punishment for inadequate rule in Castile and because he fought an unworthy battle against another Catholic kingdom at a time when Christendom could not bear infighting. Such a troubled understanding of Spain's predicament and of Philip's failures became a constant in Ribadeneyra's worldview, even if he never lost hope that things could change.[19]

Despite Ribadeneyra's qualms about intra-Catholic animosity, he did not reject force altogether. In armed battle, as in other things, God's glory should be the king's primary concern. He argued early in Philip's reign that "the ends of war should not be revenge, nor to see the enemy beaten and destroyed, nor reputation and glory, nor expansion, nor the growth of kingdoms"; the goal should only be "peace and calm among Christians and the defeat of heretics."[20] The Portuguese expedition did not meet these criteria and would, in fact, accomplish the opposite.

The launch against Portugal was especially troubling because of Philip's other diplomatic entanglements. At the time he fought his Christian neighbor, he was negotiating peace with the Ottomans.[21] Ribadeneyra's criticism might have been part of efforts to focus the king's energies back to Muslim threats or toward England, like so many other missives coming from Rome urging him to reassess priorities.[22]

Just a few years later, after Portugal had been conquered, Ribadeneyra would feel no shame or qualms about cheering the Armada. The Armada itself, as an act of faith and a sacrifice in God's name, might be enough to atone for past sins. Had he been younger and healthier, he would have set sail and spilled his own blood for the cause.[23]

Ribadeneyra's instincts and desires were his own, but his public utterances were not. He did not speak or write for himself but as an important representative of the Society of Jesus. Much to his dismay, superiors in Toledo and Rome found his *Scisma* troubling.[24] They questioned, among other things, the propriety of a priest writing on potentially inflammatory political matters. Four decades into their existence, the Society's detractors—both Catholic and Protestant—portrayed them as a troupe of scheming Machiavellians. Not surprisingly, Jesuit general Claudio Acquaviva hesitated to use print for what might be construed as "secular" ends. He believed, as he said in a different context, that "things touching affairs of states or kingdoms" were best avoided because they "offend and are of little use."[25] The *Scisma* posed dangers because it was a document of war and it stepped into the morass of anti-Elizabeth polemic. Acquaviva did not seem to mind the most salacious parts of Sander's arguments, but he did not want such a narrative to have a Jesuit label. He wondered if Ribadeneyra should just write a straight translation of Sander's book because, after all, it had the advantage of being "very accurate, and has been very well-received, and it would be better to promote it by making it more readily available."[26]

Ribadeneyra disagreed, pushed back, and eventually got his way (with help from William Allen).[27] Unlike his superiors, he believed that the loudest argument for a fight against England should be written by a Jesuit and insisted that the *Scisma* should be read as a Jesuit book. After all, had not so many great martyrs to the cause been his brethren? If a member of any holy order was obliged to "favor and promote" all things "touching our sacred religion," the duty was doubled for Ribadeneyra as a Jesuit because the Society was expressly sent by God in "these miserable times to defend the Catholic Faith."[28]

Ribadeneyra may have been sure of his anti-Elizabethan efforts, but he ultimately understood the need to choose his words carefully. His certainty about the English Catholic cause in 1588 could not be divorced from misgivings about the king's motives, nor could his public statements remain insensitive to the misgivings of his Jesuit superiors. The trick would be to write a book that would help England, stay true to Christian principles, serve the king's immediate objectives well, benefit his readers (in the short and long term), and best represent—and speak to—the Society of Jesus. This was no easy task.

The Right Words

To understand what Ribadeneyra tried to do, we should first understand what he did not do. Not long before the *Scisma* was printed, he wrote a letter to Anna de Guzmán, cousin of the Armada's captain, the duke of Medina Sidonia.[29] He attached a document that had been written as an afterword to the *Scisma* but was left out "for just respects." He wanted the paper to be passed along to the duke, although he pleaded that relatively few should read it and that it not be printed; Ribadeneyra insisted that the text should remain anonymous.[30] The document in question survives today as the "Exhortación para los soldados y capitanes que van a esta jornada de Inglaterra en nombre de su capitán general."[31] In its fury, it was among the sternest attacks against Elizabeth written in Spain and among the most impassioned (semi)public justifications for the Enterprise of England. Yet it was not another articulation of the *Scisma's* central points. Though both this manuscript and Ribadeneyra's history were meant to promote the Armada and ensure its success, their divergences are revealing.

The "Exhortación" focuses on sustaining the king's *reputación*. As Ribadeneyra bluntly put it, "The world is governed by opinion, and war even more so." A powerful king should care about nothing more (save for God and his kingdom) than his own reputation. Once lost, it was hard to reclaim, but when held, it provided stability and security. "The whole world fears our power and disdains our greatness," Ribadeneyra wrote, and consequently, Spain had many "open enemies, and many more hidden ones and feigned friends." Should the king's stature in the eyes of others falter, known enemies would act on their animosity and secret ones would surely reveal "what is hidden in their chests." With time, Ribadeneyra warned, enemies would "alter and revolt against us." More chilling still, external challenges would lead to unrest and rebellion among the king's own subjects. Elizabeth tried to lessen the king's glory by fomenting revolt among his subjects in the Low Countries, attacking interests in the New World, and pillaging the Iberian coast itself. Putting Elizabeth in her place would ensure that "beetles would not want to fight against eagles, nor mice with elephants."[32] Showing Elizabeth who was boss, in turn, required the exaction of old debts. As if decades had not passed, Ribadeneyra asked, "Who is obligated to revenge the troubles and death of the most serene Queen Catherine, our Spaniard, daughter of the illustrious Catholic kings Don Fernando and Doña Isabel?"[33] Her countrymen, of course. In riling readers to punish English heretics, Ribadeneyra warned that inaction might imply that, as he put it, "we do not want to, or that we are not able to take revenge."[34]

Ribadeneyra underscored matters of coin and purse. While he admitted that "gain and interest" should not be as motivational as faith and honor, they nevertheless "move most men and stir them in their consultations and deliberations." Those required to defend the "republic"—the king—should tend to the kingdom's success and fortune.[35] Elizabeth and her regime clearly posed threats to Spanish solvency by impeding good governance on the Continent and by hampering trade, especially with the New World. These two spheres of peril melded in the Dutch Revolt. War in Flanders was necessary, but it was a costly drain on Spain and its subjects. As many contemporaries argued, to end wars in Burgundian territories, the problem should be cut at the root: England. Doing this would protect Christendom, but it would also stop the hemorrhaging of gold and silver from Spanish coffers, most of which came from the Americas. American troubles had other English dimensions.

Ribadeneyra reprimanded Elizabeth and her men, saying they had "infested our seas, stolen the goods of our merchants." Because Spain's "wealth and greatness" depended on such precious goods, because it seemed that the "sustenance and life of these kingdoms" hinged on American trade, English prodding should be batted away.[36]

Aside from many justifications and incentives for war, the "Exhortación" made fighting for a just cause seem relatively easy. Not only did Ribadeneyra tell of how the prayers of Catholics everywhere and the intercession of fallen martyrs would ensure victory, but he described the advantages of numbers and superior competence. It was well known, he said, that the greater part of England was Catholic and that oppressed brethren would rise in arms to help their saviors. Moreover, England's proven inability on the battlefield should spur Spain's gleaming warriors. History showed that the English were prone to embrace change; consequently, there was no other Christian kingdom so prone to rebellion. Citing Gildas's sixth-century *De excidio et conquestu Britanniae* (On the ruin and conquest of England), Ribadeneyra caustically argued that the English were neither valiant in war nor loyal in peace—a lethal combination of inadequacies, for it led England to much inner turmoil when all was well and to certain defeat when confronted with challenges from abroad. When they faced no real threats, the English touted their bravery, but when they were put to the test, they showed their weakness.[37]

These arguments are striking because they seem to go against the kinds of admonitions Ribadeneyra is well known for. The "Exhortación" emphasized all those things that he often inveighed against. He had once warned the king that war should not be about revenge, destruction, reputation, or empire. Yet here he submitted to what he understood to be man's natural inclinations, presumably because this was the best way to appeal to men of war. Or maybe he assumed that his advice was appropriate for a more limited, more exalted readership that would not value secular goals over spiritual ones. Perhaps after some arm-twisting from his superiors, or perhaps because he did not want to indulge man's baser instincts, he decided that such arguments would not do for the masses nor were they totally appropriate from the hand of a holy man—except in the shroud of anonymity.

The Right Mission

The *Scisma* was ultimately written as an antidote to the human proclivities that the "Exhortación" promoted. In print, an image epitomized the

Armada's purported goal: readers holding the 1588 Madrid edition of the *Scisma* would have stopped to inspect the hard lines of a small engraving depicting a boat with sails drawn, stuffed with men who had just cast a fishnet to sea.[38] In the middle ground, a bearded man jumps overboard and runs toward the shore, his body half immersed in water, his arms outstretched, his mouth agape, his eyes ecstatic. The wading man reaches for another standing on terra firma in the foreground; his bearded face is inscrutable, but the hatch marks radiating from his head suggest divine light, and his right arm is extended in a paternal gesture. This man is Jesus; the man clambering toward him is Peter.

The image has no explanation, but anyone privy to the visual rhetoric of the times could decipher it as a depiction of events found in the Gospels. In John 21, Jesus appears to the apostles at sea, after his resurrection. The group is fishing, unsuccessfully. They do not recognize Jesus. He tells them to cast their nets, and soon, fish abound. John then recognizes Jesus, and Peter leaps into the water to race toward him. As Ribadeneyra's confrere Jerónimo Nadal explains in a gloss to an image like the one found in the *Scisma*, the fish being netted are allusions to man, the sea represents the world, and the boat signifies the Church. By casting the net at Jesus's command, the apostles (and their descendants in the priesthood) carried out God's will to save men from the sins and evils of the world. The fish caught are reminders of the nourishment only God can give; the picture is a reminder that only through his guidance can man expect salvation.[39]

England's salvation similarly depended on the recognition of the true Church and its gifts, on the efforts of holy men to net Catholics and schismatics alike so that they might receive God's bounty. Although the ships that set sail for England would be filled with few men of peace, the enterprise was undertaken in hopes of defending Christendom and saving souls.

All other considerations should be rejected. In the book's conclusion—a conclusion that presumably replaced the "Exhortación"—Ribadeneyra gave this warning: anti-English efforts should *not* be a quest "for temporal quietude, or so that our seas might not be infested, nor our armadas be robbed by English corsairs . . . but so that our lord might be honored, and his Holy church might prosper."[40] Not money, not pride, not Elizabeth's temporal offences should spur Christians to fight.

To keep intentions pure, Ribadeneyra avoided any significant discussion of Philip's political interests. As discussed before, *De schismate Anglicano* (1586) finished with a succinct defense of Philip against Cecil's polemical attacks. Tellingly, while Ribadeneyra mentioned recent affronts by Elizabeth and Leicester, his edition avoided any direct response to Elizabethan propaganda. He made a vague allusion to a book "much worse . . . than the war undertaken," in which English propagandists gave reasons for helping Dutch rebels, "but they are so frivolous, false, and unworthy, that there is no reason to refer to them here."[41] He does not mention Cecil's *Defense* by name. By passing on the opportunity to highlight differences between Elizabeth and Philip, by refusing to use Netherlandish troubles as a justification for forthcoming battles, Ribadeneyra tried to stay on lofty ground.

If Ribadeneyra soft-pedaled Spanish (or Philip's) secular concerns, he did not fear chest-thumping patriotism. The enterprise should be executed under a Spanish banner because doing so would ensure Spain's godly mission. Ribadeneyra wanted to convince readers that the defeat of heresy was a national responsibility. He did not harp on the inevitability of success as he did in the "Exhortación," instead underscoring Spain's duty as a realm that had benefitted from divine mercy. The destruction of heretical tyranny in England would demonstrate thanks for God's protection of the *patria* against infection. Because Spanish conquests would be carried out on Christ's behalf, victory in England would help destroy heresy in other "Christian provinces" too. He touted that such success would be no less honorable than ridding the Indies of Satan.[42]

Just as Sander and his editors tried to rouse readers, Ribadeneyra encouraged compatriots by offering positive and negative *exempla* that would minimize inhibitions and inspire courage. Ribadeneyra enjoyed the opportunity to tell his countrymen about Catherine of Aragon, "nuestra Española";[43] he hoped her stoic suffering would serve as an example of sanctity for readers. Martyrs were even more compelling. In general, Ribadeneyra believed memories of these glorious warriors were imbued with a mysterious, vivacious energy that taught "more through acts than through words."[44] There were no more exemplary lives than those recently executed by the Elizabethan regime, most notably Edmund Campion and others involved in the 1580–81 mission to England. Could Campion's end help illuminate other lives? Ribadeneyra hoped so. Through righteous death, he overcame "all the miseries of this fragile and mortal body" and enjoyed "the triumphant crown of his fortunate confession."[45]

The lives and actions of the persecutors were important and showed the extent of heretical corruptions. To this end, despite concerns about propriety, Ribadeneyra could not avoid mentioning Henry's incestuous relationship with Anne, which, as in Sander's book, served to delegitimize Elizabeth and provide shocking proof of heresy's corruption. More broadly, describing enemies of true faith and their attacks on good Catholics should inspire rage that would make shedding enemy blood seem a "divine mercy."

Ribadeneyra expected visceral reactions to the atrocities presented; readers who were unfazed would prove themselves deficient. True children of God were discerned by a "lively and feverous desire that his holy name be glorified." Who would not cry at the many injuries inflicted on Christ? Who would not "melt in tears" after seeing so many souls go to hell? Who could not but pity all those afflicted by the satanic abuses? If the reader were in English Catholic shoes, would they not want to be rescued?[46]

Assuming the *Scisma* got men's hearts pumping, what then? Ribadeneyra wanted to inspire fighters of body and spirit. Big ships and heavy cannon could only do so much. Ribadeneyra believed that prayers were the "strongest weapons" kings could use, weapons with which men "won when they won."[47] Unsurprisingly, he expected readers who could not contribute body or cash to seek divine aid for the consolation of English Catholics so that tyranny and heresy might be defeated.[48] Ribadeneyra envisioned the campaign of 1588 to be more than the affair of a courtly and military class but that of Spain as a congregation of beggars before Christ.

This sort of pitch makes sense given Ribadeneyra's own objectives, but it also melded with Jesuit interests. Ribadeneyra reinforced the pro-Jesuit inclination of his Latin template, picking up a loose thread and weaving it into the fabric of the book. From the start, he claimed that the principal victims of Elizabeth's wrath had been English Jesuits "who preferred pure torments" over separating "one hair from the confession of the true Catholic faith."[49] The order, as Ribadeneyra imagined it, was a standard-bearer of true piety and holy submission. Despite general European laxity and even amid Luther's heresy and Henry's tyranny, the Society of Jesus was founded and subsequently spread around the world.[50] The *Scisma* both spread this message and proved its truth by contributing to the fight against demonic forces.

The *Scisma* also aligned with the order's support of Philip's efforts. As the great fleet formed in Lisbon and the city swelled with soldiers preparing for war, the Jesuit Simão Cardoso described the key role his brothers played in battle. Aside from Spanish and Portuguese Jesuits who went on board, those in Lisbon cared for soldiers seeking penance before their departure.[51] In Rome, while Acquaviva might have been wary of Ribadeneyra's book, he embraced the cause. He avidly supported Philip's call for pro-Armada intercessory prayers and thought the king's goals "so just and universal, that we are all obliged to ask the Divine Majesty for its success."[52]

Ultimately, the king's desires might have been even more important than Jesuit acquiescence. Philip II did not commission Ribadeneyra's book, but he adopted it for his public relations onslaught. The *Scisma*'s publication in 1588 across the most important Iberian printing centers—Barcelona, Madrid, Zaragoza, and Lisbon—must have been centrally coordinated.[53] In letters written by the famed printer Christophe Plantin, there is also clear evidence of Madrid's involvement in the 1588 Antwerp edition.[54] Royal co-option is also signaled by the inclusion of the Habsburg crest in some versions. In the Plantin run, it was placed on the title page; in the first Madrid run, it has a page of its own, adjacent to the *tassa*. The Madrid version also had various official pronouncements that, despite their banality, demonstrate the regime's sure endorsement. Pedro López de Montoya's official approbation talked up the book's revelations on the evils of heresy and the glories of martyrdom. He concluded that it "can and should be printed, and that it should be supported for the well-being and good use of the Republic."[55]

Part of the regime's enthusiasm for the book had to do with its author and what he represented. Though tensions between king and clergy were not new in the 1580s, around the time of the Armada, Philip found himself in disputes with the Society, born of strife within the order. These tensions could not be hushed; criticism of the king's involvement had become public thanks to Ribadeneyra (among others). Such talk made for bad press and, more importantly, could arouse divine anger. Having a Jesuit as the fleet's promoter could be something of a boon for the crown. By 1588, Ribadeneyra was already a grand figure in ecclesiastical circles and was a powerhouse among Jesuits in Spain. Indeed, he was one of the order's most visible living symbols. Not only was he among the dwindling number that had known and worked closely with the Society's founder, Ignatius of Loyola, and not only had he been entrusted with writing a biography of the future saint, but contemporary iconography made implicit links between the two.[56] In this light, having the royal crest near or on a title page bearing Ribadeneyra's name along with his affiliation to the order served to gloss over—or hide—an adversarial stance between Jesuits and the monarch.

More importantly, the regime wished to use Ribadeneyra because the text he wrote conformed to its larger propagandistic program. When Philip II petitioned representatives of the Castilian *cortes* for funding in 1588, he emphasized the Armada's religious impetus. He asserted that he faithfully carried out all things "pertaining to the service of God Our Lord and the defense of his holy faith and Catholic religion and the obedience and authority of the Apostolic See" and thus sought assistance "in the defense of our Holy

Catholic Faith and to defend the obedience to the Roman church and the conservation of his kingdoms."[57] Such public statements attempted to disseminate a stance taken in private. Philip frequently emphasized his efforts to ensure England's return to Catholic obedience: he insisted that all other aims and "particular conveniences" were "very far behind."[58]

While the king's elevation of spiritual over secular objectives was sincere, such public utterances were undoubtedly purposeful and were echoed in a range of performances. The regime wanted to underscore royal conformance to contemporary ideas about the correlation between ethical intent and positive outcomes preached by men like Ribadeneyra. It is no surprise that Philip would promote, as Carlos Gómez-Centurión has pointed out, "the religious ritualization" of the Armada. For example, the king asked the archbishop of Toledo, Gaspar de Quiroga, to take the host on procession to inspire greater devotion and prayers from the people for this enterprise. As one contemporary chronicler revealed, Quiroga complied, "entrusting this matter to God, and there were many prayers, processions, and rogations and mortification of the flesh for this journey."[59]

If some readers were inspired by the Armada's aims, if Ribadeneyra's admonition against the temptations of worldly goals elicited requisite prayers, neither he nor his readers could have lost sight of imminent dangers; neither he nor they would have forgotten their misgivings about the regime. Quite the opposite. While the Armada was a great opportunity, it would be for naught should its leaders and promoters (not to mention the king's subjects) not stay true to ideals displayed in the *Scisma*.

History's Distorted Mirror

Even as the Armada prepared to set sail, aspects of court life in Madrid continued as usual. During the summer of 1588, Prince Philip (who would become Philip III), then ten years old, received an education fit for a future king. In a surviving exercise book from that time, we can observe, as Martha Hoffman describes, "his childish hand first copying out rules of Latin grammar, then a short version of the instruction of St. Louis to his son, and selections from Aristotle in Latin and Spanish."[60] Language, politics, and philosophy intertwined. The proper instruction of any prince, especially the immediate heir to the throne, was always important, but we can imagine that young Philip's tutor felt a greater sense of duty that heady summer. His father had not yet fallen into the gout-ridden recumbence of his final years, but even as that annus mirabilis unfolded, many knew they lived at the dusk of his reign. The young prince's education was thus doubly important, not only because he was successor to the crown, but because his call to duty was imminent. And so it is no coincidence that Ribadeneyra decided to dedicate the *Scisma* to the prince, making it one of the first books during the last decade of Philip's reign meant to instruct the future monarch.

In his effort to advise the prince, Ribadeneyra entered a "political" terrain. The potential awkwardness of a holy man entering a worldly scene seems to have caused some discomfort, perhaps because of Jesuit injunctions against political engagements of the sorts mentioned above.[61] Whatever the reason, Ribadeneyra wanted to justify the path taken to achieve his didactic ends, and in so doing, he described a set of assumptions that undergirded but had been left mostly unsaid in Sander's original book. Invoking Ciceronian commonplaces, he said the book demonstrated what "one should flee, and what one should do."[62] These goals were not reserved for "profane histories which have been written by many grave authors" but were also at the heart of "ecclesiastical histories by most saintly doctors and admirable men who were the light and ornament of the Catholic Church."[63] He continued with obvious solicitude: if in the Bible the Holy Spirit provided stories of Abraham's obedience, Isaac's sincerity, Joseph's chastity, and David's trust and devotion, it also spoke about David's adultery, Samson's weakness, and "innumerable examples of cruel kings, and most pestilent tyrants."[64] Dominican friar Luis de Granada emphasized a similar point in a freshly printed letter attached to a later edition of the *Scisma*. He compared the book to other "sacred histories where . . . the misdeeds of bad kings are told, as well as the troubles of the faith, as in the time of Manassas and Zedekiah and in the first book of Maccabees."[65] Amid nervous justifications lay a hardened belief in the benefits of providing the historical materials from which readers might discern political prudence. Ribadeneyra surely felt that by doing so, he fulfilled the goals of the Society as defined by Ignatius of Loyola, who had encouraged close bonds between members of the order and potentates: the Society's constitutions ask members to provide "public persons" spiritual aid for the good of Christendom.[66] By framing the *Scisma* as an advisory tool, the project fell well within the proper bounds of Jesuit activity.

More importantly, Ribadeneyra believed matters of the republic and matters of faith were inextricable. He stated his central argument clearly in a dedicatory note to Prince Philip.[67] He emphasized the duty of all the king's vassals, especially clergymen, to pray that God keep young Philip in his hands. Divine gifts given unto princes were not theirs alone but benefitted their subjects. Undoubtedly, the young dedicatee had the benefit of an exemplary father who would leave behind an immense empire and, more importantly, the inheritance of having been "the defender of our holy Catholic faith." So that he might fully benefit from these ancestral gifts, he must learn that "there is another king in heaven who is the king of all kings," and before him, all other kings are like "little worms." Ribadeneyra warned that greater princely power comes with greater divine expectations. God's judgment of the strong would always be stern: the "powerful will be powerfully tormented if they do not do what they should."

In the *Scisma*, reflections of princely virtue wore feminine garb. As Ribadeneyra put it, the book might be considered "a mirror of princesses."[68] Reflected feminine virtue would serve other female rulers most, but inevitably, the lessons learned would benefit the prince as well. Indeed, while the book occasionally nods at Philip II's stewardship of England in the 1550s, true exemplars of royal prowess could only be found in a queenly trifecta: Catherine of Aragon, Mary Tudor, and Mary Stuart.

Ribadeneyra's depictions of the two Marys are revealing. While he wrote about Catherine's fortitude and piety and while Catherine's story was crucial for inspiring Spaniards, his take on her is largely derivative. Aside from bits and pieces—notably a couple of letters written by the queen that were not in *De schismate Anglicano*—Ribadeneyra stayed close to Sander's narrative.[69] The Scottish queen required more space and writerly energy, especially since Sander's history had predated her execution. Mary Tudor also received more attention, perhaps because he had met her and had established a direct connection. More importantly, both Marys appear in a different light from Sander's history and thus reveal Ribadeneyra's own "spin." His depiction of their lives will show how he tried to promote proper (royal) comportment.

By the time Ribadeneyra got to England in 1558, Mary Tudor was near death. Nevertheless, what he saw or heard of her must have been impressive to explain his sympathetic rendering of her life. Ribadeneyra followed Sander's saintly description, but Mary transcended any simple notion of feminine piety. Using common contemporary language for uncommon women, Ribadeneyra claimed that "her voice was deep, more of a man than a woman."[70] She was intelligent, resolute, and prudent, a model of temperance, piety, strength, and constancy. The queen was clement but capable of stiff resolve: she was "very severe and rigorous in punishing those who acted against God, and against the Catholic faith."[71] Mary believed her cause was just and firmly rooted in God's will, and she had "the spirit and valor to undertake and finish a task which according to human prudence was very difficult."[72]

Rejection of worldly prudence also marked the account of Mary Stuart's life. Mary's death brought Catholic Europe together in a chorus of outrage. Drawing on manuscript reports from England and France, together with printed accounts in French and Latin, Ribadeneyra provided an impassioned description of the queen's martyrdom. Her troubles began upon returning to Scotland after the death of the French king Francis II, her husband. Scotland was filled with heretics who had, with Elizabethan assistance, destroyed the Catholic Church. Corrupt Protestant leaders expected the young queen to rubber-stamp their heretical innovations, but she, being "just and Catholic," would not.[73] Resistance to heretical entreaties marked the beginning of her protracted, pious, unblemished end. Hounded by enemies, she sought refuge in England—a damned land that would be no refuge at all. Elizabeth imprisoned her. In subsequent years, the Elizabethan regime tried to convince Mary that if she promised to "preserve the false sect," she would be named legitimate heir to the English throne. They extended the offer because, although she would be otherwise slandered, Protestants feared Catholic rule. Protestants believed she would "punish the heretics that now ruled over her (just as the other Queen Mary, of sainted memory, wife of the Catholic King Philip had done)."[74] She would not bend. A series of letters written by the troubled queen reflects eagerness to stay true to her faith, to sacrifice her life for it, and to devote her remaining days to prayer and spiritual edification. She requested a confessor, but even at death's door, her nemeses only offered the spiritual help of Protestant ministers. She refused such false kindness. Condemned on spurious charges of promoting Elizabeth's murder, Mary faced it all with resolve and even joy: "Oh strong queen, oh constant queen, oh queen illuminated and moved by the heavenly spirit!"[75] Ribadeneyra resorted to histrionics as he recounted her repudiation of the world. She set aside her noble lineage, her beauty, her power, her servants, her armies, and her people to accept gladly an unjust fate. She knew that "this world is but a comedy, and all those that live in it, even if they be kings, are players, and because she loved what was eternal, and desired what she loved, and was dying for the Catholic faith," she did not waver.

These models of princely virtue set before Prince Philip all led tortured lives, and in the end, none of them succeeded in halting heresy's spread. They were paragons not because of political accomplishment but because religion, not crude politics, dictated their behavior. Because she was the most disenfranchised of the three, Mary Stuart may have stood above the rest. News of one monarch killed by another was hair-raising and upped the ante in terms of what a good prince should endure. But Mary's demise meant more than this. Ribadeneyra decoded the divine message in spilt royal blood: God allowed her murder "so that we all understand that there is another life." There is no security, he continued, in crowns or scepters, because ultimately "such a great queen of Scotland and France died at the hands of London's executioner."[76] Even monarchical authority, as he had argued in his dedication to the prince, is pathetic in light of divine will.

The exemplary lives of dead queens spoke to core values and sempiternal truths, most of which would have received approving nods even from those who failed to live up to the ideals presented. Though unoriginal, Ribadeneyra clearly thought the lessons worth repeating for the benefit of Prince Philip, who would soon assume important responsibilities. As an instrument of royal education, the *Scisma* would have a long afterlife and would find a prominent place in royal libraries, including those of Philip III and his son Philip IV.[77] But as Nicholas Bomba has rightly pointed out, books of royal instruction should not be narrowly construed: they often offered an ethical matrix that served as "instruction to all of mankind."[78] Though it was a tool to promote the Armada, the *Scisma* was also a tool to awaken a political class and perhaps even a nation. It aimed to promote a logic that was often lacking among men driven by self-interest, marred as they were by the frailties of original sin and resulting human weakness.

Because the *Scisma* is a mirror of princes, we can also assume it contains the genre's ambiguities. If authors described how the prince *should* behave, how society *should* be ordered, these lessons implicitly suggested that things were *not* as they should be. Just as his son's prepubescence inspired some to write about what made a good prince, there was a similar impulse during Philip II's youth. Take, for example, Pedro Mexia's *Historia imperial y cesárea* (Imperial history). It had at least two goals. One was propagandistic: it tried to portray Charles V as heir to Roman imperial glory. The other was didactic: it tried to instruct Prince Philip through positive and negative examples of ancient rulers.[79] Other works tried to guide the young prince—but at the emperor's expense. When Philip II took the throne, several advice books were written in the Netherlands, one of which—Felipe de la Torres's *Institución de un rey Christiano* (Education of a Christian prince)—asked him to turn his back on Charles's errant religious policies.[80] A similar dynamic would emerge prominently after Philip II's death, when advice to Philip III sometimes contained severe criticisms of his father, but such a polemical strategy did not always await the king's passing.[81]

As we have seen, Ribadeneyra had never been a wallflower, nor had he been blind to Philip's deficiencies. His misgivings before and after 1588 were not suspended during the months leading up to the Armada's departure. The situation was too dire for him to have lost sight of all the dangers that threatened even good causes. Ribadeneyra felt he lived "during such a time . . . that most of the world is occupied by infidels or infected with heretics." Worse, it was a world where even Catholic kingdoms were afflicted by vices. Heresies could spread everywhere, and "with them all that which is left in Europe could be lost."[82] Living in such a corroded world, we can understand why, as one contemporary put it, Ribadeneyra cried "tears of blood" at the idea that Spain would fall.[83] If Spain did not see the kinds of horrors witnessed in France and England, there is no doubt that contemporaries often had only tenuous faith in the cordon sanitaire of the Pyrenees. Placing the *Scisma* within this context reveals an embedded discursive potential much more incendiary than scholars have previously noticed. By deciphering elements of criticism in it, we can better reconcile Ribadeneyra's immediate propagandistic impulse and his more transcendental didactic goals discussed above.

If viewed through a lens of Spanish troubles, Tudor corruption takes on different significance. As Ribadeneyra told the prince in his dedicatory note, Henry's story was marvelous because in it, one could observe how a monarch "who having once been a just and brave prince, and a great defender of the Catholic Church, was later blinded with a dishonest desire, turned his back to God and was transformed into a feral beast."[84] The violent transformation of a great Catholic kingdom—some Spaniards would even argue England had once been the greatest—seemed to widen the maw of heresy.[85] If such a transformation was possible for a man who had once been deemed Defender of the Faith, could the Catholic king stray too?

Philip was no Henry. And yet the language of tyranny used to attack the English king and his successors could be superimposed on the Spanish monarch. More broadly, Sander's description of English troubles rooted in the tepidity and corruption of all Englishmen seems to parallel symptoms attributed to contemporary Spanish society by Ribadeneyra, who compared his homeland to Rome at its fall. Talk of self-interest, atheism, abuses against clergymen (and Church property), clerical corruption, vicious overtaxation, evil counsel, prevalent injustice, corrupt upstarts, a declining nobility, and overall religious laxity could become more than a discussion of English horrors. The *Scisma* could metamorphose from a description of problems out there into a prognostication for the effects of homegrown evils.

Ribadeneyra ensured that readers would not miss the point. Amid pages of direct translation from *De schismate Anglicano*, he augmented the Latin template by suggesting specific lessons to be learned. This was in part due to a prevalent belief that Latinate readers could understand these independently, while vulgar audiences needed more guidance. But such edificatory inflections also built on an extant popular discourse suggested above; it underlined those points of criticism that formed a dark penumbra around the Spanish king and the Spanish nation. Thus Henry VIII and Thomas Cranmer's schemes to legitimize divorce were used as a platform to offer the following insight: "The laxity of subjects and the ambition of kings . . . often cause very bad effects when God, reason, and justice are not involved."[86] Elsewhere, commenting on the stark differences between Anne and Catherine, Ribadeneyra suggested that the reader should understand "how secret and incomprehensible God's judgments are": as soon as the good (Catherine) are afflicted by tribulation, the bad (Anne) are bereft of fleeting prosperity. By these means, God "perfects the gold of virtue" while providing a "knife for the sinner."[87] In a discussion of Henry's oppressive taxation and his theft of Church property, Ribadeneyra reminded readers that the more the king stole from the Church, the poorer he became.[88] At another key juncture, the *Scisma* strayed from *De schismate Anglicano* to emphasize Ribadeneyra's strong support for clerical power. He believed it necessary that "churches and ecclesiastical prelates be rich, and that they have authority." He noted the situation in Germany, where Catholicism had been conserved in those parts "subject to Bishops and church prelates."[89] The case of Cardinal Wolsey allowed the author to elaborate on the evil minister theme, emphasizing that *privados* should "keep God above all" and avoid offending him in order to please men on earth.[90] Later, after picking Thomas Cromwell apart, he urged all "mortals, and particularly ministers to kings always to have before them the eyes of justice, and to pay more attention to God's will than that of man, even if they be kings."[91]

Just as Sander's lessons had been clear to Ribadeneyra, they were not missed by Ribadeneyra's readers. Alonso Gregorio, vicar general of the University of Zaragoza, wrote in 1588 that the *Scisma* should be read because it taught how easily men forego reason in favor of sensuality: Ribadeneyra underlined the dangers of heresy "giving wings to vices and thwarting virtue," revealed the doomed fate of those who despoiled the Church, and exalted the "glorious triumphs" of saintly martyrs.[92] Similarly, Luis de Granada encouraged the book's use for royal advisors, who would see that those who try to rise through artifice "and by human means without fear of God, eventually take great falls."[93]

As Ribadeneyra surely knew, the lessons he provided readers would live on after he died. In 1674, Florian Anisson published a new edition of the

Scisma because older ones had been long "consumed." He presented the book to the count of Villaumbosa, first minister under Charles IV, as a tool of good governance. Anisson appealed to him as a patron of erudition to circulate a book that served "public and common use."[94] He claimed that the *Scisma* was "for people of all kinds and status," a "clear mirror of God's punishments for those who stray from the flock and the union from this our Holy Catholic Church."[95]

Good Works

While Ribadeneyra's dim view of Spanish affairs had emerged prior to 1588, just before that summer, there may have been a glimmer of hope. Would the balance tip toward good faith or worldly attachments? By supporting the Armada, he tried to make sure that it stayed a spiritual affair and not one of lucre. He was circumspect, supportive of a good cause, but wary of the uncomplicated triumphalism typical of wartime propaganda. Thus the *Scisma* asked that all Spaniards "emend our lives and . . . show our faith through works."[96]

Ribadeneyra's appeal to "works" is crucial. His book was not simply about "othering" English heretics, demonizing them on the eve of war to facilitate violence and destruction. This was no doubt an important element carried over from *De schismate Anglicano*, but now that the gauntlet had been thrown, Ribadeneyra could also expand upon those aspects of Sander's history that suggested that holy war depended on a new way of seeing (and even feeling) things. The worldliness of before should be discarded in favor of godly blood- and tear-shedding and prayer. The Armada was a test, a crucial moment when the general ideals of good kingship and good Christian behavior could be practiced and observed.

The *Scisma* successfully awakened spiritual fervor. Around the time of its first printing, the papal nuncio in Madrid reported that the book inspired in its Spanish readers a "great compassion for the poor Catholics of England, and a deep desire to punish that horrible queen."[97] Luis de Granada reported having "cried many tears in some places, especially in the death of the queen of Scotland."[98] One tantalizing clue suggests that the book's horrors really inspired devotion. On a blank page of a 1589 Portuguese edition, a reader hastily wrote down an intercessory prayer to the Virgin, an indication that the book rallied some to spiritual combat.[99] There is no way to get into this one reader's mind, but it is easy to believe that English sufferings triggered a blend of fear and pity that could only be assuaged by divine intercession.

After the Wind Blew

And yet the Armada blew up in smoke. If God was on Philip's side, why had he lost? Philip looked at the situation with a heavy dose of Christian stoicism. God deserved thanks for "everything he wants to do," and so he gave him "thanks for this, and for the mercy he has used." The outcome could have been worse amid such inclement weather and such turbulent times.[100] English Catholics also found solace in providence. In Robert Persons's first pamphlet after 1588, he acknowledged that recent troubles were "punishment for our sins." He reminded the reader that wars were not won by the "puissance of man, but by the power of God." This message was meant to encourage Catholics. Despite defeat, they should wait for God's eventual mercy. Persons looked to the Bible, pointing to the initial loss of Israel against the tribe of Benjamin, and in the secular realm, he evoked Caesar's initial misadventures in England before his ultimate success.[101]

Ribadeneyra had a more forward response. He wrote a scathing letter to one of the king's counselors in which he dwelled on key problems I have suggested lay just beneath the surface of the *Scisma*.[102] Although the letter purported admiration and devotion to Philip, assuring that recent failures were just bumps in the road set by God for the benefit of king and kingdom, it also described specific failures that informed providential designs. In language that could have been lifted from the *Scisma*, he insisted that God wanted to "sanctify the king and give him the opportunity to humble himself before His powerful hand, so that he [Philip] might know well the great power he has been given, and the very little that this power is worth without Him."[103] Moreover, Ribadeneyra suggested that Spanish governance was on the edge of tyranny, even if the *t*-word was not used. Avaricious tax collectors squeezed the king's subjects, especially those in charge of collecting funds for the Armada in Granada. Consequently, contemporaries grumbled that success was impossible amid such corruption. The Armada could not succeed if "weighed with the sweat and curses of so many miserable people whom God tends to judge and hear."[104] Nobles were no better than thieving bureaucrats; they too were prone to scandal and corruption. The king shared their blame because he had failed to rein them in. Ribadeneyra warned Philip that a kingdom is not measured by its wealth in treasure but in the "abundance of valorous and magnanimous men." Such men are "not born made" but must be cultivated. Proper rewards for good servants would ensure that a monarchy is run effectively, a necessity at any time, but especially then because the king was old and sick and his son too young to rule.

Ribadeneyra also zeroed in on Philip's tense relationship with clergy, especially regulars. The king might seek to meddle in ecclesiastical matters out of religious zeal, but the dangers of doing so outweighed the gains. Royal intervention sowed division within religious communities. Worse, it set a terrible precedent in Spain and abroad.[105]

God punished Philip and his subjects because they had lost sight of God's primacy, and reform required the rejection of self-interest and the one-dimensional quest for "temporal quietude." This general problem could be best observed in the Armada's particulars. The mission failed because the king's heart was not in the right place. Since Philip's brief time as an English monarch, Ribadeneyra suggested he cared more about the "security of his state" than anything else; indeed, Philip tried hard not to offend Elizabeth at the expense of English Catholics.[106] The king had chosen earthly logic and turned what should have been pious princely prudence on its head.

That such forthright criticisms echo those I have described in the *Scisma* suggests that the book had tried to warn Philip and the nation about troubles ahead. Ribadeneyra may have viewed the campaign's defeat as the failure of his admonitions within the walls of Philip's court and indeed the confines of the king's soul. This must have a hard blow for the old Jesuit. Even after 1588, however, his disappointment did not inspire fatalism. Just as he told the king's counselor in his letter, he told the much broader readership of his 1589 *Tratado de tribulación* (Treatise of tribulation) that trials should catalyze renewal. He likened God to a good doctor who prescribed unpleasant medicines.[107]

His English Catholic brethren would have agreed. They had no choice.

Sander and his colleagues identified a central problem and a solution to important contemporary quandaries. The problem—English heresy—was tied to moral failings. Men and women, high and low, had become slaves to "human prudence," to a politic philosophy or a form of Machiavellianism that would lead to atheism, further suffering, and damnation. The solution to past failures required a change of direction, action predicated on pious intent and certainty in God's providential design (as defined by Catholics). In other words, even if calls for assertive action did not pass a political smell test, those in power should know that seemingly imprudent decisions from a "secular" perspective should be taken in firm confidence that God would provide in time.

Though such an argument might seem banal given typical early modern pieties, its rhetorical force cannot be undermined if we consider the ways it was attenuated in other circumstances. Peter Lake has shown how secret histories like *Leicester's Commonwealth* and the *Treatise of Treasons* attacked the enemy's Machiavellian schemes even as they employed a Machiavellian logic to encourage certain kinds of future behaviors. This dynamic is similar to that in Spain, where Keith Howard has argued that anti-Machiavellian discourse embraced Machiavelli's modes of analysis, even in works produced by purported enemies like Pedro de Ribadeneyra.[1] "Reason of state" had seeped into the realm of public discourse partly as a result of the growing cognizance of how things really worked behind the curtains. Knowing the inner workings of government perpetuated its (immoral) behaviors. Those in the know could strategize according to the rules set by the game of politics, no matter how dirty—if only to avoid being eaten alive.

Nicholas Sander and Ribadeneyra in their histories of England encouraged a different kind of political engagement. They showed the enemy to be a cagey manipulator and highlighted their twisted logic but suggested that the corrective to these successful manipulations required overturning perverse political doctrines. The solution did not involve hard-boiled scheming; only Christian resolve would do.

Martyrs mattered. Sander's history, especially in its 1586 version, offered Edmund Campion and other glorious dead as the highest exempla of piety for Catholics across Europe. Their motivations served as counterpoints to both heretics and many idle Catholics who had let England burn. Ribadeneyra took this central theme and politicized it further by focusing on the exemplarity of Mary Stuart. She allowed him to discuss princely ideals without having to wade in realpolitik waters. In her, the reader could appreciate someone who fought against heretics despite real-world demands or political consideration. The importance of this Marian narrative cannot be overstated, both because her story exhibited Elizabeth's tyranny and because Stuart's exemplarity hinged on her monarchical status. Not only would her noble death edify the masses (who were supposed to follow the examples of their rulers), but it would send a powerful message to other monarchs as well.

The texts discussed here tried to inspire changes of behavior intimately linked to the workings of the soul. Sander's and Ribadeneyra's narratives reveal the historical means used to inspire certain types of action, be it prayer or war, based (primarily) on a godly logic. The success or failure of these books depended on whether readers were convinced, by means of positive and negative exempla, that all (political) activities should be tightly linked to pious goals. This in turn required a fundamental shift in reader interests and preoccupations, a reshuffling of priorities based on a resolve to follow God.

If all this is true, we must understand Sander's history as part of a broader "spiritual" discourse. Just as *De schismate Anglicano* and the *Scisma* must be placed within the context of a Tacitean trend, they also resonate with a strand of Catholic devotional literature receiving intense attention at the time. During the 1580s, English Catholic exiles (mostly in France) published a series of manuals on good Christian living. The most important of these had Iberian ties: Friar Luis de Granada's *A memoriall of a Christian Life* and the Jesuit Gaspar de Loarte's *The Excercise of a Christian Life*. These efforts culminated in Robert Persons's own wildly popular *A Christian directorie*, a book inspired by Loarte.[2]

Together, these texts tried to reconcile the theoretical aspects of good Christian behavior and action. As Persons saw it, men understood how one should behave but could not act on that understanding. They "hath lesse difficultie, payne, and resistance in hym self to knowledge, than to good lyfe, where our corrupt affections make warre against us, and so doe make the matter unpleasant for a tyme, until they be conquered."[3] His book, like Loarte's and Granada's, tried to bridge the gap by suggesting that activities—meditation, prayer, reading, Communion—helped cleanse sordid vessels to better engage God. Granada asked, If there are books on the ideal prince, the ideal courtier, the ideal magistrate, why should there not be a book on how to be a good Christian? Without this knowledge, there was little hope of spiritual or earthly successes, as both were predicated on God's grace.[4] Books such as Granada's *Memoriall* offered a road map for focusing energies on God and devotion to him. These books called on men to resolve in his favor (Persons's primary focus), but they also lingered on the pragmatic. Rituals of everyday life would reflect individual resolve or at least focus the reader's attentions in such a way that he would, through hard work and effort, alter the intensity of his devotion and even achieve a truer understanding of God.

Forms of "Spanish" spirituality that resonated with Persons were not only, or even primarily, for export.[5] If figures such as Granada became important across Europe and among English Catholics, their voices were just as powerful and necessary in Spain. This almost goes without saying except that the rhetorical power of such devotional texts in *times of crisis* is worth pointing out. It is not surprising that around the same time that Granada, Loarte, and Persons were being published and republished, there was a renewed push to bring one towering figure in Spanish spiritual life, the famous Granadino preacher Juan de Ávila, back to prominence on the Iberian Peninsula. Around 1586, Ribadeneyra thought seriously about writing his biography, a task ultimately taken by Ávila's disciple, Granada.[6] Ávila's writings were meant to inspire rigorous asceticism and forms of discipline that would facilitate a proper and fruitful relationship to God. His regimen of abnegation and fervid prayer was meant to be followed by all: men and women, rich and poor.[7] Indeed, rulers themselves would reap benefits from his work. Granada pointed out with amazement that Ávila's advice is just as important for spiritual matters as it is for things pertaining to "the good governance of a Christian Republic."[8] Such a renewed embrace of Ávila's spirituality was meant to influence rulers as much as anyone else. It is not by chance that the 1588 edition of his letters is dedicated to the Portuguese viceroy Cardinal-Archduke Albert at a time when the Armada prepared to sail and was released by the same printer that published the *Scisma*.[9]

Clearly *De schismate Anglicano* and the *Scisma* belong to different genres than spiritual manuals, but the ultimate goals promoted are fundamentally the same. Moreover, because these texts were all being produced at essentially the same time, it seems that publishers, editors, and authors saw them as deeply related. While Sander's and Ribadeneyra's histories might seem far removed from the realm of spiritual edification, I have argued that both authors (unsurprisingly) used history to provide pious lessons. To some, it might seem that "spiritual" books cannot be placed on the same plane as books so imbued with salaciousness and tonal harshness. This seems misguided. Though these books might seem far removed from bald polemics, they were not. Questier and Lake have shown how Persons's *Directorie*, because it was a guide to good Christian living, could and did have a polemical edge amid ongoing debates about how English Catholics lived or failed to live. Far from mending fences, it had an exclusionary function that rejected irresolute Catholics.[10] More broadly, the species of Iberian spirituality briefly alluded to here was not innocent of promoting and establishing a mind-set that could lead to the crudest sort of real-life violence. As Denis Crouzet has suggested within the context of the French Wars of Religion, the works of Juan de Ávila, Teresa de Ávila, and Granada became popular in France during religious strife and helped create a mental world that allowed neighbor to kill neighbor.[11]

Aside from thematic resonances, histories and spiritual guides share a similar relationship to the reader. Authors like Loarte or Ávila expected audiences to act on their advice, to do certain things, to say certain prayers. Sander and Ribadeneyra also wanted to inspire activity. Histories could elicit certain types of real-world actions—discussion, commonplacing, note-taking—that informed how people behaved in public life. Sander's and Ribadeneyra's histories expected people to change their ways of thinking but also to do things based on this change, be it through prayer or war. These actions impinged on the salvation of not only individual readers but Christendom as a whole.

And yet while I would like to suggest that Sander and Ribadeneyra were more than "mere" propagandists, I cannot undermine the profoundly political nature of their projects. After all, changes in worldview and heart were to be in the service of Elizabeth's deposition, the punishment of heretics, and the bloodshed of warriors. To disentangle the spiritual and the political

PART I   HISTORY IN ACTION

workings of these books would be foolish. The Anglo-Spanish moment around the time of the Armada allowed the priests discussed here to explore where these two worlds—the spiritual and the political—could and did meet on paper.

The publicness of these books deeply influenced their vitality. A survey of private letters and memorials to the Spanish crown during periods of potential anti-Elizabethan action would reveal many of the discursive activities I have described above. Moralist clarions, historical scare tactics, and pointed critiques abound. But these were things read by candlelight in privileged spaces: the king's study, for example. By 1585, because the political moment allowed and required it, a Sanderian narrative and its interpretive implications involved a broad reading public. For them, editors tried to weed out worldly objectives that might have been tied to Anglo-Spanish strife. This is clearly the case in Ribadeneyra's decision not to publish the "Exhortación," and it is equally true of the tone taken by Spanish Elizabethans who had previously (in private correspondence) championed the conquest of England in terms of its benefits to Philip II's efforts in Holland and advertised the *ease* of the enterprise.[12] By accentuating spiritual imperatives, authors and editors tried to publicize a righteous cause and exhort proper responses to critical problems. These books tried to create a community of readers who might compel—or participate in—certain royal efforts like the conquest of England. In doing so, authors tried to ensure that this broader community would also have the tools to judge those who participated or stayed behind, who failed or succeeded based on a providential logic.

English history as promoted by Sander and his editors became embedded in the Catholic imaginary, a tool to be used to work out pervasive problems of the day—evils that (from a Catholic perspective) often had roots in England or at the very least English echoes. This is particularly true in the Iberian world. As Deborah Forteza shows, the publication of the *Scisma* was a game changer, influencing all writings about England.[13]

Aside from examples of times when authors mined the *Scisma* extensively—as, for example, Calderón de la Barca did—perhaps the most important proof of its pervasive influence are those moments when English history appears out of nowhere. In the early seventeenth century, we find strains of Ribadeneyra (and Sander) as far away from Madrid as Mexico City, where the German printer Heinrich Martin published a long astrological treatise with historical elements used to prove what was written in the stars. Much of his choppy historical narrative deals with religious matters, especially the horrors of heresy, including Sander's take on Henry VIII's incest.[14]

Back in Spain, when polemicists battled over the status of Teresa of Ávila as patron saint, they evoked the fragility of Catholic security amid the challenges of heresy and corruption by pointing to England's past.[15] In general, debates about ecclesiastical authority in Spain immediately brought to mind Henry VIII's overreach. Juan de Mariana, in a pungent pamphlet on monetary policy, evoked Sander's discussion of Tudor coin debasement as a form of highway robbery. He admonished the "prudent reader," asking him to think about "whether we are getting on the same road; whether that historical moment is a portrait of the tragedy certainly threatening us."[16]

In the years around 1588, English Catholics had knocked on Spanish doors, and they were let in. English Catholics had written a book to influence Catholics everywhere and Spaniards in particular. They succeeded. By finding amplification in Spain through Ribadeneyra's voice, an exile version of the English past—their interpretations of English history and its lessons—became deeply rooted in the Spanish world. *De schismate Anglicano* and the *Scisma* would cast their shadows on Spanish affairs, much like they would over the rest of Catholic Europe, as reminders of the nightmare that came true.

PART II

THE KING'S MEN

Alonso Sánchez could not have pitched his plan to conquer China at a worse time. The Jesuit stood before Philip with memorials in hand just as the king received news of the Armada's defeat. Both men went through the motions, knowing that nothing would come of the meeting. If God had ordained defeat at the hands of heretics in a runty island near Spain, surely an attempted conquest of a distant, powerful state like China was out of the question. In retrospect, Sánchez's bellicosity seems foolish, and his appeals for war seem little more than bluster.[1] And yet as Manel Ollé Rodríguez has shown, he was not a lone wolf. His devotion to the Chinese enterprise emerged from the hopes and plotting of several interest groups in Manila with their eyes on Macao, the riches that Canton had to offer, and a new missionary zone.[2] Sánchez did not ignore material desires but framed potential conquest as a spiritual mission ordained by God. The Philippines had become a providential entryway to China, and he urged the king to "note that God put that grain in the midst of such a vast and deserted field to multiply."[3] The king could now undertake an enterprise bigger than any other by any "Monarch of the World." If he chose to do so, he might "achieve riches and perpetual renown" as well as "the salvation and repair of so many souls created for Him (God) and redeemed by his blood, who are now deceived and possessed by the devil and his blindness and vices."[4]

Plots to promote the conquest of China exemplify the heightened providentialist tone of Spanish political and religious culture. Geoffrey Parker has emphasized the messianic qualities of Philip's reign and argued that he and many of his supporters were driven by a belief that the end was near and that the king (as a new Solomon) could usher in a transformative age.[5] Such a vision had inspired Philip's effort against England, ensuring its execution despite tactical concerns among his closest advisers.

Some close to the king pushed against the rampant providentialism that they blamed for clouding the king's judgment, but messianic discourses did not die.[6] As we will see, after the Armada, the king's attentions increasingly turned to France, where the succession of Henry IV, a Protestant, seemed unacceptable. Some goaded Philip with terms such as those used by moralists like Pedro de Ribadeneyra. As one would-be advisor put it, the battle, though difficult, had to be put in perspective: What, after all, was better, "God or the state or the company of infidels?" France had allied with Satan, and anyone who made peace with them was equally damned. God would surely protect Spain, "to the loss of infidels and corrupt, envious men."[7]

Just as providential arguments were used to support the king and his aspirations, they could be employed to suggest Habsburg demise. The place of Spanish monarchy within millennial eschatology was fragile. In the 1590s, the rogue Italian Dominican friar and eclectic philosopher Tommaso Campanella saw that the end was near and reckoned that Spain would play an important role. Writing from Naples, a Habsburg territory, he asserted that Spain *might* be a positive force in the process but that the Spanish monarchy could only grow if it submitted to the papacy. There were signs that Spain would be crucial in defeating the Ottomans, but success depended on decisions made by its rulers. The jury was out.[8]

In Castile, individuals could easily slip between fervent support and serious doubt. Juan de Herrera, for example, designed El Escorial—an emblem of Philip's Solomonic aspirations—while he also helped outfit caves for a select few who would survive the cataclysm that would usher in the rule of a future, pious king after Philip's demise.[9]

This section will explore ambivalences at the heart of Spanish political culture through the lens of an important "English" discourse. We will see the ways in which Spanish Elizabethans became integral to Iberian politics and how they held to the Spanish line in addressing the rest of Europe. Most of the books treated here were not written in aggressively messianic registers, although they all try to construct an image of Philip as the good Christian king, often in the guise of the providential savior. However, the goal was not mere adulation; even in books easily identified as pro-Philip propaganda, we can discern the combination of praise and critique we saw in part 1. Even when deeply embedded in Spanish affairs and while on Spanish soil, the English Catholics discussed here were not minions but spoke in multifaceted ways befitting their exile.

Philip knew the benefits and liabilities of English Catholic polemics. The next three chapters reveal how the Habsburg regime absorbed, refined, and reacted to English books to promote a version of itself relevant to the series of challenges, real and rhetorical, that it experienced in the early 1590s. While the king himself had messianic impulses, his hesitancy to embrace all aspects of Spanish Elizabethan discourse on Iberian soil speaks to the regime's sophisticated understanding of providentialist propaganda and its discontent. Such nuanced engagement with "foreign" discourses in Spain proves the extent to which these helped constitute Spanish political culture.

4

ENGLISH VOICES IN SPAIN

In April 1591, something miraculous happened over the skies of Norfolk. At midnight on the Feast of St. George, three blazing suns appeared surrounding a resplendent image of a cross within a circle accompanied by a dimmer one beneath it. News of this prodigy spread, and one report, though uncertain of what it all meant, read it as a good sign. The reporter recalled that England had last been reconciled on the feast of St. Andrew (Scotland's patron saint).[1] Perhaps something similar was afoot. Later that year, more formal interpretations circulated broadly. Alonso Chacón, a Dominican antiquary in Rome, wrote a book in which he placed the event within a historical context reaching back to Constantine's *Chi-Rho* miracle. Just as the emperor's vision spoke to his imperial destiny, Chacón implied that recent prodigious signs prefigured Spain's future successes against heretics. The timely publication of Chacón's book shows how quickly rumor and news sheets from English Catholic centers across Europe could spread.[2] Through these reports, English Catholics wanted to amaze, edify, and maintain anti-Elizabethan sentiment. Such efforts intensified in Spain after the Armada, partly because the Iberian Peninsula had become a new node of English Catholic activity. Young English Catholic men would train to become zealous missionaries in Castile while some of their older, more established compatriots and teachers worked to ensure that Philip II resumed efforts against (English) heresy.[3]

Life for Englishmen in Iberia was complicated, especially during years of Anglo-Spanish strife. William Arte would learn this one Lisbon summer while holed up in a chamber where few people, especially an English merchant, wanted to be. Suspected of heresy, he stood before the Inquisition. Asked whether Lutherans were right to break away from the Church, he predictably answered no. In fact, he continued, it seemed that "God punished them [English heretics] by putting together the Armada."[4] Like modern scholars, contemporary ecclesiastical authorities were doubtful. The Inquisition was interested in Arte because he, like many of his compatriots—and those viewed as rough equivalents, such as the Irish and Scots—could not be trusted.[5] In those days, Catholics worried "lest perhaps the cancer of the plague of heresy be injected and circulate through the hidden veins of the republic."[6]

English priests did not escape humiliation. John Blackfan, Henry Floyd, and John Bosville learned this when they were unceremoniously put in chains upon arriving in Burgos. Spanish eyebrows were first raised when the strangers visited a famous local shrine. It was May 1589, and England had recently attacked Iberian shores. Rumors spread "that some of Drake's agents had arrived, who having donned the habit of ecclesiastics in order to conceal themselves, were feigning prayer and devotion." As authorities dragged them off, crowds shouted, "These are kinsmen and friends of Drake in our midst!"[7] These were not isolated incidents, nor were they simply the overheated acts of an unruly mob. One anonymous informant wrote of the "great pity" he felt toward an "English bishop" who had been mistreated at the hands of the archbishop of Burgos.[8]

At court, things did not go smoothly either. Much as Nicholas Sander had found the regime hard to deal with, Robert Persons felt fury after fury when it was his turn to represent English Catholics in Spain. At times, he could not hide his anger. In a letter to Philip's secretary Juan de Idiáquez, the Jesuit linked endemic distrust of Englishmen to recent failures. For success, Persons insisted, the Spanish needed to nurture alliances with Catholics in England. They had failed to do this. Did this betray a Spanish aversion to the English? In that case, perhaps Spain's recent defeat was a good thing; English Catholics may have been spared Spanish abuse.[9] This tough talk was hyperbolic, but the sentiment came from a plausible assessment of reality. Persons rightly intuited that those whom English Catholics relied on most did not always trust them.

Many in and around Spanish circles expressed wariness. The papal nuncio in Spain grumbled about "the many exaggerations concerning the great need" experienced by Catholics in England.[10] The count of Olivares, Spanish ambassador to Rome, tended to be less cynical but no less of a realist. Though burdened by unending petitions by the likes of William Allen and Persons, he understood they were moved by Catholic zeal. Overstatements were not duplicitous but colored by the experience of exile. Despite their well-meant optimism, however, he understood conquering England would not be simple and that the English—Catholic, Puritan, or neutral—would not greet Spaniards with open arms.[11] Philip himself assumed Catholics in England would be "of little or no help."[12]

And yet the regime did not leave English Catholics stranded. From the start of the Elizabethan regime, Philip had been a benefactor of exiles. After the Armada, his attentions increased. He publicly and privately, metaphorically and at least once literally, embraced those English Catholics in Spain who sought his protection and assistance. The king's piety ensured charity and paternal warmth. Diego de Yepes, Philip II's confessor, recalled reading and telling him about persecuted Englishmen to "help relieve his infirmities." Yepes chose to read him the lives of English martyrs because of the "particular affection" the king had for them.[13]

The regime also had politic reasons for helping. It subscribed to a precept promoted by Bernardino de Mendoza, Philip II's longtime ambassador: military success depended on developing opportune if often fragile relationships with desperate men. In England and France, Mendoza had courted Catholics who, finding themselves amid religious, political, and economic upheaval sought his king's protection. Many of these foreign allies became some of Philip's staunchest supporters. They were motivated by the firm belief that their lives and property were in danger, and they were thus innocent of Machiavellian scheming. Unlike malcontents who were moved "more by the present ills, than by the uncertain future," the truly desperate acted on a fatalism that made change within the current regime seem impossible. Malcontents looked for an easy fix; they compromised with whoever wanted to cut a deal. Desperate men wanted revenge at any cost. Among them, seeds of "universal displeasure" flourished, as did the thorns of civil war.[14]

Olivares offered a less nuanced, if still utilitarian, analysis. He, like Mendoza, deemed exilic passion an asset. English Catholics were well-versed in English affairs and guided by "necessity, that great teacher."[15] They would do the king's bidding and would be good informants when needed. Even if the regime often ignored English Catholic suggestions, stacks of "white papers" in Spanish archives show that it took their advice into consideration and greedily accepted intelligence.

The usefulness of English Catholics depended on circumstances. Should Spain go to war with England, a small coterie might help with strategy and the mechanics of conquest. More importantly, they would become key propagandists for Spain, as they had intended in 1588 when they published English pamphlets and broadsides to accompany the Armada.[16] But even outside the context of active Anglo-Spanish war, English Catholics stayed relevant. During times of low-grade or indirect combat, by word and body, they helped support the regime.

Bring Out Your (Future) Dead

The English college in Valladolid became an important institutional vehicle for developing close relationships between Spaniards and their Elizabethan allies, but cementing the connection took some work. When Persons reached Madrid at the end of 1588, he probably did not plan to establish English colleges and hospices in Iberia. But in response to a growing English Catholic presence in Spain and the instabilities experienced by exiles elsewhere on the Continent, he ultimately helped create such institutions at Valladolid, Sanlúcar, and Seville.[17] At first, he had to quell fears caused by Englishmen on Spanish soil. Some Spaniards thought so-called students might spread heresy; a "traitor" might very easily hide "beneath a student's gown."[18] The Inquisition was especially leery, partly because of xenophobia but also because many exiles were Jesuits. Tensions between the Holy Office and the Society of Jesus in Spain had recently reached a peak.[19] Eventually, city and religious authorities grudgingly gave in. They offered the seminarians rooms in the hospital of St. Cosmos and St. Damian as temporary refuge. But more protests ensued. Some complained the hospital did not have enough resources to take on English exiles. Foreigners would take away from the public services offered, especially those for the poor. When the king got involved in favor of the exiles, some dug in their heels. They questioned whether the king could force assistance without papal approval.[20] By September 1589, the Englishmen left their temporary quarters and got funds to rent a house of their own. It would become the seminary that still stands today: the Royal English College of St. Alban.

These birth pangs produced the first printed acts of persuasion by English Catholics in Castile. In September 1589, Persons published a pamphlet showcasing the importance of seminaries in the post-Tridentine world to fend off critics and establish financial stability for the fledgling college.[21]

As Leo Hicks has suggested, such advertisements may have been necessary because the seminary was still something new in Spain at the end of the sixteenth century; Persons wanted to underscore the continuities between the new Spanish school and others like it in Rheims and Rome. Both were noted orthodox houses of learning, and like them, the new college was an approved institution in service of Catholic renewal.[22] As evidence, he pointed to the English situation: once a seemingly lost cause, seminarian efforts offered new glimpses of hope. Young priests helped convert heretics, and Catholics who had been afraid to express their faith were empowered by them to profess the truth openly. This made heretics lose hope; they feared debating Catholics because their ignorance might show. The most learned heretics "begin to doubt, although for honor's sake and in order not to lose their property, they do not want to convert."[23]

Such assurances did little to ease local concerns about possible heretic infiltration or the role of an English college among competing religious houses. Persons offered cynics his promise that the college would not be a disturbance: the seminarians only wanted to finish their studies and return to England. He also underlined the traditional alliances between England and Spain. Persons recalled past diplomatic relations and the recent aid provided by English Catholics after the Armada's failure, when they tried to care for Spanish prisoners.[24]

Persons outlined a procedural scheme to prevent the infiltration of heretics. First, there would be a rigorous selection process that would require evidence of each potential student's faith. Spanish authorities would examine the students. Second, the students would have a Spanish rector, would live publicly under the watch of all, and would go to confession frequently. Third, Persons argued that Valladolid was an auspicious place for a college because it was a seat of the Inquisition. Surely the Holy Office would be vigilant.[25]

The most powerful rhetorical moments in Persons's pamphlet juxtapose meekness with defiance. He insisted that the political situation in France and elsewhere required another center of English Catholic activities. Beside God, English Catholics could only rely on Spain. After this whimper Persons let loose a bark. Why would the Spanish refuse to help? If French and Flemish exiles received Spanish aid, why not the English? The reader should recall God was always pleased by works of charity done unto strangers, especially those who were fighting in His name.[26] Persons finished by asking Spanish elites (*nobles y principales*) for money, though he added that the English had no intention of disturbing "other pious works" in town.[27] The result of Spanish kindness would be the victory of Catholicism in England and peace between the two kingdoms.[28]

English Catholics had no greater argument for their cause than their martyrs. As Hicks has pointed out, the lives and valiant deaths of recusants went a long way "to stimulate the generosity of the faithful."[29] In Spain, news of their heroic acts spread widely in diplomatic correspondence, newsletters, and books on the Continent. Iberian lands inevitably became the center of a communication network that made English martyrdom a source of edification on a global scale.[30] The presence of English Catholics, their deeper immersion into Spanish society, and their more exacting efforts to gain Spanish support ensured the specter of England's suffering would become more important than it had been in previous years. The establishment of English colleges in Spain led to an uptick in vernacular books on the country's martyrs, culminating in a long compendium of English sufferings published by Yepes, Philip's confessor, in 1599.[31]

Early in 1590, leaders of the English college in Valladolid promoted the dead. A broadside by Juan López Mançano (the new rector) listed martyrs from English seminaries across the Continent, a preview of what was to come for some of the young men in his care.[32] Persons compiled his own short martyrology, the *Relacion de algunos martyrios, que de nuevo han hecho los hereges de Inglaterra* (Relation of some martyrdoms once again committed by English heretics).[33] Broadly, the collection provided the faithful with a mirror where, as Persons put it, "we can see ourselves and fix ourselves, and reform our lives." The glorious dead reminded readers that recusants, especially those who fled from England and ended up in various colleges, were exemplary. Martyrs had long been placed before the faithful to fortify them, but reading about holy men and women of the past was less effective than news about contemporaries: "Present things are very moving and that which we see is much more of a stimulus than those things that we read or hear about."[34] English martyrs allowed for the participation in a kind of holiness that otherwise required a sophisticated historical imagination. Now martyrdom became more communicable. Their deaths also had immediate significance. Persons encouraged readers to understand English Catholic gore within a providential framework as God's way of guiding worthy men and women at a moment of great need.[35]

Persons wanted to tie his mission to a Habsburg destiny. Although the book was published after Philip had already cast his lot with the exiles, clearly more work needed to be done. Having already tapped her father, Persons appealed to the infanta Isabel Clara Eugenia, the book's dedicatee. He suggested his book would speak to her Christian and royal interests. Not only did he offer her spiritual edification, but he also showed that Philip's past benefactions to English priests had "sustained, protected, and favored these servants of God." In return for royal protection, the English had given their blood, and "there in heaven we should believe that they [martyrs] intercede particularly for those who have favored them here on earth." He asked the infanta to "imitate" the protections given by the king, especially toward the new English college in Valladolid.[36]

Persons also suggested that a debt was owed to English Catholics. The failure of the Armada *increased* Spanish responsibilities toward the English. The first account of English martyrdom in Persons's book pointedly deals with the aftermath of Spanish defeat to show the connection between English suffering and Spanish disappointments. After 1588, a once nervous Elizabethan regime became assertive. Fears of possible Spanish conquest disappeared, and the regime "turned into ferocious lions and raving tigers against Catholics."[37] Now Elizabeth and her advisors thought their crimes were justified. Together with unfair questions about papal allegiances, interrogators asked Catholic prisoners if they would support a Spanish invasion. This was done to give their religious persecution a secular appearance.

Persons emphasized that English Catholics *did* support the Spanish on spiritual grounds. They had never stopped supporting Habsburg efforts. He reminded readers that the count of Arundel was killed because he had prayed for the Armada's success. Help had come in more direct ways too. Despite imminent dangers, despite poverty and affliction, English Catholics showed remarkable courage in their protection of Spanish prisoners of the Armada.[38] Why should Spaniards not sacrifice gold and silver?

Stories of valiant Englishmen were told against the backdrop of contemporary geopolitical strife. Aside from the Elizabethan regime, with whom tensions had already exploded, the *Relacion* also took aim at France, especially Henry IV, who was then fighting with English forces in Brittany against the Spanish-supported Catholic League. English Catholics were casualties of these troubles. Persons underlined the point by including a letter by Elizabeth Sander (Nicholas Sander's sister) that provided information about the exiled nuns of Syon Abbey, who, having just arrived in Rouen, were in dire straits. Toward the end, she described how two English priests were sent to Philip to secure support for the holy women. The king promised money, but on the way back to France, things soured for the priests as Huguenots (French Calvinists) captured them in La Rochelle. There Henry IV interrogated and tortured them. Because the priests were poor and had no useful intelligence for Henry, he shipped them off with English heretics for even crueler treatment across the Channel. The vignette depicted English Catholics caught in a Franco-Spanish conflict and how the French thwarted Philip's best wishes.[39]

The king surely believed that helping exiles was the right thing to do but was doubtless also aware that support could be a public relations boon. In the summer of 1589, he openly gave his "favor and protection" to English Catholics when he allowed them to collect alms in all his realms.[40] By doing so, he took a stand against the naysayers who thought there was little to gain from an English presence on Spanish soil and thumbed his nose at heretics abroad. Philip must have understood the payoff for his aid in terms similar to those Cardinal Allen used in a thank-you note: Philip's efforts would garner heavenly and earthly rewards through "the souls of Catholics."[41] Support for Catholic exiles was an act of personal piety, but it would also have effects on earth, where God would support his efforts against heresy. If God was the primary cause for success, the king's alignment with past and future martyrs might also galvanize support among his own subjects and allies, providing an example of charity for those who, through prayers and war, would be the secondary cause of Habsburg victory.

The Iberian connection with English Catholics ensured Philip's good works toward them became more prominent. After his death, English and Spanish Catholics would hearken back to the king's kindness to inspire his son.[42] Indeed, some would suggest that support for English Catholics had become a defining feature of Habsburg rule. Yepes argued that Philip III, through his father's efforts, held a stake in English martyrdom. The martyrs themselves had become something like "an inheritance and legitimate patrimony."[43]

Such a significant relationship was actively nurtured. During the last decade of Philip II's reign, English exiles hoped for the best, but certainty was elusive in those days and with that monarchy. Still, no one could deny that things had improved for Persons and his men after the woes of 1588. Three years after a band of exiles showed up in Valladolid, unwanted and disliked, they would stand in the flesh before an approving king. The bond was cemented, and the spectacle of that encounter would be enshrined for Spanish and English readers to behold.

The Strong Embrace

By 1592, Philip II was past the point of enjoying travel. He was old, sick, tired, and evermore tied to the familiarities of his beloved palace, El Escorial.

Only a sense of duty and an understanding of the fragility of his authority made his voyage to Tarazona feasible. He left in May of that year for the *cortes* of Aragon, to pacify a kingdom that had grown weary of his rule. Philip traveled there in the aftermath of a rebellion in Zaragoza, inspired by Antonio Pérez, the king's former confidant turned fugitive in England. The incident unleashed pent-up pressures of social and political unrest that led to bloodshed and cutting polemics. Rebels defended Aragonese freedoms against perceived Castilian oppression and against a king whom they considered a tyrant.[44]

While the political significance of his visit to Tarazona could not be matched by any other stop along the way, his stay at Valladolid stands out for being the most pleasant. The city was eager to live up to its grandiose self-image and wanted to ensure a proper reception. It did. The city's various institutions gave Philip the most spirited greeting, the most joyous entertainments of his journey. Their fireworks disrupted the gloom of the enterprise.

Amid festivities and solemnities, Philip visited the English college. Like everything else on the trip, the event was highly choreographed and laden with meaning. Jesuit José de Acosta described festivities, which had been consciously planned for a jubilee day that would be celebrated with "great and universal devotion."[45] Students and faculty at the college also recognized the importance of this unique opportunity to speak to Philip and his children, Prince Philip and Isabel Clara Eugenia. They hurried to make their home amenable. Fresh coats of paint were applied; unfinished nooks were hidden behind elegant drapery, colorful emblems, and large posters with poetry on them. In later years, the day would be remembered with due reverence as "that most glorious and shining day, the brightest that ever was seen in this our College."[46] While two well-known manuscript accounts of Philip's travel mention the visit briefly and without much fuss, those involved ensured that its importance would be preserved in print.[47] The resulting pamphlets were more than news reports; as scholars have recently suggested, they were forms of "commemorative literature." These texts "preserved and disseminated the College's literary activities and . . . highlighted their political and ideological significance."[48]

The remembrance of Philip's visit benefitted both the king and his hosts. This is true of the English version by Persons, *A Relation of the King of Spaines Receiving in Valliodolid* [sic], and of the Spanish version prepared and expanded by the English Jesuit Joseph Creswell, the *Relacion de un sacerdote ingles*.[49] In the latter, Creswell explained the origins of the college and placed it within a providential framework while highlighting the worthiness of its students and their earnest efforts. Readers were even given a full summary of daily activities and a transcript of the solemn oath students took upon admittance. This, for a Spanish readership, would reinforce the worthiness of the cause and would inspire continued support.

The first half of the pamphlet contextualizes Philip's visit to the college. It points out the political significance of the voyage to quell rebellion in Aragon and describes the king's many, mostly pious, public activities before visiting. Creswell predictably emphasized the latter theme. By underlining the king's piety rather than the turbulent political circumstances, he signaled that the book meant to fly in the face of political realities.

Interests and destinies of king and exiles then united in a memorable embrace. After a flattering opening oration before the king, a young student approached Philip to kiss his hand. The king refused. Instead, he wrapped his arm around the young man's neck as "a sign of love."[50] Toward the end of the festivities, the king would embrace all the students as he had the first "as a sign of his Royal benignity, love and clemency."[51] These gestures were signs of familiarity that had compelled Philip to visit in the first place. Creswell revealed that Persons had only petitioned to meet the king; Philip himself suggested going to the college. Indeed, he chose to prioritize the visit over other state matters: some were surprised that he came on the day he did because he usually reviewed "extraordinary mail" then.[52] When Philip arrived, he went out of his way to show English Catholics high regard. He came without the normal retinue of guards "to show love and trust."[53] Such details underscored the bond between English Catholics and the king and implied by extension that the king's "natural" subjects should be supportive.

The optics of the event would boost Philip as well. Throughout, the king was depicted as a savior of oppressed Catholics. In this he was like another Constantine or like Joseph, who in Hebrew Scriptures gave nourishment to Jews in exile (indeed, to brothers who had once betrayed him).[54] Such allusions only reinforced the providential quality of the story students and teachers told. The king's awesome power was a divine gift to ensure his battle against heresy: "For this reason he has placed at his [Philip's] feet so many kings, and he has humiliated so many glorious men on earth, and he has raised up your monarchy no matter how much heretics and evil men have schemed." The wealth of the Indies and "the secrets of other kingdoms no matter how far away they might be" were connected with the king's great efforts to protect English Catholics and to "restore them to their *patria* someday."[55] In turn, English martyrdom reflected the king's own piety. Should some of the students at Valladolid suffer the gift of martyrdom, their glory would fall on the king both in heaven and on earth. Moreover, martyrdom would be great publicity. The blood of the fallen would, as Persons described it, "write in the squares and streets where they are spilled the great deal we owe to Your Majesty, as it will seem to say that this is blood that was made of those who spill it with the support and mercy that Your Majesty did unto them."[56]

Such bloody propaganda would be useful at any time, but it was particularly helpful given the political situation Philip faced. English Catholics doubled down on the basic pillars of Habsburg self-imaging: namely, an emphasis on the king's piety and providential role. And yet the significance of these platitudes was enhanced as the king traveled to quell a rebellion that challenged such royal pieties.

The Aragonese jealously protected their local *fueros*, or laws, that distinguished them from neighboring kingdoms like Castile.[57] Tensions between local autonomy and Philip's will to keep his "composite empire" united created serious problems throughout the era of Habsburg dominion. These were crystallized in the controversies surrounding Antonio Pérez. When Pérez fled imprisonment in Castile for the murder of Juan de Escobedo, he not only accused Philip of having masterminded said murder but also set off a jurisdictional battle. A squabble between local Aragonese judiciary authorities and the Inquisition (seen by some as Philip's foreign tool) led to violent altercations between those who wanted to keep local authority pristine and those who supported the legitimacy of transferring Pérez and his allies to Inquisitorial holding.

During and after his escape from Aragon to France, Pérez cemented his place as a symbol of the Aragonese revolt. He trumpeted the king's violent tyranny far and wide and self-servingly insisted his release from wrongful imprisonment was consonant with God's will. Pérez also emphasized his martyr-like role by highlighting the fact that "when God gives many tribulations and persecutions to one man, it is not only for his own good, but as an example and lesson for all."[58] Contrary to what Pérez and his supporters tried to suggest, the king insisted he was the protector of proven martyrs. Their support deflected Pérez's attacks because unlike his nemesis, Philip claimed some portion of true martyrdom.

Because of the spiritual capital the English Catholic mission had already accrued before Philip's arrival, the spectacle at the college did not devolve into mere back-patting. To the contrary, Persons and his students felt emboldened to offer up a cocktail of praise and exhortation of the sort that defined *De schismate Anglicano*.

During the opening oration that led to the noted embrace, the speaker compared Philip to two biblical figures: Obadiah and Cyrus. Obadiah had hidden Jews in caves and fed them water and bread when Jezebel killed the Lord's prophets. The contemporary resonance scarcely needed explanation, but it was stated anyway. Obadiah's actions paralleled "what the king has done when the English Jezebel expels priests and Catholics from her kingdom." But Philip was much greater than Obadiah because he had saved not just a hundred but many hundreds from death. Moreover, he did not hide them away but "received them publicly and put them in cities, giving them houses and support not only of bread and water."[59]

The verdict of Philip over Obadiah is notable, but the comparison—for those familiar with Scripture—was not simple. Many would have known that Obadiah had been a reluctant player in God's narrative. Indeed, after the efforts just mentioned, he had to be convinced by the prophet Elijah to continue fighting the enemy despite dangers posed by King Ahab, Jezebel's husband. After having done good once, Obadiah wondered why he should face further risk. He asked incredulously of Elijah, "And now thou sayst: Go and tell thy Lord [Ahab]: Elias is here that he may kill me?" (1 Kings 18:14).[60] As the sixteenth-century authors of the Douay-Rheims Bible put it in their commentary, Elijah only "hardly perswadeth him [Obadiah] to tell Achab that he [Elijah] is present."[61] Should readers (or listeners) have wanted to see (or hear) it, there might have been a less flattering comparison to be made with Philip. Having taken up the English cause so forcefully with the Armada, why did Philip now hesitate?

The example of Cyrus seems to confirm this double edge. The orator argued that he and his peers were like the Jews forced by providence to endure a Babylonian captivity only to return under the protection of a new Cyrus. He reminded Philip that the ancient king was chosen by God so that the world might fall at his feet and other kings might submit themselves to him. God humiliated the glorious and gave Cyrus secret treasures. Yet he ultimately failed to recognize these gifts as divine. The orator suspected that if God gave so much to a gentile, Philip was poised to receive more, since he was moved by "piety, religion, and virtue."[62] Why should the English not expect a similar fate as the Jews, since God had already rendered so many heretics subject to the king, had enriched the king with money from the Indies, and had so magnificently increased his power?

Comparisons to Cyrus surely flattered Philip, but there was a more menacing message embedded too. The orator, by invoking the great liberator, also evoked Cyrus the conqueror, thus calling for the conquest of England—a point so evident and combustible that the passage was omitted from the English version. This militant note adds a level of ambiguity to the praise for the king. The success of English Catholic efforts depended not only on support for the college but on further action of the sort that in 1592 was only aspirational.

The key event of the day's festivities involved several scholars showing off their oratorical and linguistic talents. These young men spoke in Hebrew, Greek, Latin, Welsh, English, French, and Spanish as they commented on Psalm 71. The choice of biblical text was not incidental; it praised Solomon, who in Scripture prefigured Christ, and thus allowed students to extol Philip by drawing useful parallels. In doing so, they drew on a playbook reaching back to the 1550s, when Charles V was figured as David and his son, soon-to-be-king Philip, was described as Solomon. Philip promoted similar imagery in his later years, as enshrined in the stone used to build El Escorial, a palace-mausoleum meant to replicate the Solomonic temple of old. The building was a vivid reminder that Philip, like Solomon, had been "granted exceptional peace and wisdom."[63]

Tellingly, at this moment of most robust potential for pro-Philip propaganda, English Catholics tried to temper the message for Spanish audiences. Christopher Highley has noted that the verses chosen for exegesis were carefully curated to avoid too close a marriage between monarchical propaganda and Christological imagery.[64] Creswell was also careful about how he described interpretations of those parts that had been included; deviations in the Spanish pamphlet and its English counterpart are notable.

During the Welsh oration, the speaker commented on verse 7: "There shall in his days spring up justice and abundance of peace as long as the moon or element shall endure." The English author explained that while this was "properly spoken on Christ and of his everlasting and ghostly inward peace and justice, as before hath been noted, yet did this man apply it also very aptly to the extraordinary peace and justice within the King's days, after so many wars of Charles the Emperor."[65] Creswell offered a slightly different description. The orator explained that although these words were spoken of Christ, "*by God's particular mercy* done unto His Majesty [Philip], the same could be said of his days, like the beautiful, clear days God had given his holy church."[66] This was both a nod at divine monarchy and a reminder that monarchical authority was a (contingent) gift.

Where the English version used particularly effusive language, the Spanish edition appeared muted. In the French speech, as described in English, the speaker comments that verse 13 of Psalm 71—"he shall spare the poor and needy and he shall save the souls of the poor"[67]—had been "sung in times past by the royal prophet David to his son Solomon, as to him that bare the figure of Christ or Savior who was indeed, the true Salomon." But, he continued, "it hath not seemed to us from the purpose this day to apply the same [to] your [Philip's] royal person, not as a figure of our Savior to come as Salomon was, but rather as to a perfect flower, royal minister, & most faithful disciple of our said savior now in heaven."[68] This rhetorical flourish was excised from the Spanish version.

For Spanish readers, the author may have wanted to add a note of wariness. The first oration (in Hebrew) discusses the first verse: "O God give thy judgment to the King and thy justice the son of the king." In English, the text recalls that "as judgment and justice were two principal pearls, and precious stones which among others did adorn and greatly beautify an Imperial crown, and for that, and for that reason were so especially attributed in this verse of the psalm unto the Royal Government of Christ our savior." The speaker continues, "By the singular goodness & favor of the same our savior," despite rampant war and other tribulations, "judgment and justice should flourish in the crown of Spain, as never by any man's memory was recorded the like."[69] In this case, the Spanish text follows much the same line, though when comparing God's kingdom and the Spanish crown, it hesitates, asking "our Lord that he always conserve these virtues in her."[70]

Pro-Philip propaganda was not always so restrained. As Adam Beaver and others have shown, the king actively promoted the biblicization of his image by subventing biblical scholarship.[71] In the popular press, the Christological parallels between Philip and Christ himself could be crude. For example, in the early years of the Dutch Revolt, Hans Liefrinck published (after an engraving by Hieronymus Wierix) a memorable double portrait of Christ and Philip, putting both on the same visual plane.[72] Closer to the events at hand, less than a month before the king visited St. Alban's, some professors at the local university offered more straightforward support for the king's power than the seminarians would. A medical doctor pointed to an anatomical model as he explained that Philip was the "head of the Republic." Later, a professor of canon law dealt with royal authority in a plainly absolutist mode by minimizing the contractual relationship between king and subjects: "Neither the prince nor the king are established by men, but are chosen by the hand of God and by him raised to such a dignity."[73] None of this is surprising or inherently at odds with what English Catholics were saying, but it shows that praise could be, and often was, thicker.

The impulse to hedge had to do with sensibilities and contexts. Men like Persons agreed with a strand of Catholic thought prevalent in Spain that emphasized the limits of monarchical authority. The Spanish translator reflected the animus of like-minded Spanish thinkers who claimed, as Pedro de Ribadeneyra did, that kings "are not proprietors of their kingdoms, they are God's viceroys and deputies."[74] (It is worth noting that Ribadeneyra was one of the men who approved the pamphlet's Spanish publication). Spanish sensibilities aside, the book's tonal shifts may also have coincided with a certain wariness based on concrete experiences: while the book extolled Philip's virtues, it also advised him. While celebrating the king, students at the college also tried to impress upon him the duties of a good Christian monarch, subtly pushing him to live up to that standard.

There was nothing subversive in taking such a tack. The regime itself saw the whole spectacle as a teaching moment. Throughout the day (and throughout the text), Philip's son was a special target of performed wisdom and many of the materials displayed were collected for the prince's later perusal. A manuscript of emblems and poetry drawn from the event survives and was clearly intended for the prince's inspection, even after he became king.[75] Much of the manuscript deals with ways the younger Philip could learn from the elder, but the texts also speak more broadly to the herculean tasks required to destroy heresy. As with the *Scisma*, the message for Prince Philip was equally relevant to Philip II on whom, for better or worse, English Catholics depended.

The Franco-English Voice in Spain

Philip's visit and the subsequent reportage is an important context for a remarkable case of polemical ventriloquism. Sometime in September, Antonio de Herrera—Philip's future chronicler—published a translation of a book purporting to be a "warning" written by English Catholics to French Catholics and first published in France: *Advertencias que los Catolicos de Inglaterra escrivieron a los Catolicos de Francia* (Warnings written by English Catholics to Catholics in France).[76] Herrera's book came a few months after another translation published in Madrid by Félix de Guzmán, a Cathedral canon in Seville.[77] Marco Penzi has suggested that English Catholics must have promoted these publications to galvanize support for their cause in Spain.[78] This is undoubtedly correct, but there is room for a little more precision. Herrera's translation is further evidence of Philip's anglicized efforts to settle matters in Aragon. As such, it shows how embedded an English discourse could be within Habsburg political culture at a moment of high stress.

Herrera's and Guzmán's interests in their French template were different. Guzmán acknowledged the book's value to "understand the particulars of the state of the things of France and the origins of the tempest that our religion suffers there." But in general, the translator did not delve into polemics; instead, the book comes off as a showpiece. An introductory letter by Guzmán's uncle talks about the difficulties of translation and the merits of his nephew's work. Guzmán himself wrote of how he had been attracted to the book because of its sharpness and ingenuity. He dwelled on the book's rhetorical delights, its exemplary apologetical style with all its "metaphors, ironies, interrogations, and other figures."[79]

Herrera's framing is more predictable given the book's content. He dedicated it to Cristóbal de Moura, an important member of the Council of State, to insinuate himself further within the king's patronage circles at a moment when he was still just outside Philip's inner sanctum. He underlined the book's central theme: how prejudicial accepting a heretical king would be to the Church. Together with the central text, he also appended a series of shorter ones—not in the original French—to further smear the enemy and show that Philip's involvement in French affairs was solely for the "conservation of the Catholic faith."[80]

Herrera's book had royal imprimaturs all over it. The title page introduces the translator as a "servant of his majesty," and the book was published in Zaragoza by Lorenço de Robles, the king's official printer. After the dedicatory epistle to Moura, the reader would have turned to see Philip's imperial crest.

Philip clearly wanted to promote an *English* voice in Zaragoza. To this end, Herrera's book did not fill the reader in on a white lie that Guzmán did not hide: as he put it, the original French book was "composed by some French Catholics under the name of Englishmen."[81] In fact, though he probably did not know the specifics, the French book had been anonymously published by Louis Dorléans, a member of the radical French League in Paris. Katy Gibbons argues that Dorléans tried to use "English examples to urge the prevention of a similar course of events in France."[82] Herrera, like Guzmán, must have known the game being played, but he played it straight. He simply told readers they held in their hands "a warning that English Catholics give to French Catholics."[83]

In Aragon, the book would have had a double edge. At the time, Spain was in the middle of helping the French League's forces against Henry IV, who asserted his rights to the French throne. The fight against Henry implied conflict with Elizabeth, who staunchly supported him, especially before his conversion back to Catholicism from Calvinism in 1593. From Philip's perspective, the French threat did not stop neatly at the Pyrenees. His cautious sympathies toward French resistance against Protestants had always been predicated on the fear of heresy's seepage from the other side. Such fears seemed especially justified during the 1590s. Antonio Pérez had already hatched a short-lived plot to take French troops into Aragon, and fears of renewed French efforts plagued the king's travels in 1592. Reports landed on Philip's desk with warnings that Spain was in danger on all fronts: through Portugal with the potential assistance of those who supported Antonio, prior of Crato (then in France), and through Aragon, a place still teeming with malcontents. Some reports suggested that the French kept a close watch on Aragonese turmoil and that they waited for the king's forces to disband "to enter with the people that wandered there [Pérez's supporters] and Aragonese *naturales* to rouse that kingdom."[84]

These threats never materialized, but they intensified tensions. Philip's regime understood that quashing a rebellion did not extinguish rebellious instincts among laity and clergy. The link between French heresy and Aragonese rebellion was magnified because of Pérez's links to heretical regimes *and* because he himself had been deemed heretical after (trumped-up) Inquisitorial persecution.[85] If hugging English Catholics in Valladolid was a defensive measure against criticisms that inspired rebellion, the *Advertencias* took an offensive stance: it used English warnings to shame Aragonese subjects.

The *Advertencias* must have felt ready-made for Philip's purposes. Because Dorléans had written it in 1586, before the League had turned on Henry III, the book does not have much to say against any "legitimate" monarch. Even if Henry III had proven himself unworthy of his throne, attacking another (legitimate) king could prove uncomfortable for Philip. As far as many Catholics were concerned, Henry IV was no king at all. The Spanish regime wanted to attack a known heretic and reveal the atheistically (and therefore cruel) habits of that brood. Henry IV stood at the center of a broad Protestant conspiracy to spread its heretical filth. From the 1560s, he appealed to foreign troops, risking the souls and lives of Frenchmen in hopes of taking a crown that was not his to take. Henry IV indulged in passions and lusts that in their lechery evoked memories of Henry VIII in terms of both his sexual addictions and the poor governance they portended. The French pretender adhered to nothing but the logic of raw power, the only tool Satan provided.[86] Misery awaited those who cast their lot with him, especially among putative Catholics.

Heretics were wily dissemblers, chameleons willing to say or do whatever was necessary to achieve their nefarious ends. Those tempted by Henry's appeals, his claims to peacefulness and sanguineous legitimacy, needed to recognize the profound heresy in his heart and heresy's incompatibility both with good rule and with the Catholic roots of the French crown. For those who still harbored hopes that Henry might—despite all his faults—at the very least end war within France, the English example seemed important. Elizabeth too had claimed benevolence toward the confessional enemy, but reality proved her lies. Persecution, execution, and all sorts of bloody abuses reigned supreme. English Catholics were Elizabeth's "slaves," subjects of constant mockery, the playthings of heretics.[87]

France stood at the precipice of such a great threat because of its moral weakness. Much as *De schismate Anglicano* implied, the *Advertencias* called for Catholic soul-searching. In France, those who should have safeguarded the Church were not up to the task. Priests had "fallen asleep," prelates had become mere lackeys to politicians, a whole clerical class had become obsessed with money.[88] As a result, society had fallen into ruins. Clerics were ignorant, nobles ambitious and vain, justice had been corrupted, and moral depravity was pervasive. Moreover, Machiavellian and politic posturing among the French had aimed to temporize against heretical threats—or worse, tried to cut deals with heretics. The book doubles down on the failures of past peace edicts and efforts to compromise instead of firmly rejecting heresy. No matter how many times French Catholics had been warned, and despite recent evident failures, they had resisted reform. Lacking the requisite fortitude, they chose meekness and sloth, the ease of avarice over charity, the lures of pleasure over chastity and temperance.[89]

Such warnings are so common as to be trite, but the anglicizing conceit of the book made the message urgent. In its French and Spanish versions, the link to England did not need consistent emphasis to be effective. Indeed, aside from the title, some early commentary, and a handful of explicit comments linking English and French affairs, the book reads like League propaganda and nothing more. The link to England and all that it implied needed only gestures because it built on an already thriving discourse of fear in which England was seen as the seedbed of Continental heresy and exemplary of how a successful tyranny necessarily proceeds. This was certainly the case in France, where scholars have shown the vitality of English Catholic propaganda, and it was similarly true in Iberian lands, especially after Ribadeneyra's *Scisma* and related martyrological texts. Herrera's book suggests that Philip's regime recognized the potential force of such an "English Catholic" discourse or they would not have nurtured it.

Herrera's translation works on at least two fronts. First, the book justifies Philip's efforts against Henry and renders them essential. Dorléans (and subsequently, Herrera) suggested that the fall of England cleared the way for the same eventuality in France should current (Catholic) torpor continue. The message had similar resonances in Aragon during its subjection to rebellious humors. Such entangled fates between France and England might make colluders with those regimes think twice of associating with heretical forces (as Antonio Pérez had done), not out of loyalty to the king per se, but because playing with heretical fire meant getting burnt. Dorléans's moralist stance also seemed applicable to Philip's own Aragonese rebellious subjects. By suggesting the moral shortcomings of French Catholics, Herrera hinted at the weaknesses of Spanish society and blamed it, not the king, for current tribulations.

Conclusion

When Philip II embarked on the Armada campaign, the history of his reign became indelibly linked to England. This had been the hope of English Catholics who promised the king success and looked forward to the reform of Christendom under a Spanish banner. In defeat, Catholic exiles and their allies worked to secure the entwinement between Spanish concerns and English Catholic desires, and they succeeded to the extent that the king actively adopted English Catholic discourses when it seemed to his advantage. This was true not only in Spain but also abroad. As we will see in the following chapter, Philip II and his advisors embraced English efforts to expand on germinal efforts in the 1586 *De schismate Anglicano* to defend the king from (Elizabethan) aspersions by pinning all aspects of bad governance on Elizabeth on a European scale.

5

AN ANGLO-SPANISH VOICE IN EUROPE

English Catholics played a crucial role in Philip II's self-promotion abroad. The king had always faced criticisms, but a mix of diplomatic bluster, a muscular foreign policy, and a series of failures ensured the end of his reign would be especially turbulent. While supporters saw the king's approach to European (and global) affairs as a key to saving Christendom from heresy, enemies saw it as a ploy to extend Spanish dominion and establish a universal monarchy. The fierce arguments among those who held these opposed views took place in a pan-European discursive space constituted and memorialized by print. No reader would have been surprised by a French pamphlet written by an anti-Spanish Portuguese exile Vasco Figueiro, printed in English as *The Spaniards monarchie and the leaguers Olygarchie*. While the booklet—one of many possible examples—described Philip's oppression of Portugal as a warning to French Catholics, its message worked just as well for English readers. The English editor connected the dots: "Is not our Island [England] the mark that Philip's ambitions especially aim at? Nay would he not repute himself an absolute Monarch, if he might but get any interest with us? And have not we a viperous brood of puritan Papists, and reconciled Leaguers, that dream upon a new invasion?"[1]

Elizabeth's counselors would have responded with resounding yeses. Defeating the Armada changed the way the regime saw itself within a providential narrative, but it did little to quell old fears. The Spanish empire might fall, but it would not go down without a fight. Many at court clenched their jaws as they received intelligence about Spain's attempted invasion of Brittany, part of a strategy to intervene in French confessional conflicts. From an English perspective, it looked like continued efforts to extend Spanish tyranny. But Spain was only part of the problem; the regime feared Rome just as much as Madrid. Not only did the pope seem to support Philip's efforts against English and French Protestantism, but he appeared on the verge of starting a new missionary assault on England.[2] New English colleges sprouting on the Iberian Peninsula looked less like educational havens and more like nexuses of Hispano-papal plots. Such fears were confirmed in reports brought by a secular priest who had spent time at one of these: John Cecil. While in Valladolid, he had been employed by Catholics to gauge the level of English support *in* England *for* Spain.[3] These reports hardened Cecil's belief that England needed to take a more proactive stance against Spain. They also provided ammunition to push back against wrongheaded efforts at home to censure troublesome Protestants. Catholics at home and abroad posed a clear and imminent threat far beyond anything posed by some (perhaps overzealous) Puritans.[4]

Cecil had long been the secret hand behind anti-Spanish polemics in England, but 1591 marked an important change. After some chest thumping in 1588, anti-Spanish propaganda generally used a range of masking techniques—anonymity, pseudonymity, and so on—that gave the regime plausible deniability and kept popular vulgarities at arm's length. In 1591, Cecil orchestrated the publication of a proclamation in Elizabeth's name that took previous tropes and made them official denunciations of specific enemies.[5] The *Proclamation* promoted a series of initiatives—the vigorous hunting of Catholic traitors who had sold their souls to Rome and Spain—and established the legitimacy of those initiatives. Cecil concocted an overcooked description of a Hispano-papal-papist cabal against which the English nation had no choice but to fight.

The *Proclamation* revisited Philip II's predatory instincts. Cecil's attack built on a central paradox in most anti-Philip bromides toward the end of his reign: while enemies expressed fear of Spanish hegemony, simultaneously they indulged in fantasies about the king's weakness and imperial decrepitude. Cecil started with a critique of the king's decision to interfere in French politics, describing his efforts as "mighty actions (as he never before attempted the like)." But despite Philip's terrifying aggression, he would not succeed. His behavior would lead "to the ruin or correction of such as will not be content in peace with their own." The providential angle emerges again with specific reference to Philip's past failures in England, "whereof

God gave him and his whole army just cause of repentance." Philip's inability to understand the writing on the wall revealed the irrationalism of his foreign policy. The king was in no shape to challenge the English and the French. His royal body itself was proof; Philip was then in his "declining years," a time "when he ought to be satisfied without seeking of more kingdoms by violence and arms." Cecil underlines the unseemly enormity of the king's empire: only the victory of passion over reason could lead the king to expand an empire already composed of "more crowns and kingdoms and countries, and more wealth than any of his progenitors."[6] This reality made his enemies tremble, but the extent of Philip's realms could easily signal something *less* troubling as well. Readers sympathetic to the Elizabethan regime heard echoes of recent Cecilian efforts to show Philip's inability to keep it all together. His empire, according to some critics, tore at the seams.[7]

Conflict with Philip had nothing to do with religion: the Elizabethan regime bemoaned the king's expansionist ambitions because they prevented friendship among all European nations. Cecil wished that Philip had "been altered into some peaceable humor, meet to have disposed him to live in concord with us, and other Christian princes his neighbors; and by such good means to establish an universal peace in Christendom." Philip's disinterest in Christian peace could be gleaned from his relationship with the pope. He intended to keep the papacy under his thumb, arranging the election of Clement VIII, "a Millanois, a vassal of his own . . . and hath seduced him, without the consent of the college of cardinals, to exhaust the treasures of the church."[8] Philip stood at the center of a vast conspiracy to oppress the Church itself and to ensure that all its energies were turned toward his political stratagems. Cecil tried to lay bare the lie that the Spanish tyrant was a religious crusader.

Cecil only let up on the king when he attacked English seminarians and their leaders. In fact, the *Proclamation* gestures at an evil-counselor trope by suggesting that Philip would have thought better of his ploys had he not been seduced by Robert Persons and William Allen. They had falsely assured him, Cecil explained, "that though heretofore he had no good success with his great forces against our realm, yet if he will once again renew his war this next year, there shall be found ready, secretly, within the queen's dominions many thousands . . . of able people that will be ready to assist . . . and by their vain vaunting they do tempt the king hereto; who otherwise ought in wisdom, and by his late experience, to conceive no hope of a safe landing."[9] The *Proclamation* does not know whom to attack: the king and pope "know a great part thereof to be false," but Catholic "fugitives" had traitorous goals from the start and had become consummate enablers. Things had gotten worse since the establishment of those "dens and receptacles, which are by the traitors called seminaries." Ensconced in these Jesuit fronts, riffraff and wayward youths were "instructed in school-points of sedition."[10]

This strongly worded attack required retribution. Persons would have preferred an invasion, but instead, he settled for taking part in a propaganda storm against the Elizabethan regime.

Would Philip play along?

The Response

Much has been said about the king's distaste for brash polemics and tactless self-aggrandizement. He famously refused to have his biography written, saving himself, in Henry Kamen's words, "from adulators, whom he hated."[11] Though personal sensibility is important, Richard Kagan has suggested that his dislike of the genre had as much to do with broader monarchical concerns. Philip believed that biographies and memoirs were beneath him and, more importantly, that they would detract from his royal dignity, the mystery of monarchy that he wanted to cultivate.[12] Still, toward the end of his reign, the king succumbed to the barbed swipes dealt by all his enemies. His advisors insisted a history of his times be written, something that, according to Kagan, increasingly seemed "a strategic necessity when the kingdom's honor and reputation was under attack."[13] After much thought, he decided to allow a history of his reign to be written. Antonio de Herrera, the man chosen for the job, reported that Philip ordered him "to investigate how one might write about his glorious life and after having discussed various possibilities, modesty suggested that it should take the form of a general history of the world."[14]

The king's engagement with English books can help us flesh out his polemical strategy. Despite the ever-growing interest in how Philip presented himself, scholars have generally ignored the fact that between 1592 and 1593, the king bankrolled a printed English Catholic campaign against Elizabeth that also provided the kind of cheerleading that the king supposedly disliked. This flurry of activity consisted of at least three Latin treatises meant for broad European consumption, together with a bevy of translations or adaptations in several languages. Although evidence is somewhat sketchy about how all these books were interrelated and the extent to which the regime knew about every aspect of the campaign, there is no doubt they knew about the most important among them. Philip's regime had long expected to hear reports on any polemical projects undertaken by English Catholics connected to court, and it took oversights seriously. In the early seventeenth century, Juan de Idiáquez would reprimand Joseph Creswell for not following norms by which "the secretary of state must be informed [of book publications] as has been the custom, and the command awaited according to your majesty's pleasure."[15] In the aftermath of the *Proclamation*, there is direct evidence that Philip took particular interest in a book written by Persons (under the pseudonym of Andream Philopatrum) commonly called the *Responsio ad edictum* (Response to the edict) or the Philopater tract.[16]

Initial talks about an anti-Elizabethan print campaign must have occurred during Philip's visit to Valladolid, perhaps on the same day of his visit to the English college. Just a few days later, Philip agreed to fund the *Responsio*. Because Persons likely completed the book before talking to the king, key royal counselors reviewed it. The book came under the careful eyes of Idiáquez and several Jesuits, including José de Acosta, Rodrigo Cabredo, and William Chrichton as well as Francis Englefield.[17] All these readers quickly understood that it was, in Albert Loomie's words, "a sympathetic defense of his [Philip's] policy toward England."[18]

The king wanted the book printed across Europe with one catch: it should be done under a veil of secrecy. Neither author nor funder should be known. Philip had learned from experience. He surely remembered how a decade earlier he had published a takedown in the form of a bounty on the head of the Dutch rebel leader William of Orange only to be hit back by one of the most effective pamphlets of the sixteenth century. Orange's *Apology*—which accused Philip of tyranny, irreligion, and parricide—would become one of the key sources for the Spanish Black Legend.[19] With the English Catholics, he saw an opportunity to publish a fiendish book without any personal dangers. Their books were of the sort some of the king's advisers had been lobbying for to little avail, the kind that Philip himself wanted to have written for a European audience as long as he was not (publicly) implicated in their production.

The *Responsio* continued and expanded a project begun with *De schismate Anglicano*. Richard Verstegan, who would pen the *Responsio*'s notorious English adaptation, talked about both in the same breath. He suggested that the Philopater book contained, as he put it, "points of curiosity and hidden histories touching our estate discovered in the same, and so many personal causes, conditions of men, and secret affairs unfolded . . . as I marvel not though printers to gain thereby, do strive in many places to divulge the same with all celerity." Publishers had learned how popular a book such as the

Responsio might be "in the late historie of D. Sanders in Latin de schismate Anglicano, which for that it contained matter of such curiosity and novelty in personal affairs, I find it printed again in Latin almost in every state besides the translations that go in other languages."[20] Although there are important generic differences—Nicholas Sander's book was a history proper, Persons's an *apologia*—the *Responsio* kept a promise made by Sander and his editors to speak out against the regime should it give birth to more monstrosities.[21] Persons returned to this vow and justified it by pointing to a long succession of churchmen like Tertullian and Clement of Alexandria who had written apologies against "the furor of tyrants."[22]

In his greatest service to Philip, Persons expanded upon the Anglo-Spanish antinomies first described in the 1586 edition. Persons described the king as a pacifist, not the power-hungry Catholic beast of Cecilian fantasies. There was no greater proof of this than Philip's longtime softness toward Elizabeth. From the moment he landed in England to assume the role of king consort, he had defended her against what would have been just punishments. Though she had conspired against Mary Tudor early on, Philip—inspired by his "singular clemency" toward a young and frail woman—interceded on her behalf, saved her life, and gave her freedom.[23] Such clemency established a pattern that continued throughout Mary's life. The regime could have disposed of Elizabeth at any point had the king not argued for mere vigilance as opposed to punishment. Not much changed when Elizabeth became queen. The king proved indulgent by allowing her to keep precious jewels and treasures brought from Spain to England, and he continued to fight gallantly for English interests on the Continent, especially its outpost in Calais. While Mary lived, Elizabeth unsurprisingly double-crossed her sister by giving the French intelligence that would allow them to take the cherished fort. After Mary's death, while Philip tried to settle a proper peace agreement that would have kept Calais under English rule, Elizabeth started her own negotiations behind his back. The king had plenty of reasons to strike back against Elizabeth, but he refused because he wanted to stay true to the alliance that had long been established by both countries.[24] He would not engage in the Northern Rebellion ignited by Catholic subjects and would only (hesitatingly) provide money for other anti-Elizabethan activities. In 1578, when appeals came from Ireland to save the kingdom from the "intolerable cruelty" of their queen, Philip felt pity but could not help because good faith and religion would not allow it. Only after much insistence did he provide some troops on the condition that the pope should employ them "where he deemed necessary."[25] Finally, after thirty years of Elizabethan insults, he decided to send the Armada.[26]

Persons also emphasized Philip's best efforts to promote friendship with sometime enemies. In Scotland, the king had been an unwavering ally to Mary Stuart and then her son King James. Indeed, Persons warned James that he should remember Philip's "singular benevolence" during his infancy and youth, lest he be thought ungrateful. The *Responsio* also discussed the king's constancy toward Ireland. He offered them access to ports and commerce even though they were Elizabeth's subjects.[27] Franco-Spanish amity also deserved admiration because it survived despite their history of war and competition during much of the sixteenth century. After settling peace with Henry II in 1558, the king, Persons said, "conserved it unassailably until the present day."[28]

Touting Philip's close ties with France took some gumption, since at the time of publication, he had troops there. The easy explanation for the apparent paradox hinged on the nature of Philip's interventions. He had not initiated aggression but responded to Catholic pleas. He chose to fight not against "the king of France, but against the enemy of France, who looks to usurp the kingdom against its laws." The fight was just and necessary for the safety of all Christendom against the threats of heresy.[29] The success of this worthy mission might set things right in Europe, something that Persons suspected Elizabeth feared because it would interrupt her efforts to "incite and support tyrants to wrap everything perpetually in sedition."[30]

By discussing the French case at length, Persons defended the king against the *Proclamation*'s insinuations, promoted efforts against Henry IV, and provided a clear justification for Spanish involvement in France, much as *De schismate Anglicano* and the *Scisma* had justified the Armada. However, the techniques used to accomplish this were different. While Sander's history worked largely by suggestion, in the *Responsio*, Persons mounted a defense for Spanish intervention on explicit theoretical grounds. Philip only helped the French effectuate the will of a greater body. Royal power was not established by civil law or by the laws of nature or of nations, but by the "people," or *civitas*, with God's blessing.[31] Conditions set by the people dictated the ongoing relationship between subject and ruler. The Christian prince had been primarily charged with the defense of the "one Roman Catholic faith," and all great theologians had shown that failure to live up to this fundamental duty provided just grounds for deprivation of "all power and dignity by human and divine right."[32] In real time, this removal could be carried out without direct papal permission so long as efforts met two conditions: (1) that there were adequate forces to resist a heretical ruler and (2) that a ruler's heresy was open and undeniable. Should these two conditions not be met, there was no expectation that individuals should take on a possibly fatal task, and if there were doubts about the monarch's religion, the ultimate decision was to be left to the pope.[33]

Luckily there was no ambiguity in France. Henry IV might claim that he embraced a purer religion, but his (potential) contractual obligations bound him to the Catholic Church in particular: Catholic princes since the start of the "Christian republic" promised to defend it in ceremonies of baptism and coronation.[34] Since Henry—a known Calvinist—refused to take traditional vows, his putative French subjects did not have to deal with the thorny prospect of deposition. Instead, they could simply reject his candidacy for failure to enter a basic agreement inseparable from royalty. These arguments were crucial to Persons's suggestion that legitimacy is not "established by right of birth or nature, but by the free will of the people" together with the confirming hand of the Church.[35]

As we will see in chapter 6, these arguments harmonized with polemics written by the Catholic League in France, to the extent that a French version of the *Responsio* was published in 1593.[36] But as much as the *Responsio* spoke to concerns commonly held by Philip and the League, it never shook off its English qualities. The French situation allowed Persons to discuss his primary concern, the Elizabethan regime's illegitimacy.

While the right of good Catholics to reject Henry IV allowed Spain's intervention to be cast in a positive light, it also provided a justification for similar responses in England (something that, again, was not on Philip's radar at the time). Using the kind of deflectionary tactics in Herrera's translation of Louis Dorléans (discussed in chapter 4), Persons depicted the English and French cases as versions of the same problems. The French situation could only be understood in its full dangerous potential by showing how bad things were in England, where Catholic resistance had not succeeded. If talk of deposition and resistance could be made relevant for those fighting against a pretender to the French throne, they were more relevant for those who had suffered under that new Jezebel. The attack on Henry's claims only reinforced and gave depth to the *Responsio*'s central threat: "All the emperors who have persecuted the church have been killed by their own hands or by that of their subjects."[37]

Attacking Elizabeth benefitted interests outside of England. The worse the queen looked, the scarier Henry IV seemed to be, and perhaps more importantly, her monstrosity brightened Philip's reputation by comparison.

Ultimately Elizabeth's own failings are key to Persons's whole enterprise because they both delegitimized the regime and helped establish the queen as Philip's inverse.

Before we consider Persons's attack on Elizabeth, a caveat is in order. Scholars are right to note that the *Responsio* deviates somewhat from Sander's history by reverting to evil-counsel tropes in which Cecil plays the role of villainous upstart and would-be usurper.[38] Catholics publicly accused him of being the author of the *Proclamation*, a text so coarse that it could not have been of the queen's own design. And yet such deflections were done so half-heartedly as to seem willfully transparent. From the start, Persons effectively dissolved the distinction between queen and counselors. In the preface, he openly accused Elizabeth of anti-Catholic animus and insatiable greed; he attacked the queen and her counsel for their impostures and artifice. Moreover, throughout the book, save when Persons singled out key advisors, Elizabeth herself is accused of this or that evil thing.

Persons unflinchingly criticized Elizabethan heresy. The queen's break with England's pious past is described by a revealing and unflattering comparison with her father. While Henry VIII had maliciously cut ties with Rome, he never embraced outright heresy as his daughter did. The king had remained Catholic, "save for the article concerning the Roman Pontiff"—a remarkable claim that goes against the line of argument followed in the 1586 *De schismate Anglicano*.[39] Elizabeth, while styling herself Defender of the Faith, rejected the very Church her father once protected to earn that title. Worse, while her father fought against Lutheranism, she embraced it. The situation was so dire, the changes wrought in a matter of decades so great, that were the king alive, daughter would have to hang father or father would have to light daughter up in flames.[40]

No line divided heresy and tyranny. The queen compared unfavorably to ancient torturers of good Christians. Like Nero and Domitian, like the Scribes and Pharisees, like Aryan kings, she chose to do away with religious enemies by sheer force. But her cruelty was far worse, as she tried to delve deeper than they did into the consciences of her subjects. Censuring Catholic freedom of belief had nothing to do with the queen's religion: she was guided by atheistic principles to which neither law nor faith applied. The logic of her persecutions was proof enough of her immorality. Elizabeth hunted Catholics and sought to legitimize her efforts by means of a glaringly false logic of treason and supposed collusion with Spain. This too was an old ruse, employed by the likes of Maxentius, Julian the Apostate, and especially the Aryan king Genseric, who persecuted on political grounds those who simply asked the pope to send them priests.[41] All tyrants have slandered "most tranquil innocent servants of god" for immediate political gains.[42] Elizabeth feared Philip and the pope, contrary to her specious claims, because of two core principles. First, she feared retaliation from both because she had offended them. Second, she was moved by greed. She hoped to inspire hatred against Catholics to justify stealing their property and wealth.

Persons's argument was simple: If Philip tried to defend Christendom, Elizabeth tried to destroy any semblance of unity. While the Elizabethan regime accused Philip of a tyrannical universalism, Elizabeth was the one who plotted away, playing a fiddle while Europe burned. The endgame was general strife, without which her power might be diminished. Elizabeth's efforts in Scotland epitomized her strategy. From the beginning, she could not abide the potential of a peaceful kingdom also ruled by a queen, and so she started to promote flimsy accusations of foreign conspiracies linked to a French presence in Scotland. Such spurious claims of imminent danger masked her own conspiracies.[43] And yet like Pontius Pilate, she maintained innocence of bloodshed. Who would be so foolish as to believe a woman who, apart from shifting her religious beliefs at will, had the gall to hurl such "obvious, notable lies?"[44]

Persons insisted it was time these offenses be called out and redressed. In doing so, he revisited the theme of Catholic fortitude. From the start, he defended his stark assessment of the Elizabethan regime by insisting that temporizing had gotten Catholics nowhere. Allen and a host of others had tempered their tones in hopes of coaxing the queen, but their sweetness had failed.[45] The point might be extended, as with *De schismate Anglicano*, to Philip himself. Although the king's gestures of friendship toward the queen revealed his clemency and magnanimity, there is also a sense that the king frequently had missed good opportunities. If only he had taken a stronger stance in the Northern Rebellion, maybe it could have succeeded. Most jarringly, Persons recalled how the first English seminary on the Continent (in Douai) had fallen victim to Spanish neglect. The king himself was not blamed, but his subjects had been deceived by the queen's claims that students were mere English rebels.[46] Seminarians were forced to leave and seek support from the Guise in France.

Such criticism, reminders of past inadequacies, are buried underneath a much more prominent effort to establish the diametrically opposed images of the good king and the bad queen. Philip belonged to the kingdom of light and Elizabeth to that of darkness. The benefit of this most basic thread in

Persons's book to the Spanish king is obvious, but the full providential-ist potential of the rhetorical stance could be more comfortably highlighted when told from behind the mask of a loyal Habsburg subject. This imposture would be undertaken by an unlikely exile: Thomas Stapleton.

Philip's (English Catholic) Subject in the Low Countries

Stapleton came to Flanders with the first wave of learned Elizabethan ex-iles and, over the years, became active on the Continental scene much like Persons or Allen. Although he cared deeply about the situation in England, after the 1560s, his efforts became less Anglocentric. He challenged heresy through huge theological tomes, but these weapons likely had more of an impact in and around Louvain than in London. Unlike Persons, who would always be primarily attached to English institutions (mainly the English col-leges), Stapleton joined the local academic establishment in Flanders, where he was awarded the Regius Chair of Theology at Louvain in 1591 after lobby-ing by his colleagues there. If he was beloved by Flemish friends and patrons, his own compatriots became a bit wary. Maybe because he did not embrace Personian pugilism, some doubted his loyalty to the cause and his feelings for Philip II. When challenged on either front, he denied the insinuations. On his Habsburg loyalty he claimed to "desire sincerely to remain a true and trusty servant to his Majesty of Spain."[47] His foray into the realm of lowbrow polemics seems to prove this without much doubt. In 1592, he joined many other English Catholic voices by taking on Elizabeth's *Proclamation* in what might have ultimately been the sauciest book to come out of that altercation, the *Apologia pro Rege Catholico Philippo II* (Apology for King Philip II).[48]

Although written under a pseudonym evocative of Stapleton's birthplace (Henfield, Sussex)—Didymo Veridico Henfildano—Stapleton tellingly chose to write under the guise of Philip's subject. In the book, he describes how he (as Didiacus) was walking around Antwerp when he bumped into friends read-ing a copy of the *Proclamation*. It was not long before he took umbrage. The text, he ranted, was a libel parading as an official edict, an attack against the king, his "most clement lord." Stapleton's framing device was an obfus-catory strategy, but as Jan Machielsen has shown, both his approach and the book's substance require that we place it within its proper Flemish context.[49] It is not coincidental, as Machielsen explains, that the title evokes William of Orange's *Apology*. When Stapleton presented inverted images of Philip and Elizabeth, his positive take on the king resonated in local circumstances, where such fawning was hotly contested. Indeed, because the Dutch Revolt had produced the most vigorous polemical lambasting of the king, Stapleton must have felt particularly empowered (or required) to enhance Catholic anti-Elizabethan mudslinging.

Though much of what Stapleton said was similar to what his compatriots had argued, contemporaries noticed points of particular emphasis. In 1593, Persons wrote a short pamphlet, *Newes from Spayne and Holland*, where he offered an advertisement for several anti-*Proclamation* works printed since 1592.[50] In his discussion of the *Apologia*, he underlined Stapleton's two most striking contributions. First, Persons told of how the book takes Cecil to task for falsely claiming that the Elizabethan regime reigned over unheard-of tranquility. Second, Persons described how Stapleton exposed Elizabethan ties with Muslims.[51]

The first theme is present to varying degrees in all responses to the *Proclamation*, but Stapleton laid it out forcefully. What the regime called peace was a mere specter manufactured out of deception and cruelty: there can be no peace where cruel laws reign, where fear is all-pervasive, where subjects are squeezed out of every penny. He likened England to a shoddy building with frail foundations, a leaky roof, and weak walls. Although such a structure could stand, it might blow over at any moment. The nobility had been subverted, taxes were high, Elizabeth had made enemies of powerful foreign powers, and the ecclesiastical realm had been replaced fraudulently by Parliament. Stapleton also proved the lie of Elizabethan tranquility by showing how the regime allowed different competing religious sects to thrive, creating an atmosphere of distrust and crime. How can there be true peace in a realm divided in its faith?[52]

When Stapleton described Elizabethan relations with Muslims, he ventured into territory lightly touched in most English Catholic propaganda. While writers often resorted to tropes comparing heretical regimes negatively with the ungodly Saracen, only Stapleton truly dwelled on the topic. He printed the Ottoman emperor's letter in response to Elizabeth's initial request for assistance against Philip II, where she apparently asked for his help in connection with efforts by Dom Antonio to take back Portugal from Habsburg control. The emperor was vague in return. He encouraged her to fight Philip and suggested that he might help once the Ottomans dealt with their Persian enemies.[53]

Stapleton used this letter as a springboard for a series of criticisms. On religious grounds, he thought close ties to the Turks proved the queen's religious impurity. If England turned from Rome to better serve Christ, how could they be in cahoots with the proven slayers of Christians? Moreover, her actions flew in the face of her pacific persona. These kinds of communications with the evil Turk had been going on for years and could not be in the name of peace. He also noted that the anti-Spanish efforts described in the Ottoman letter occurred four years *before* the Armada, clearly proving that Elizabeth was the first aggressor. Such chicanery would ultimately lead to the demise of Christendom as a whole, including England: Stapleton reminded readers that fighting among Christian rulers in the past had been the key to Islamic successes in Africa, Greece, and Asia Minor.[54]

Although plenty of Christian monarchs established diplomatic ties with the Ottomans, plotting a joint invasion would have seemed a step too far. The Elizabethan regime could try to justify its actions on politic and even religious grounds, but such coziness was controversial in England itself.[55] Fear of the Saracen on European shores tended to be one of the last remaining unifiers among confessional enemies, as shown most famously by the happy bells rung everywhere from London to Madrid when the Catholic League defeated Ottoman forces at Lepanto (1571).

This communal fear of Muslims also united confessional enemies in negative ways. They all employed the label of Turk, much like that of Machiavellian, as a catchall dehumanizing tag. The confessional enemy was easily associated with a Muslim threat, and by extensions, the workings of the Antichrist. Thus from the start of the Reformation, Martin Luther could be easily placed on the same plane as Mohammad.[56] Philip II and Spain, because of its "Moorish" history, could suffer similar slurs. William of Orange's *Apology* frequently made the link between Habsburg and Turkish tyranny.[57]

Stapleton underlined Elizabeth's demonic qualities. The link to Islam is reminiscent of William Rainold's attack against Calvinism, the *Calvino-Turcismus*, which puts Protestantism on the same level of Muslim demonic perfidy. Jan Machielsen has also shown Stapleton's efforts to depict the queen as a witch. The language of *maleficium* swirled around her throughout the text, most notably when Stapleton suggested her link to a circle of witches in Berwick who stood accused of causing a storm to harm James VI's Danish wife. Ultimately, Stapleton likened the queen to Satan himself when he accused her of trying to usurp God's throne.[58]

Such negative stereotyping of Elizabeth reflected on Philip himself. Elizabeth hated Philip so much because in him she saw another David chosen by God to bring her to submission. The king was so feared because there was no fiercer crusader against novelties of the age and no greater protector of the Church.[59] If Elizabeth stood for the workings of the devil, Philip must then be on God's side.

Again, the extremity of such a polemic, especially in Stapleton's Netherlandish stomping grounds, was related to the specific developments of religious tensions and war there. From the 1560s until after Philip II's death, the king's territories were mired in religious strife. They witnessed the ritual desecration of sacred objects, the Inquisitorial bloodshed of Calvinists, and a civil war that combined religious animus with protonationalist zeal. Unlike anywhere else in Philip's empire, a violent discourse—and indeed, actual physical violence—created an environment for polemical harshness and conspicuous grandstanding. By contrast, the final sections of this chapter will show the way that many of these themes were packaged for English and Spanish audiences and the adjustments deemed necessary in these venues.

England, Spain, and Who's to Blame

The price for direct attacks against the queen and her regime in England was steep. The 1591 *Proclamation* itself signaled the hardening of anti-Catholic sentiment, so any response had to avoid aggravating an already bleak situation. Things said with a vengeance on the Continent required softening for English audiences.

Robert Southwell had been a student at Douai and returned to England as a missionary in 1586. Not long after the *Proclamation* went into effect, he wrote a newsletter that circulated among English Catholics on the Continent telling of the horrors faced by recusants and how the Elizabethan regime became more violent by the day.[60] His letter was a long list of Elizabethan corruptions as they related to Catholic subjects, who were excluded from public service, lacked access to fair justice, faced exorbitant fines, and experienced many indignities including naked interrogations and vicious tortures.

Amid such darkness, there were providential signs of God's imminent punishment for Elizabethan wrongdoings. Southwell found it "strange to see how God maketh the whole realm to taste of the same scourges that Catholics are wronged with."[61] Internationally all major powers deemed England evil: "No nation of Christendome is this day so infamous in all countries as the English for vice, for cruelty, for unfaithfulness and breach of all leagues with their friends and confederates, and for all other odious parts—and this to requite their infaming of Catholics." Only the Turks looked kindly on all this.[62]

Southwell's newsletter contains an important opinion on the root of all English troubles. The manuscript takes an aggressive turn back to evil-counselor tropes of the kinds published before *De schismate Anglicano*.

While Southwell had no kind words for Elizabeth, who appeared to be a dupe, Cecil is shown to be the source of all evil and the "full owner of Her Majestie's determinations";[63] he sowed distrust and hatred of Catholics to enhance and secure his own authority. Amid the uncertainties of succession, he wanted, in Southwell's words, "to have the realm so much at his own commandment and to be so mightily backed by the faction that he privily fostereth, that he may be able to command the best competitor and to make his own composition with him for his most commoditie, which is the only ground of his love, and god of his devotion."[64] Southwell surely believed Cecil and bloodthirsty minions like the priest-hunter Richard Topcliffe were villains, but this renewed emphasis was also a strategic decision. The document shows Southwell thinking through the complexities of how to respond publicly to the *Proclamation* without confirming the imputed seditious qualities of English Catholics. Indeed, the newsletter was essentially a rough draft of a more formal composition ultimately printed after his death: *A Humble Supplication for her Majestie.*[65]

In preparing the book for publication, Southwell was self-conscious about its function within an English sphere. Though dedicated to the queen herself, he was aware that he (as a Catholic) did not have access to her. He thus appealed to a broader public—he was "forced to commit it [the book] to the multitude." By explaining Catholic troubles to a varied readership, he hoped, he wrote, that God would "touch some merciful heart to let your highness understand the extremity of them."[66] The other justification for this turn toward publicity had to do with the regime's own tactics. The publication and distribution of the *Proclamation* was itself a maneuver akin to "racking of publique authority to private purposes."[67] Since elements of the regime had committed sins of publicity, Southwell now had to shape public opinion in such a way as to delegitimize that violent attack on Catholics.

To this end, Southwell padded his book with language that sweetened the message purportedly aimed at the queen. By leaning on tropes of evil counsel, the appeal intended to coax a range of potential supporters, including hardened Catholics and perhaps some of the nonzealous (church papists or Protestants of convenience) who would be appalled by the violence he described.

For this to work, Southwell established loyalty on several fronts. He described the queen as the last hope for English Catholics and acknowledged her "goodness." He fawningly suggested she was "perfect in all Princely virtues."[68] Those around her had skewed facts so that she could not fully act on her own instinctive justice. If only, Southwell insisted, she "would vouchsafe to behold our case with an unveiled eye, and not view us in the mirror of a misinformed mind," Catholics would be treated kindly. With proper information she would show more clemency as befitted, in his words, such a "gracious judge as your sacred self."[69]

Having established the queen's goodness, Southwell exposed the conspiracies and coercions that had misrepresented the Catholic community. The demonization of Catholics required covert efforts to incriminate them. Thus the infamous Babington Plot was not a Catholic-hatched plan to murder Elizabeth and raise Mary Stuart to the throne, but a case of entrapment perpetrated by Elizabeth's spymaster Francis Walsingham. His double agents planted the seeds of the plot and promoted its execution. Indeed, the more that the plotters were enticed into the anti-Elizabethan activities, the more distanced they became from mainstream Catholics: the closer the Jesuit John Ballard got to Walsingham's agents, the more "he became a stranger to all Jesuits and priests, being limited by the politique Rules of his prompter, to such company as Master secretary knew to be of dim sight to see through so many mists as he by his instruments had already cast before his eyes."[70] Like these misguided conspirators, Catholics who suggested they would take part in anti-Elizabethan actions under a foreign banner did not represent Catholics in general. Theirs might have been words uttered under the extremities of torture "or else they were spoken by some unskillful lay man, not knowing how to answer such captious questions."[71]

Southwell's case also rested on the unlikelihood of Cecil's accusations. To think that Catholics would be involved in the treasonous activities they stood accused of in England and abroad defied logic. Why would Catholics scheme when they knew that their efforts would be in vain? They understood there was little hope for foreign aid, and they recognized the Elizabethan regime's brute force. Should there be some attempt at general rebellion, local authorities would be unforgiving. After all, the regime had already proven bloodthirsty. Indeed, because instruments of justice had been so aggressively employed, English Catholics were generally weak and dispersed. Given these realities, why would Catholics scheme to help Philip? "Do we not see that they are scattered one among thousands, and to wish them to stir in the King's behalf were to train them to their undoing, and to expose them to a general massacre by domestical fury?"[72]

Although Southwell wanted to skirt direct attacks on the queen, he did not avoid forward critiques of the regime's general policy. He not only tried to underline the fraud of anti-Catholic polemics but emphasized the primacy of the Catholic Church. Part of his defense against accusations of treason hinged on the idea that reintroducing Catholicism to England was not wrong. To judge harshly the return of Catholicism would be to reject English history itself: it was "the faith of your [the queen's] royal ancestors this 14 hundreth years, is the faith of the greatest part of Christendom; and for the defense whereof your majesty's most worthy Father attained the glorious title of *Defender of the Faith*."[73] To deem missionaries traitors would be akin to suggesting that "all the glorious saints of this land . . . were no better than traitors, and their abettors felons."[74] Strikingly, he suggested that such a position, together with a general disrespect shown to the Catholic Church, could have dire consequences if, in his words, "it should please God to allot the day of general resurrection in your Majesty's time." He asked, "What would so many millions of prelates, pastors, and religious people think, that both honored and blessed this kingdom with the holiness of their life and excellency of their learning?"[75] Though Southwell might have been working on presuppositions of evil counsel, the threat of damnation for the queen and the Protestant establishment was jarring.

Southwell's defense of Spanish activities was even more so. In part because of Persons's hard work, Spain remained welcoming to English merchants, priests, and students despite general Anglo-Spanish strife, but still, that strife must be accounted for. Whereas the *Proclamation* argued that forms of Spanish aggression were spurred by Persons and Allen, Southwell insisted that "it is not the authority of two private men that carry away such princes so readily to employ their main forces, if they had no other motives of greater consequence." Philip's actions were in self-defense, considering, as Southwell described it, "our surprising of the king's towns in Flanders, our invading of his countries in Spain and Portugal, our assisting his enemies against his daughters rights in Brittany, our continual and daily intercepting his treasure, warring with his fleets, and annoying his Indies."[76] Southwell did not provide the kind of inversionary narrative that Persons (and others) would, but he has no qualms about justifying anti-English activities.

Writing from the Continent

A Humble Supplication established some basic patterns later adopted by others who wanted to enter the English polemical scene. The onus of those efforts in the wake of the Philopater tract fell on the exile Richard Verstegan. Verstegan was in contact with Southwell and, from his base in Antwerp, had become a key facilitator of English Catholic polemical activities as an author, editor, engraver, and printer.[77] In 1593, he wrote English pamphlets that were precis of the *Responsio*, such as *An advertisement written to a Secretarie of my L. Treasurers of England* and *A declaration of the true causes of the great troubles, presupposed to be intended against the realm of England*. The first was a summary of Persons's *Responsio*, supposedly sent to Cecil from the Continent; the second was addressed to the "indifferent reader" and purported to explain England's many travails.[78]

Verstegan emphasized troubles experienced during the Elizabethan regime. His project focused on the idea that England had lost standing internationally. From where the supposed informant of the *Advertisement* sits in Germany, he says, "where both parties [Catholics and Protestants] live in peace together, our course of England hath diverse that approve it not."[79] This malignant course is marked by political disarray, confessional discord, fears of international warfare, increased poverty, and abuses of power, especially toward Catholics. In the *Declaration*, Verstegan painted another dreary picture, claiming that the "cries and complaints of the oppressed multitude" fully exceeded "all those of all past ages, in the memory of man."[80]

Despite such claims, the author insisted on Catholic loyalty, much as Southwell did. This involved roasting Cecil in order to forgive Elizabeth. In striking language Verstegan compared Elizabeth to Eve and Cecil to the serpent who "did sometime seduce the first woman and Queen of the world, to break the commandment of God, whereby herself was forced to exile, and her posterity made subject for ever after to such infinite calamities."[81] In fact (and this is a marked departure from the *Responsio* or *De schismate Anglicano* before it), Verstegan suggested that the queen was actually a Catholic at heart. Whereas past commentators saw her acceptance of Catholic rituals at her coronation as a front, Verstegan said that she showed early on that she might have been "contented to have continued the faith of her ancestors."[82] Cecil impeded this, and in Verstegan's telling, he attained all those tyrannical attributes that had elsewhere been pinned on people like Elizabeth or her father.[83]

To stay out of trouble, Verstegan sanitized issues that might cast shadows on English Catholic activities. For example, he implied that Catholics did not promote Spanish causes and avoided the topic of papal authority. Thus in his summary of the *Responsio*, Verstegan felt comfortable discussing Henry IV's illegitimacy but purposefully dodged the possibility of papal intervention.[84]

Yet if he sidestepped any suggestions that English Catholics were at the head of a Hispano-papal cabal, Verstegan, like Southwell, could not resist defending Spain. He did not hide Philip's positive qualities or the fact that the Elizabethan regime was at the helm of anti-Spanish activities. Though the language was somewhat muted, Verstegan provided evidence that the regime had gone over to the dark side. He even added a new perspective on Elizabeth's slippery relationship with Islam. The regime promoted efforts to compare Philip to a Turk on the playhouse stage, in public preaching, and elsewhere; they even suggested that a Turk was better than a Catholic. But even as they used Islam as a cudgel, the regime tried to destabilize Spain by promoting a "moorish" rebellion on the Iberian Peninsula. Even worse, partly because they now saw themselves isolated in Europe, they formed alliances with the Ottomans.[85] Verstegan thus generally picked up on the theme of Spanish pacifism and English bellicosity. The schemes of one man—Cecil—were at the root of England's rut and could only awaken Spain's furor.

The King's Visit in England

While Verstegan resisted suggesting that English Catholics would help Habsburg retribution, the alliance with Spain was always just beneath the surface. Indeed, it was exposed by the publication of Persons's *A Relation of the King of Spaines Receiving in Valliodolid*. Although it was substantially shorter than the Spanish version, within an English context, printing the book was a gutsy move. The positive portrayal of exiles and their activities rebutted Cecil's caricature along the lines of previous defenses of seminary activities, but the close relationship described between the exiles and the king had no precedent in the pamphlet literature up to that point. Neither the support for the Habsburg mission nor the genuflection of the students to the king was denied. The book left unchallenged the *Proclamation*'s suggestion that Philip and the seminarians were close, rejecting only the Elizabethan regime's interpretation of their relationship. Bonds were cemented not by some tyrannical impulse but by concerns for England's soul.

This was understandably a tough sell, and contemporaries clearly saw the text's treasonous potential. Nearly a decade after its publication, one critic—secular priest Christopher Bagshaw—discussed Philip's visit to the college to highlight Persons's "deadly malice." Bagshaw was familiar with both Spanish and English accounts of the king's visit, to the extent that he could fill readers in on a key part of the Spanish text that had been omitted: namely, the first orator's promise of submission as well as the vows made on behalf of "their [Seminarians'] whole Country, their parents, and friends, with all their Allies, confederates, and acquantance."[86] Though precise on this point, the rest of Bagshaw's summary is hazy and provides little insight into what the orator actually said. According to Bagshaw, the young scholar described how "her majesty is by all means depraved: the kings honor an excellency is extolled above all measure: her Highness downfall, and his victories are prophesied, and nothing is omitted that might advance the one and depress the other."[87] Persons's *Relation* does not spell all this out, but Bagshaw's account is evidence that the pamphlet's implications were obvious to contemporary readers.

Conclusion

None of these texts—except perhaps *A Humble Supplication*—was an actual attempt to communicate with the duped queen; they were appeals to a public that might be amenable to a critique of the regime. By and large, the goal was not to proselytize or enlist new conscripts in the battle against Elizabethan heresy. Instead, these books tried to sow doubts about the regime and its competence. Who was running the show? And to what end? Were the regime's international engagements worthwhile, or would it simply prolong war against Spain? And should the regime really be at the beck and call of Muslims? To insert these types of questions into public discussion was, of course, extremely tricky because the texts described here had to do this while supporting a Habsburg regime that many considered an existential enemy.

While one would think that such complications would be specific to Catholic efforts in a Protestant kingdom, this was not the case. As the next chapter will show, the Philopater tracts and Philopater-like books fit somewhat awkwardly in a Spanish sphere as well.

6

BETWEEN "ENGLISH" PROVIDENTIALISM
AND REASON OF STATE

In part 1, we saw how Pedro de Ribadeneyra's adaptation of Nicholas Sander's *De schismate Anglicano* caused concern in Jesuit circles, while the Habsburg regime promoted it. Here we will see the reverse in the case of Robert Persons's *Responsio*: efforts to bring the Philopater tract and related texts to a vulgar audience in Spain seem to have gone unchallenged by many outside court, while Philip II and his counselors had doubts. The appropriation of English Catholic texts in the aftermath of the Armada sometimes fit uncomfortably within the regime's changing discursive preoccupations. Identifying these tensions will confirm two themes explored thus far: the ambiguities of English Catholic polemics and the care with which Philip II engaged with it and its possible effects.

Toward a Strategic Shift

After the failures of 1588, Philip decided to pursue a particular strategy directed at Spanish-speaking subjects. As Kagan has described in rich detail, Philip sponsored historical research and writing to produce *historiae pro patria*. Instead of having a congratulatory life written, he wanted history to reflect the greatness of the "nation." The burden of this enterprise fell on Antonio de Herrera, whom we have encountered as the translator of the *Advertencias*. Herrera would not become an official *cronista* until 1596, but he had entered court circles in and around Madrid by 1585 and started producing books for the king that circulated in manuscript around that time. His *Historia de lo sucedido en Escocia e Inglaterra* (History of that which has occurred in Scotland and England), published in mid-1589 on the eve of an English expedition to Portugal, arguably counts as Herrera's first book to deal with immediate Spanish concerns. It described events in England and Scotland during the life of Mary Stuart, largely in response to George Buchanan's anti-Marian narrative, the *Rerum Scotaricum historia* of 1582.[1] The *Historia* deals with the machinations of Stuart's enemies and their fraudulent accusations against the queen, who was only guilty of staying true to her faith. In arguing this, Herrera unsurprisingly attacked Elizabeth. He wanted "to show the world how much the devil can accomplish when dressed in a human body, even if that body belongs to a woman [Elizabeth]."[2] He concluded the book with a damning portrayal of the queen as another Diomedes, king of Thrace, "who taught his horses to eat human meat so they could tear apart his guests." Like Diomedes, Elizabeth would meet her reckoning as required by "divine justice" at the hands of another Hercules, Philip II.[3]

Despite this harsh tone and the invocation of Mary's godliness, which contrasted with Elizabeth's demonism, Herrera insisted his account was fundamentally different from recent histories of Britain, most notably Ribadeneyra's *Scisma*. He indicated that his interests were "temporal." He had in fact worked up "spiritual" elements, but as Ribadeneyra had covered all those themes "with much elegance," his was the *political* complement to the Jesuit's *ecclesiastical* history.[4]

For our purposes, Herrera's "temporal" orientation is crucial. In a recent dissertation, Kiri von Ostenfeld-Suske has shown that attacks on Philip's rule influenced Spanish historiographic developments so that humanistic principles and polemical objectives became mutually reinforcing. Both the historical methodologies employed to attain "truth" and the thematic emphasis on "reason of state" ideology were powerful tools in defense of the regime. Herrera's publication of the *Cinco libros* [. . .] *de la historia de Portugal* (Five books on the history of Portugal) in 1591 exemplifies this dynamic. It was published in response to Girolamo Conestaggio's *Dell'unione del regno di Portogallo alla corona di Castiglia* (On the union of the Kingdom of Portugal with the Crown of Castile), a book written to urge the maintenance of the Genoese republic and the dangers of "losing liberty." To counter Conestaggio's negative take on Philip and Castilian rule, Herrera defended Philip's Portuguese inheritance and described his benevolence. As Ostenfeld-Suske has argued, the book did this through a demonstration of Philip's ideology and style of governance written in a self-consciously *political* vein that allowed for the exploration of his prudence and kingly *dignitas*.[5] This inclination affirms the suggestion by other scholars that while Herrera did not reject religious principles or theological virtues, he also did not see religion as the cornerstone of a reason-of-state system. Instead, he understood reason of state as a set of political behaviors based on prudence that complemented theological ideals. As such, he did not write history through an exclusively or even primarily providential lens.[6]

Philip's self-promotion at home did not end at Clio's gates. In 1591, at the king's own request, Herrera published a translation of a popular book by the Italian statesman Giovanni Botero, the *Diez libros de la razón de estado* (The ten books on reason of state).[7] Though some important work has been done on Botero's long-lasting influence on Spanish politics, little has been done to show how this book played an important role as royal propaganda when it was first printed.[8] Herrera translated Botero to promote Philip II's statecraft innocent of Machiavellian or Tacitean goals.[9] These evil authors were guilty of separating matters of governance from matters of conscience, a move Herrera deemed "bestial" and that the king, by association, rejected as well.

Botero understood reason of state as a tool primarily for the conservation of polities, not expansion or conquest.[10] This emphasis was important because it subtly rejected those who claimed the king wanted to achieve world dominion.

Botero also provided a temperate idiom for discussing tyranny. He dealt with evils perpetrated by past rulers but did not linger on recent failures or providential punishment. Though readers might find some historical material that could be pinned on Philip himself and although they might not recognize their own king in Botero's ideals, the book is not overtly castigatory. There are no comparisons between kings and worms, à la Ribadeneyra, and no mention of the Armada either. Botero believed that following Christian ethics was "practical" because political success depended on divine assistance, and he even suggested that Spanish imperial power depended on it. But while the idea undergirds the whole text, it is understated. There are key moments when Botero expressed concern about Spanish stability, but these moments are *not* linked to any providential narratives, only to material contexts. Most famously, he expressed concerns about a dwindling Spanish population. Thus embracing Botero's reason of state allowed the king to flaunt his embrace of prudence, justice, and overall good Christian principles without giving enemies any rope.

Again, such a pivot did not preclude godly or religious elements. To the contrary, the regime's approval of Herrera's works hinged on the fact that his books proved Philip helped Catholics "only in order to protect the faith."[11] Nonetheless, that Philip wanted to shift away from thunderous messianic, providential discourses seems important. It is not that the king believed such narratives were useless but that they were not useful at the moment.

This discursive pull and push is evident in Philip's only known personal engagement with a Philopater-related text. Evidence that the regime actively promoted a Spanish translation of an English Catholic book in response to the 1591 edict comes to us a few years after the fact. In 1599, Philip's confessor, Diego de Yepes, published an extract from a letter purportedly sent to Cecil as part of his large compendium of English Catholic texts, the *Historia particular de la persecución de Inglaterra* (Particular history of the English persecution).[12] The text is drawn from a book published by Joseph Creswell in 1592, just a few months prior to his arrival in Spain: the *Exemplar literarum* [. . .] *ad D Guilelmum Cecilium* (Example of letters [. . .] to William Cecil).[13] Creswell's book is similar in tone and polemical approach to Persons's and Thomas Stapleton's books, but it above all others seems to have struck a chord with Philip. Yepes reported that the king asked him to print it for the "public good."[14]

Philip seems to have been interested in a tiny part of Creswell's original book. The excerpt that ended up in print ignored all the complicated anti-Elizabethan arguments discussed in previous chapters, preferring instead to praise the king at the expense of Elizabeth. The short text underlines the providential signs of the king's role as protector of Christendom; the breadth of his empire was itself evidence of divine grace. Though most rulers would blanch at the enormous responsibility and would fail, Philip thrived not—and this is important—by human prudence but by God's will: "This is not a business that can result from human prevention, but it is manifest providence from God." So long as his intentions stayed pure, further success—indeed, further expansion—seemed certain.

Creswell's text also emphasizes the ties that bound Philip to his subjects. Though the king had inherited many of his lands from his forefathers, the assemblage of territories required good governance that, again, depended on godliness above all else. His domains had been left to him united by "justice and piety and supported by the Catholic faith . . . in such a way that the temporal state is bound to religion." Though fear might ensure power for others, the king's authority was based on the pious nurturing of divine law and the love consequently secured by the Catholic Church between him and those he ruled. Such love was thus not a result of "human prudence" but underlined "Christian obedience that the catholic religion plants in people's hearts." Realms established on Catholic principles promoted *love* (not fear) to "captivate the will and engender fidelity in their [the subjects'] hearts." Subjects would be enticed by the love shown toward them and, more importantly, by the love rulers showed God. As the king labored on behalf of religion, his subjects would labor on behalf of the king. All worked together, sacrificing money and lives, for the public good.

Philip's empire was stitched together by faith and a common Christian morality. This dynamic extended beyond the realm and united the king to all his allies as well. Though some, like the Germans and Swiss, might seek Spanish Habsburg alliances out of convenience, Creswell tells of "many who love and serve him only because he defends the Catholic religion." In sum, Philip was the glue that kept what remained of Christendom together.

Elizabeth was thus Philip's opposite. If he reaped the benefits of his faith, she suffered from following a "Calvinist sect." While he conformed to God's laws, she went against them. While he enjoyed the comfort of security, she was plagued by danger and fear. He chose as "friends" the best men that he could find; the queen saw the "best servants of God [Catholic priests] as the most untrustworthy of men." These dichotomies were determined by ancestry. If Philip's forefathers had left him a good Christian empire, Elizabeth's father had left her heresy. Though the text betrays some hope that Elizabeth might reform, that she might be another Magdalen, there is a sense that nothing could overcome her putrid roots. At their core, her anti-Catholic policies were the means by which she tried to hide her illegitimacy. Were she to join the Catholic camp, Elizabeth would have to recognize her bastardy and give up the crown. She made enemies of Catholics only to maintain her own fragile authority.

These arguments are not new, but if we trust Yepes's claim that the king wanted its publication, this brief translation of Creswell gets us close to Philip's own polemical and propagandistic desires. Creswell's text supports Spanish monarchia but shows personal piety as the cause of imperial success. Moreover, it underscores how Philip's defense of the Church created bonds of mutual affection with subjects, providing the context for stability. Here we have, in brief, the anti-Machiavellian king and, as such, the anti-Elizabethan ruler. Here is a vision of political integrity dependent on the king's goodness and his proper relationship to the Church as both proof and argument for past and future success.

And yet this pamphlet (in its Spanish form) was not printed during the king's lifetime, likely because of a growing awareness of the dangers implicit in the polemical tack taken therein. To better understand the regime's desires and its fears, we would do well to dwell on one perceived misappropriation of English Catholic polemics by none other than Ribadeneyra.

Ribadeneyra Again

In 1593, Ribadeneyra once again wrote to support the English cause and to offer Spanish audiences important lessons. His continuation of the *Scisma*, the *Segunda parte de la historia ecclesiastica de Inglaterra* (The second part of the ecclesiastical history of England), was first printed as a stand-alone book and subsequently integrated with the original 1588 narrative in later editions.[15] It draws on a range of texts produced by English Catholics after 1591, including the description of Philip's college visit, the prodigious sighting mentioned at the start of part 2, and various responses to the *Proclamation*, especially Persons's *Responsio* and Creswell's *Exemplar*. Despite the combustible material from which it drew, Ribadeneyra took pains to extricate the book from politics. He claimed to have "cut everything that touches the state and political government" so that contemporary and future readers would benefit from the spiritual fruits of English Catholic torments. He wanted readers to understand such torment "as a singular work of the Lord and the triumph of his wife the holy church."[16] As ever, Ribadeneyra wittingly or unwittingly tried to minimize complex political and polemical intentions. His claims of political innocence contradict the book's effort to contribute to politico-religious discussions in a way that Philip and his regime found vexing.

Philip and his closest counselors did not like the *Segunda parte*. Such was the regime's displeasure that Persons had to intervene on Ribadeneyra's behalf in Rome to mitigate the rumors that were circulating against him. Persons pointed out his help to the English Catholic cause and the injustice of royal snubs.[17]

People at court were very unhappy that Ribadeneyra had chosen to include a translation of the *Proclamation*. Just a few months after the book's publication, the king himself ordered it removed from circulation, and the Jesuit provincial of Toledo even feared the regime might call on the Inquisition to collect all copies that had been sold. The king and his counselors thought it inappropriate that the queen's edict "should circulate in the Castilian vernacular, to be read by all sorts of people."[18] Such displeasure is unsurprising, as Spanish authorities tended to react swiftly when they discovered books that allowed (or worse, promoted) an Elizabethan voice.[19] Further, Ribadeneyra offered only a muted defense of the king, insisting that the attacks against him were so ludicrous that they need not be refuted.[20] Ribadeneyra said something similar in *Scisma* in response to Elizabethan propaganda, but there he did not advertise Cecil's words in as much detail.

Times had changed, and Ribadeneyra's double-edged message (against Elizabeth with warnings to the king) that may have seemed appropriate leading up to the Armada seemed less so just a few years later. Philip and his regime knew, and justifiably feared, that the entrance of Elizabethan attacks against Spain left too much room for interpretation and appropriation. Spanish audiences might be receptive to Elizabethan slander, especially among those increasingly critical of the king. Ribadeneyra did not endorse these attacks, but his own critical efforts against the Habsburg regime helped create a discursive space in which Elizabeth's words could become dangerous.

To better understand the significance of the *Segunda parte*, we should read it alongside a book that Ribadeneyra must have deemed its companion in 1593: not the *Scisma* but his *Tratado de tribulación* (Treatise of tribulation), which had first been printed in 1589 and was reprinted, along with the *Segunda parte*, by the same printer in Alcalá. This double-publishing venture is reminiscent of Ribadeneyra's 1588 efforts in that, as then, he chose to intervene forcefully at a delicate moment in Habsburg international efforts. As we have seen, after the failed Armada, France topped Philip's agenda. Like 1588, 1593 came with the promise of success and the threat of failure. Henry IV continued to consolidate his authority while the Spanish lobbied the French Estates-General that had just convened to choose Isabel Clara Eugenia as queen of France.[21] Ribadeneyra had long followed French affairs with interest, especially since the threat of a heretical king became more likely.[22] What happened in England now threatened to happen in France, and Ribadeneyra once again tried to find a way to encourage fortitude against the great enemy.

To this end, the *Tratado* was a powerful statement against despair. Written in a highly Christianized, neostoic voice, Ribadeneyra argued for courage in the face of life's vicissitudes based on an understanding of providential benevolence: Tribulations are caused not by natural circumstances or the function of human will, but by God, whose designs are inscrutable yet undoubtedly just and good. Though there is a punitive element to hardships experienced, they also offer opportunities for moral correction and a turn toward virtue. Efforts to live a holier life may or may not be rewarded on earth but would undoubtedly be rewarded in heaven. Faith in this certainty helped explain why bad people sometimes thrived. Ribadeneyra insisted that God treats his flock like a parent and heretics like slaves. A father might not marvel that a prostitute behaves as she does and thus lets her continue a life of sin, but he would quickly punish his daughter or wife for much smaller indiscretions "because the love and care he has for them makes him take note and punish very small faults, while dissimulating grave faults in others [prostitutes/Protestants] who advertise what they are on their foreheads."[23] Punishments should be taken as acts of paternal kindness, and so adversities should not be met with apathy, self-pity, or saggy faith. Instead, good Christians should thank God and scrutinize their own failures. Through prayer, various forms of purgation (such as the Eucharist), and thoughtful action, they should reject sin and live conformant to God's laws.

Ribadeneyra clearly used the *Tratado* to advocate Spanish reform in the wake of the Armada.[24] In the years after its first printing, Spain still bore the marks of corruption that would continue to elicit God's punishment. In a telling moment toward the end of the book, it cites St. Salvian, bishop of Marseille, and his discussion of Rome's fall. Salvian describes a general turn from God, signaled by the "neglect and tepidness of priests, the theft and tyranny of lords, the insolence of nobles, the dissolution of courtiers, the poverty and insatiable greed of the rich, the calumnies of plaintiffs (*pleyteantes*), the extortions of ministers of justice, the cruelty and heartlessness of soldiers."[25] Among other things, he harps on the unjust taxation of the poor, the corruption of tax collectors (often with the tacit approval of clerics), and the immorality of idle spectacles, especially theater. For this and more, God destroyed the Roman Empire. Readers would have understood the parallels between ancient imperial demise and Spain's situation.

Although the *Tratado* does not focus exclusively on monarchical corruption as a source of divine displeasure, the theme is prominent. Ribadeneyra insisted that monarchical authority is not in itself a guarantor of saintliness and that God's justice may visit the king as it might any other man. Kings and queens have been eaten up by fleas and worms like everyone else, a lesson on how "frail and of little esteem is all that sovereignty and majesty that we admire and adore in men."[26] The king's humanity ensured that he might be subject to divine punishment, but his status as "head" of the kingdom imbued such punishments with special significance. For example, the king might be allowed to become a tyrant to punish the corruptions of his subjects; it was thus incumbent on "each member of the community to consider himself, not as separate, but as a member and part of the Republic." Each part contributed to the success or failure of the whole.[27] Just as the king's sin might emerge out of his subject's sinfulness, subjects might be punished for the king's sins, a fate that might seem unfair but that was in fact miraculous and should harden the resolve of the entire republic to fortify its faith.[28]

Amid tribulations, amendments should be communal, but those in power played a particularly important role. "The heads and governors of the Republic" had to reform themselves as a matter of individual salvation but also to set an example of how to lead an "honest" life. Rulers should also ensure that others lead good Christian lives insofar as they could. They had to oversee matters of public behavior, though Ribadeneyra insisted that political leaders should not interfere with the workings of the soul under ecclesiastical jurisdiction. Rulers should try to make sure "that there are no public scandals, nor grave offenses against our Lord."[29]

Although there are historical elements to the *Tratado*, the *Segunda parte* was meant to concretize his discussion of divine tribulations. By focusing on English suffering, Ribadeneyra both explained why God allowed heresy to thrive and provided a set of exemplary lives for the reader, who might draw from them the courage to reform. To place the valiant in high relief, Ribadeneyra spent time echoing English Catholic narratives of English rot. Stories about the queen's evil counselors, her own usurpation of ecclesiastical authority, and her self-serving persecution of English Catholics were important vehicles to underscore the slippery slope of heresy and tyranny and to promote many of the politically pointed messages he offered in the *Scisma*.

But the queen abided, and this needed some explaining too. Following the logic of the *Tratado*, Elizabethan success despite atrocious behavior signaled divine wrath as she fell further into her sinful ways. Her evil (and that of her counselors) also offered English Catholics an opportunity for real purification.[30] Whereas they had once been weak, now Catholics understood the dangers of half-heartedness and the virtue of intransigence against godless rule. Now "by God's mercy all Catholics understand that it is not enough to believe in the Catholic faith, but that it is also necessary to confess it out loud."[31]

Most importantly, Ribadeneyra emphasized that God allowed tyrants to thrive so that there would be no lack of martyrs.[32] Slain English Catholics epitomized a holiness on par with (if not greater than) "our ancient and fortunate martyrs" and as such would reap divine benefits in heaven. On earth, they would serve as examples for the faithful and for heretics, "who often convert and die of the same faith [as the martyrs] because they saw Catholics die with such fortitude and meekness."[33] Ribadeneyra asked Spanish readers to consider English Catholic suffering when they lamented their own plight. Those who faced poverty should cast an eye toward the rich and noble in England who had been stripped of everything they once had; the ill should consider the torture and suffering faced by women and priests. When readers tired of working and felt the pangs of hunger, they too should think of English persecutions to make it through the day. English suffering was a gift, Ribadeneyra explained, to help "confirm our faith, awaken our hope, inflame our charity, teach us of divine grace, fortify our patience, awaken our devotion, condemn the gift of our flesh, feel shame of our weakness, and finally to confound our negligence."[34]

Ribadeneyra meant these lessons for all Spanish subjects as eternal truths, but he also underscored their value within the context of current political affairs. He called on readers to help those most hurt by heresy—presumably a pitch for English Catholics—and to work hard against the threat of heretics knocking at the door.[35] To avoid infection, foreign affairs required attention; more than once, he described the benefits and justifications for fighting confessional enemies. Perhaps more importantly given the times, Ribadeneyra wrote against Henry IV using talking points given by Persons and others.

Ribadeneyra no doubt saw his writings as supportive of the king, and there is much in them that conformed to the king's own worldview. In general, Philip could not help but agree with much of what Ribadeneyra said—he undoubtedly believed that a providential hand was behind his successes and failures. In a moment of deep despair after news of the Armada, Philip confided in a key counselor his fears of worse to come and how he wished to die before that day to avoid seeing future misery. He hoped he was wrong, but unless "God returned to his cause," all signs pointed south, as recent failures seemed to imply. He admitted that the main cause for divine neglect had to be, as he put it, "our sins."[36]

But Philip and his regime knew that public statements of this sort could be dangerous; he had no interest in advertising his own sinfulness. Thus the king's displeasure about having Elizabeth's voice (via the *Proclamation*) amplified was probably only part of the problem. What Persons wrote to Rome in Ribadeneyra's defense suggested that a general pall had fallen over the latter's publications. Ribadeneyra likely felt the monarchy's cold shoulder because, as discussed above, the tone of his books rubbed against Philip's desired polemical tack at the time.

That said, Philip was clearly not out to silence Ribadeneyra. The *Segunda parte* was, after all, published and then republished without the offensive Elizabethan edict in subsequent editions. But the regime was discriminating in its embrace of Catholic materials at home. It did not have to decide on one kind of polemical strategy to the total exclusion of the other, but it had to be scrupulous in its tactical decisions and deployment of polemical techniques.

CONCLUSION TO PART II

The utility of exile polemics depended on the relevance of their stories (and their lessons) to Catholic Christendom in general. Appropriation of English Catholic texts in Spain by men like Ribadeneyra is evidence of a much broader European dynamic: the 1590s witnessed many books outside the English or Spanish orbit that took the fight to the queen. Perhaps most importantly, in 1591, a Dominican monk in Florence, Girolamo Pollini, published another (much expanded) version of Sander's *De schismate Anglicano* to promote tears and resistance among Italians. In it, he encouraged readers "to over-power once and for all this hydra, to hunt these infernal monsters, to chase away the rapacious harpies from the world, and finally purge the sad English Church."[1] The message also made it to more general accounts of Catholic suffering, notably Tomasso Bozzio's *De signis ecclesiae dei*, a book that re-produced anti-Elizabethan slander to better highlight the glories of English martyrs, whose sufferings helped prove the Church's righteousness.[2] Once English Catholics started producing Philopater-like tracts, they became com-mon currency and helped expand a growing anti-Elizabethan animus; thus, for example, news chronicles incorporated Persons's *Responsio* into their up-dates on English affairs.[3]

The efforts described throughout part 2 were extraordinarily successful. The *Responsio* and related books wreaked havoc in England. As ever, Cecil kept a close watch on what was being written against the regime both at home and abroad through his many contacts there. For example, between

1591 and 1592, one Lord Darcy, then traveling in Italy, sent his master frequent notices of spurious books, including Creswell's *Exemplar*, and worked with local government officials to destroy slanderous material.[4]

The Continental assault seems to have shaken the regime. The viciousness of the attack—and perhaps more importantly, the sharp elbows swung at Cecil himself—left them at a loss as to how to respond, even if some of the queen's advisers insisted that a response was necessary.

By 1593, many felt that enough was enough. Steps were taken to initiate a rebuttal. Such efforts seemed necessary, according to the archbishop of Canterbury, John Whitgift: "We are all sought to be dishonored by these libels whereof there are many and dispersed anywhere and yet no care [is] taken for answering them, and men willing to do it are discouraged without cause." Cecil and Whitgift were not always on the same page, but they were this time. The chancellor wrote the archbishop thanking him for facilitating "a confutation of the multitude of slanders dispatched in books against the state and government."[5] Shameful hesitance must end, but prudently. Although a more ample set of responses was still to come, the regime did not first aim at Persons and his colleagues directly; instead, it combatted Sander's *De schismate Anglicano* in the guise of a Latin tract written in Cambridge: the *Antisanderus*.[6]

That Cecil and others took English Catholic attacks so seriously suggests that contemporaries thought they worked. Not only could such propaganda reinforce Catholic prejudices against the regime, but they could and did play a role in further poisoning divisive discourses in a broader political sphere. This made responding to English Catholic polemics frustratingly complicated. Francis Bacon—then an important part of Cecil's circle—got to the nub of the problem when he observed how the effectiveness of slander limited the utility of responses against it: while malicious pamphlets "are thought to be the flying sparks of truth forcibly kept down and choked by those which are possessed of the state," rebukes "are for the most part taken and deemed to be but colors and pretenses, set forth rather to instruct in a formality of speech those which are otherwise followers of the time, and demand but what to say though they neither examine or believe it."[7]

Catholics predisposed to hating the regime would believe the worst, but even Protestants loyal to the queen used Catholic polemics when it seemed useful. Books produced by Persons and his associates helped deepen divisions in England because many believed elements that were convenient in their own courtly battles. As Alexandra Gajda has shown, the earl of Essex understood the value of anti-Cecil invective and even saw it as a point of contact with loyal Catholics as he tried to counteract Cecil at court.[8] There is evidence that a range of Protestant readers happily cited Catholic bromides against mutual enemies.[9]

Success was palpable in Spain too. Philip II may not have been thrilled by Ribadeneyra's book, but he supported (and funded) English Catholic efforts: he co-opted them to push back against critics at home and abroad. As suggested here throughout, the regime was keen on employing an English discourse (even by way of France) at especially sensitive political moments. Between 1591 and 1593, tactics and strategies of image-making and image-breaking coalesced around the mutual desires of Spanish Elizabethans and Philip. English Catholics became, if briefly, the voice of the Catholic king.

And yet what looks like anodyne patter about Habsburg greatness turns out to have, upon deeper inspection, more contentious potential. From an English Catholic perspective, this work had to push the king in the direction of action while at the same time providing credible tools to support and enhance Spanish authority in Iberia and elsewhere. While it is true that we can use books by Ribadeneyra or Persons as evidence for a messianic mentality, they also contain within them elements of discontent, fear, and critique.[10] Indeed, the regime fully understood the dangers of these highly providentialist narratives within a turbulent Iberian landscape, an understanding that mitigated the regime's enthusiasm for Spanish Elizabethan works when they were meant for audiences closer to home.

The books described here underscore the strength and fragility of English Catholic exile. We can observe the skill with which they could place their books in various contexts by embracing a universalizing message, yet they struggled to promote the conquest of England in particular. Spanish Elizabethans thus had to be aware of public discussion(s) and identify ways to mold it when possible.

I have dwelled on ambiguities. Despite these, however, Spanish Elizabethans ultimately argued that Philip had been endowed with a holy mission and that the Church might be supported on his shoulders. To be sure, they had misgivings, but they also had textual answers that might help allay such reservations. The following chapters will examine the practical measures taken by English Catholics to effectuate benevolent Spanish governance.

PART III

(HABSBURG) ENGLAND AND SPAIN REFORMED

Robert Persons's efforts to promote the invasion of England took many forms. Among other things, he tried to gather and distill important intelligence for Spanish authorities to develop an effective strategy against Elizabeth. For example, in the spring of 1594, Persons received papers written by an English sailor and shipbuilder then stationed in Cádiz, N. Lambert (via one Jonas Jones). The documents—drawings of the English coast with accompanying commentary—argued for Milford (Hampshire) as the most convenient point of entry for Spanish ships. Persons seems to have held on to these papers until 1596, when he sent them to Madrid at a moment more conducive toward anti-Elizabethan action.[1] Once these documents landed on official desks, they were likely read and piled on top of others like them that survive in archives today. The contents of such memoranda provided by English Catholics varied but were unified by their efforts to provide practical information for use by strategists. They were meant for an extremely limited group of people trusted with state secrets.

By contrast, this section will outline how certain kinds of strategic documents were written for public consumption. Though maps and specific tactical plans remained necessarily top secret, I will show how English Catholics transformed policy papers into forms of ideological armature to promote and ensure successful Spanish intervention in England.

The following pages focus on two books by Persons, *A Conference About the Next Succession to the Crowne of Ingland* and *A Memorial for the Reformation of England*, along with a host of related texts.[2] I will show how, apart from providing a road map for success, "going public" was part of a strategy to guide Philip's regime toward behaviors and actions consonant with the ideals discussed in previous chapters.

These books appeared between 1593 and 1597, a period of turmoil and renewed plotting. James VI, Mary Stuart's son, had, after some earlier signs of wavering, come firmly under the influence of Protestants and eagerly asserted his claims to the English throne. For people like Persons, the possibility of his succession was a death knell for British Catholicism. In this context, schemes to remove Elizabeth were resuscitated. Scottish nobles and some clerics plotted to help Spain invade England through Scotland, which ended no better—perhaps worse—than previous schemes. In Ireland, things went similarly awry. Hugh O'Donnell and Hugh O'Neill, key clansmen, signed an alliance on the assumption that lobbying in Madrid would soon pay off and that Spanish aid was on its way.[3] It was not.

English Catholics stayed on the margins of these efforts while, as seen in chapter 2, they supported Philip and promoted an English cause. But Persons was sharp enough to know that despite his efforts, Spanish intervention required a shift in geopolitical contexts. While France topped Philip's agenda, England would have to wait: in the best-case scenario, England would topple after France had been won. Instead, however, Spanish failure across the Pyrenees ultimately provided an opening. By 1593, prospects of Spanish success in France dimmed, and this raised hopes that England might become a renewed area of focus. Such desires seemed more certain by the summer of 1596, when news came that the English had attacked Iberian soil in Cádiz.

Advocating for and shepherding England's liberation by Spanish forces was, as ever, complicated and required finesse. English exiles had to remain supportive of Philip's many geopolitical interests while promoting specifically English Catholic ones. They also tried to establish (by embracing ideas circulating in Spain) a plan that would ensure proper Catholic restoration while dealing with conflicts within the English Catholic community (partly) caused by disagreements over the role Spain should play in England's future.

7

POLITICS OF SUCCESSION

Justification for Philip II's foreign policy in Europe hinged on dynastic claims. The last two decades of his reign witnessed reinvigorated polemics centered on competing genealogies concerning Spanish rights to the thrones of Portugal, France, and England. Philip did not need English Catholics to tell him that archives should be scoured. Plenty of evidence survives that the king employed his own subjects to figure out his English rights based on Castilian (and Portuguese) lines.[1] Still, English Catholics became crucial participants in these investigations. Apart from enhancing ongoing research, they helped frame how genealogical polemics should ensue.

They ultimately tried to conjoin separate spheres of heredity into one textual package. Contentious spats about Habsburg succession across Europe often overlapped so that, for example, fights over the Portuguese succession could be inserted into English or French political squabbles, or the French lines could be a matter of serious concern and discussion in England. However, within Spain, these realms of genealogical contention had tended to remain separate until Spanish Elizabethans brought them together.

Initially, Mary Stuart proved problematic for melding English Catholic and Spanish dynastic interests. Since Philip's time as king consort of England, there was a well-established link between Habsburg blood and English monarchy going back to Edward III, but most Scottish and English Catholic intrigue after the first wave of exile centered on the fate of Mary Stuart.[2] John Leslie, bishop of Ross, became Mary's representative on the

Continent and her most avid defender. English Catholics followed his lead. But as some—William Allen and Robert Persons among them—forged attachments to Spain, defending a Scottish succession became a liability. Philip II trusted Mary as much as he trusted any statesman: very little. He trusted her son, the heretically raised James VI, even less. The king wanted to keep his options open. As the Armada came together, Philip thought seriously about installing Mary, so long as her final testament or papal fiat secured him the right to choose her successor. Such plotting evolved even as he contemplated his own claims, which, as contemporaries knew, were incompatible with Stuart ones. In the end, Philip's advisers were happy to sidestep blood altogether, noting that many in England would gladly accept a king regardless of it. Some would take "whoever released them from their captivity." Brute force would suffice should Philip or anyone else want to use it. Rights to the English crown, one report argued, had historically been asserted by arms, "and he who wielded them best became king, justly or unjustly."[3]

Knowing the king's distrust and recognizing the fluid nature of the regime's justification for replacing Elizabeth, Allen and Persons scrambled. They argued that Mary would reward Spanish efforts by affirming succession rights. Were the king to rescue her, "bestowed in marriage by His Majesty, this same Queen's authority and acquiescence can . . . be used in setting up negotiations for the succession of His Majesty." But such plotting seemed increasingly quixotic, especially as 1587 proceeded amid rumors of the Armada and the ax over Mary's head. Allen and Persons predictably tried to sidestep complications by suggesting that Spanish success did not depend wholly on Mary's good graces. Were Philip to conquer England, Elizabeth was likely to have her killed, "believing that the Enterprise is undertaken because of her"; however, Philip's subsequent pretensions would then easily materialize. Allen and Persons considered Mary's death and Philip's imperial ascendance a small price for England's Catholic renewal. And yet they urged caution. All claims should be kept secret, particularly from the pope. Sixtus V could not keep a secret, and worse, he might "for reasons of state . . . indulge in diverse reflections and conversations and suspicions in reference to His Majesty's actions." Necessary allies such as the French and Mary herself would also be turned off by such talk.[4]

Mary's death provided clarity. When news of her execution got to the duke of Olivares in Rome, Allen and Persons sent Philip a report buttressing the king's claims. Despite not having all the pertinent sources, a sufficiently sturdy set of genealogical arguments was fetched out of available tomes.[5] In doing this, Persons and Allen parted ways with the bishop of Ross and his pro-Stuart stance. They explained that while Ross argued for claimants from three family lines, there were only two: they disproved contemporary orthodoxy that held there was a Yorkist line, a Lancastrian one, and a mixed third. The duke of Huntington claimed Yorkist, the kings of Castile and Portugal Lancastrian, and Henry VII's heirs mixed blood. The last of these, they insisted, was considered "mixed" because while Henry's wife was a Yorkist, he was said to be of Lancastrian stock. But in fact, the king was not. According to Ross, Henry's claims were based on his familial links to John of Gaunt and Blanche (who was the original bearer of the title), but Allen and Persons pointed out that the king descended from John and Catherine Swynford, his third wife. Henry VII and his heirs thus had no claim on Blanche's blood. For the true Lancastrians, contemporaries should follow the descent of her children, especially Henry IV and his two sisters, Philippa and Catherine, both of whom married into Iberian royal families and were thus Philip II's ancestors. Allen and Persons suggested that claims might be pushed by the descendants of Henry IV's daughters: Blanche, who married the duke of Bavaria, and Philippa, who married the king of Denmark. But this was uncertain. They were unsure if the current rulers of Bavaria and Denmark were of the same line, and they did not want to know. They hoped the issue remained "secret and unknown by them."[6]

On the eve of the Armada, despite their effort to construct convenient family charts, Persons and Allen could countenance a more turbulent future. Even if the Lancastrian claim was pristine, Allen and Persons argued that with heretics in power and with Spanish enemies across Europe, Philip's ascent had to be violent.[7]

This harsh reality was no less true after 1588 than before, but Persons's stance on secrecy had changed, leading to the publication of several texts touching on the issue. Such a change of heart was informed by evolving dynamics of Spanish geopolitical engagements. Philip's bid to have Isabel Clara Eugenia elected by the Catholic League in Paris had failed. Worse, amid League "betrayal," Henry IV officially converted to Catholicism on July 25, 1593, and was crowned at Chartres early in 1594. The new king could now promise to "expel from all lands under my jurisdiction all heretics denounced by the church."[8] By September 1594, a further blow to the Spanish cause came from Rome, where Clement VIII, despite reservations, accepted Henry back into the Catholic fold. In a letter to Philip, the pope reported, "As to the true or feigned conversion, this is something that troubles us greatly, as it does not only touch on the health of one person, but the whole kingdom, and consequently millions of souls." Considering this, he argued that God alone could know man's heart. Presently, he continued, "we are forced to follow conjectures and signs which in this case are very important."[9] Given the failure of Philip's French efforts, it seems that Persons and his colleagues decided it was time to push dynastic matters as a way to reorient Spanish foreign policy.

A first move in this direction came in the summer of 1594. On August 29, Pedro de Ribadeneyra approved the translation of a report written by the exiled nuns of Syon Abbey, as prepared by Charles Dractan, a priest at the English college in Valladolid. The book describes the hardships experienced by these Bridgettines after their expulsion from London under Henry VIII and their subsequent forced peregrinations around the Netherlands and France until their recent arrival in Portugal. The text was a fund-raising tool for the nuns, but it also offered Spanish audiences an English view, as advertised on the title page, "of the state of things in France, after Vendome [Henry IV] was accepted as king."[10] As mentioned in chapter 5, English accounts of French troubles could help build a case for anti-French aggression, but the Bridgettine narrative was different. It emphasized that, whether the Catholic world liked it or not, Henry had taken the French throne. The nuns decided to leave France to avoid involvement in succession politics: they did not want to voice their opinion on Henry's legitimacy. In fact, after his coronation, they seemed to accept him. They even thought he would provide passports for their escape. The king's governor in Rouen tried to convince the nuns to stay, largely because he wanted to shore up Catholic support, but the women were resolute. Despite any possible good intentions on the part of royal governors, they doubted safety could be assured. The nuns' distrust lingered primarily because of the prevailing threat from Elizabeth and English Protestants.[11] France was too close to home and the English threat too palpable. Subtle though the message was, the narrative thus pushes pious Spanish readers from concerns about France back to the real English threat.

The book tries to focus on the needs of Philip's subjects. After describing the history of Syon Abbey, the author(s) argued providence had brought the nuns to Lisbon. They had found a haven in Portugal, they explained, "under the protection of the descendants of the house of Lancaster and of the royal blood of Henry V. For it is known that the kings of the house of Portugal . . . are direct descendants of the house of Lancaster, because they come from the queen doña Philippa, daughter of John of Gaunt, duke of Lancaster, and sister of his son king Henry VI of England, who was the wife of John I, king of Portugal."[12] The Bridgettines had found a path back to their legitimate ruler: Philip.

Tying Lines

This gesture might seem insignificant except that it is part of a much more comprehensive project to publicize Philip's English inheritance. Sometime in 1594, a manuscript, the *Raçonamiento y parecer de los letrados ingleses sobre el caso de la sucesion del Reyno de Inglaterra* (The reasoning and opinion of the English lawyers about the succession of England), began circulating in Spain.[13] The book summarizes part 1 of the aforementioned *Conference* (on theories of political authority) and translates most of part 2 (on English succession wrangles). The *Conference* and in turn its translation were probably authored by several contributors in and around the English college at Valladolid.[14] If there were many hands involved, however, Persons spearheaded the project. He was likely the main author of the Spanish and future English and Latin iterations, though these books officially appeared as the work of one R. Doleman. Not only was Persons the head of English Catholic activities in Spain; he also never quite denied at least partial responsibility. Moreover, there is no convincing reason to assume men like Englefield (Persons's ally) would attribute the project to him had he not been the principal author.[15]

Persons tried to take succession out of the shadows. The formality of the manuscript, with its proper introduction and title page, not to mention its survival in several copies, suggests that it was intended for "public" consumption. There is a slight chance it was printed, but it was more likely meant for a select, elite audience in courtly circles. Its immediate purpose may have been to garner support for a version that would soon be printed in English with Spanish support, the aforementioned *Conference*.[16] More broadly, it was meant as a statement about the compatibility of several Habsburg claims to European hegemony, conjoining English matters to those realms of dynasticism so vital to the Habsburgs at the time: France and Portugal.

The *Raçonamiento* is framed as an unbiased account of open and frank debates concerning English hereditary rights. As such, the interlocutor, "a civil lawyer," provides a subtle, multifaceted discussion of rival claims to the English throne with no explicit conclusions drawn. It did not take much, however, for readers to notice that Habsburg legitimacy was strongly implied.

In treating the infanta's claims to the English throne, Persons provided a thorough examination of her rights to the French crown. While sketching England's succession since the Norman Conquest, the interlocutor offers a brief excursus on French affairs because, he insists, those who defended the infanta's English claims based their arguments on the Breton succession.[17] Luckily for Spain's supporters, France and England had become indelibly linked when Henry II married Eleanor of Aquitaine and their son (Geoffrey) married into the Breton clan. The successor to one crown could claim rights to the other. Arguments for the infanta's descent were thus multifaceted. First, the book regurgitated what had become dogma in Spanish circles: the eventual descent of Brittany into Valois hands made the infanta a natural successor. Second, the author provided an argument that established a "direct" link between Philip's daughter and Henry II of England.[18] Henry's daughter, Eleanor, had married into the Castilian monarchy, eventually giving birth to Blanche of Castile, who in turn married the French king, Louis VIII of France, and so on. Some also suggested that England belonged to France—that the English had once subjected themselves to French rule. Having grown tired of King John, they chose Louis VIII to be their king. This arrangement, however, never came to fruition because upon John's sudden death, the English changed their minds and elected Henry III. Despite this, some said the infanta, as Louis's legitimate heir, could nevertheless claim the English crown. English subjects had legally selected Louis, and so his heirs could legally reassert their old rights.[19] As queen of France, Philip's daughter could very well claim the English throne.

The infanta's name had been floated as a possible English successor since the days leading up to the Armada, perhaps because Philip did not want the weight of another crown on his aging head. He probably also thought promoting his daughter was a prudent compromise: denials of imperial pretensions might ring truer. Nevertheless, at least until the *Raçonamiento*, English Catholics seemed to lean on the king's own inheritance. Persons left that argument for last.

Philip's claims hinged on Portugal's Lancastrian ancestry going back to Philippa (John of Gaunt's daughter), who had married João I of Portugal. As Isabel of Portugal's son, he was thus grandson of Dom Manuel, to whom several other claimants were also linked. As with the French succession, in discussing the Portuguese one, Persons dipped into a series of important contemporary Iberian debates. While most other Portuguese claimants relented to Philip's might, Antonio, prior of Crato, did not. Fancying himself the true king, he spent the rest of his life looking for both popular support and occasional aid from foreign powers, mainly the English and French. Philip, on his side, strained to assert and reassert that his conquest of Portugal was based on the certitude that his claim was "the most just."[20] Persons echoed the Spanish court by taking direct aim at Antonio's pretensions, pointing out he was a bastard and ineligible for the throne.[21] Beyond blood ties, he also raised an alternative argument for Philip's claim to Portugal. He suggested, as the crown had since the 1570s, that Portuguese monarchs themselves had given succession rights to the Castilians as part of a dowry.[22] In sum, as with the infanta, who possessed dual legitimacy in England and France, Philip had dual claims to England and Portugal.

Persons did not hide critiques of Habsburg claims to England. Critics raised two major objections against arguments dependent on the Portuguese succession. First, they insisted that "old and forgotten titles should not be admitted." Second, they said that as a foreigner, Philip endangered the commonwealth because being "a great Prince and powerful monarch, as he truly is, [he] could put English liberty at risk."[23] Having said this, however, Persons was sure to mention the potential weakness of these arguments. He rejected the idea that Lancastrian rights through the Portuguese line lessened with the passage of time; to the contrary, "no royal title ceases or perishes" but can be justly claimed when "he to whom it belongs can recover possession."[24] Against xenophobic sensibilities, the author lamely reminded readers that most Englishmen do not mind foreign rule; they remember the good that came of French-born monarchs like Henry VII and even of Philip II's own time as king consort—many even speculated about the benefits that might have come if negotiations with the French during the late 1570s and early 1580s to match Henry III's Catholic brother and heir, the duke of Anjou, with Elizabeth had succeeded![25] This is a shocking claim that others present at the *Raçonamiento*'s mock-discourse cannot let slide. Were Anjou and Philip not universally unpopular in England? The interlocutor agrees but insists that this popular disapproval is unreasonable and unfounded, "raised by some restless, rambunctious, seditious men who did not approve of the religion of these princes." Their logic is not founded on "reason of state," because *that* logic called for the acceptance of a foreign ruler.

Of course, the infanta's claim was no less complicated than Philip's. The *Raçonamiento* reveals that her critics also censured Spanish backers for supporting "old" collateral lines over direct ones. Like Philip's nemeses, others argued that the infanta could not be crowned because she was a foreigner. Most importantly, the infanta's opponents insisted that religious strife would increase under an inflexible Catholic monarch. As to the antiquity of the claim, the infanta's supporters again said it could be dusted off. As with Philip, Persons rejected antiforeigner sentiment, this time through a curt statement that no English laws called for such a prevention. The matter of Isabel's Catholicism was probably most troubling to Persons, but through the interlocutor, he suggested that such fears were overblown. Not everyone in England would be put off by the infanta's religion; in fact, many would love her more for it.[26]

There were other claimants, but the historical context rendered their arguments untenable. The *Conference* and its Spanish version mark the sputtering end of the Wars of the Roses.[27] Strife that had once been quelled by the ascent of the Tudors—the marriage of Henry VII and Elizabeth of York—was revived by Persons and his colleagues, who portrayed English history since the reign of Henry VI as a story of Yorkist usurpation. As mentioned above, in their formulation, the Lancastrian kings all descended from John of Gaunt, though the familial title did not derive from John himself but from his wife, Blanche, and this assertion allowed Persons to argue that Henry VII had no legitimate Lancastrian blood. Since the Lancastrian claim was the legitimate one, it stood to reason that the entire Tudor line was illegitimate, thus precluding (on a purely genealogical basis) the legitimate succession of any contemporary claimant—James VI, Arabella Stuart, and so on—who descended from Henry VII's sisters. If the only legitimate Lancastrian claim was in Portugal, the bulk of the *Raçonamiento* was moot. Only the infanta, whose roots sank back to a time before Edward III, could challenge Philip's pretensions.

Although on the face of it, genealogical arguments seem to be part of a pro-Habsburg propaganda campaign, things were not so simple. To be sure, as I have argued, it did not take much to notice the author's support for various Spanish dynastic claims, but in this, Persons deviated from the regime's polemical strategy. Prior to his intervention, talk of the Portuguese or French successions was independent of English affairs. Even after Persons's book(s), the genealogical inquiries emphasized by the king's Spanish servants would focus on French claims to the exclusion of English ones.[28]

Nevertheless, the *Raçonamiento*'s limited circulation in Spain was important because it served two important functions. First, it tried to capitalize on Philip's perceived goodwill. As Joseph Creswell wrote from Madrid in 1595, "The king is old and we don't know if those that will govern after His majesty will be as well disposed" to English Catholic activities.[29] English matters needed resolution "during the life of the Spanish King," Creswell reiterated later that year, "because his intention is saintly and good."[30] Thus the book provided a set of arguments for when the regime decided to act against Elizabeth. Indeed, sometime around 1595 or 1596, Persons argued that Philip could assert his dominion by gathering the "principal Catholics in a sudden parliament as has often been done in extreme situations." Once assembled, the group would easily agree with the king's succession as lobbied for "in the newly published book."[31]

The *Raçonamiento* also tried to save English claims from negligence. Persons placed them on par with other areas of Habsburg interest to suggest how the English succession could fit into a bigger network of pretensions. In doing this, however, Persons did not push too hard on the theme of "monarchia" or its defense. That sort of apology would be saved for the *Conference*.

Imperial Benevolence

Apart from genealogy, Persons made several implicit arguments favoring Spanish (more broadly, Catholic) pretensions. To begin, he presented conquest as a legitimate way to assert control. The clearest example of this was the Norman Conquest, which served as the starting point for the book's historical reconstruction of England's succession. In 1066, William the Conqueror had taken England by means of "force and arms, although he tried to show that he had been elected by the will and testament of Edward the Confessor." The legitimacy of William's rule was not important; what mattered, according to Persons, was that "in whatever way this [William's ascendance] occurred, what is certain is that his line continues until this day."[32] This interpretation of the English monarchy melded with the aforementioned notion circulating in Spain that force in itself was the ultimate arbiter of English affairs.

Persons scrutinized the possibility of foreign rule—most explicitly when discussing James's claim. Here a disproportionate amount of ink was spilled challenging censures against foreigners.[33] Many arguments against the Scottish king were ignored or perfunctorily questioned, but Persons wanted to ensure that his foreignness did not preclude him from the throne. Persons recalled Leslie's arguments in favor of Mary Stuart to highlight this principle. The bishop of Ross had argued that statutes frequently raised to deny foreign inheritance had been glossed incorrectly. If prohibition existed, it applied only to individuals and excluded royal inheritance, which was never mentioned in any laws. Because "the crown has and enjoys of many privileges," he said, it was not subject to laws judging everyday quarrels. While statutes referred to "inheritance of dominion," the crown was not part of common vassalage schemes because it "is received from God, our lord."[34]

In the *Conference*, Persons pushed further than the *Raçonamiento* by adding a chapter on the *benefits* of foreign rule. Admitting the ingrained prejudice against foreigners from Aristotle to the Bible to more recent critics of the Habsburgs and the Guise, Persons asked English readers to set aside such impulses in favor of reason. A good government should be measured solely "by the effects thereof, that redound unto the subjects, for whose good it was ordained." Where justice is preserved, where subjects live well, where peace is maintained, and above all, where the true faith is kept, the good ruler's provenance did not matter.[35] It is much better to live under the yoke of a stranger than to live under a local tyrant. Indeed, the homegrown governor becomes a de facto stranger once he falls into tyranny: "Little availeth it to me, whether he be of my blood and country or no."[36]

Persons offered a nuanced discussion of "strangeness." In the fragmented political landscape of early modern Europe, identifying those in or out of a given group was subjective. Some might "be of the same nation, and language" and still seem foreign. Thus Frenchmen despised the Guise though they were culturally similar. In Italy, Florentines and Sienese could not get along, though they lived thirty miles away from each other and were of the same "nation."[37] On the other hand, peoples culturally divided could be well integrated. Biscayans did not consider Castilians strangers; Bretons and Normans got along, as did the English and Welsh.[38] Persons rejected the notion that a foreign king should be snubbed outright when the concept was so contested.

The *Conference* insists that there is nothing sinister about having an outsider for a king. There are several ways by which a foreigner may come to rule, but even the least palatable of these—conquest—was not very bad. Though the conqueror might be brutal against hostile subjects at first, the prudent king often needed to be gentle and sweet for the sake of "policy." Even doctors after administering "a vehement purgation doth minister levities and soft medicines."[39] Indeed, history showed that invaders resorted to brutalization only against the recalcitrant. William the Conqueror longed for peace and was eager to grant his new subjects freedom; he only shed blood to avoid rebellion. When the conquered accepted their lot, however, foreign rulers were clement. Some admired Roman rule so much that non-Romans often sought it. According to many, "the world was never more happily governed, than under the Romans, and yet were they strangers to most of their subjects."[40]

Persons peddled imperialist fairy tales. He emphasized Habsburg activities in the Low Countries and asked readers to take a broad view of the past. For hundreds of years, "a man shall read nothing almost, in their stories, but war, sedition, and blood shed among themselves." However, since the first days of Austrian rule (starting with Philip I, Philip II's grandfather) down to the recent outbreak of Dutch rebellion, it was "incredible how those states increased in wealth, peace and dignity."[41] As far as government was concerned, Spanish Habsburgs demonstrated an abiding respect for local custom. If they ever tried to implement anything that went against it, Flemish representatives in Castile would quickly voice concern and "by this means they obtained lightly what they would . . . so as in effect they were absolute kings in themselves."[42]

Spanish rule in Italy further proved imperial benevolence. Italians were not subject to the same taxes as Spaniards, and they were not subject to the Inquisition. Nor were any laws passed externally. None of their old rights and privileges had been eroded.[43] Light-handed rule in Italy resulted from a buffer system—rule by governors helped mediate what might have been unmitigated oppression. Homeborn kings were absolute and could execute their laws forcefully and unremorsefully, having "to give accompt to no man." Rule under a royal representative was, by definition, not direct and thus required more circumspection. Decisions were not made unilaterally but needed approval of councils and the crown. Bureaucratic necessities aside, governors, knowing they would eventually be private citizens, were wary of antagonizing their momentary subjects, according to Persons: they "take heed what they do and whom they offend."[44]

The bigger the empire, the less dangerous it is. Persons argued that a great monarch would be able to defend his dominions without squeezing his subjects. The mighty king would not take but give: he would reward the valorous and virtuous.[45] The "little king," on the other hand, needed to maintain his royal dignity but lacked personal resources and would be more dependent on the populace. More troubling, he would not have the means to keep subjects happy. Persons supported this premise by showing the deficiencies in Geneva as opposed to kingdoms like France and Spain. Individuals living in a Swiss canton could expect little more than what the "commonwealth and state can give." Larger polities could be more generous. The Roman Empire "had the preferments of all the world to bestow."[46]

That Persons provided such apologies for conquest and imperial expansion to English readers, not Spanish ones, is noteworthy. Perhaps only an English audience needed to be convinced that absorption into a larger imperial unit would be painless and beneficial. But perhaps this absence speaks to the Spanish situation as well. As suggested in part 2, if the regime struggled with how to depict its imperial might amid widespread aspersions, it seems unlikely that they would have embraced promoting expansionist logic, even if consonant with what Philip and some of his advisors would have believed. Persons may have been sensitive to this and censored himself, either because he originally wanted to publish the book in Spain or because he did not want to clue the regime in to what he had prepared for an English audience.

Of course, Persons must have known that English readers, except for a very small number of recusants, would have been hostile to such arguments. To mitigate this, Persons emphasized earthly politics and reason of state as rationales to help decide the succession. However, such arguments could only work within the context of a purportedly neutral discussion, devoid of the confessional animus that had become prominent in Spanish Elizabethan polemic.

From League to London

The *Conference* was a carefully calculated risk based on an opening provided by the political situation in England. Persons (and his colleagues) started working on the book sometime in 1593, just as London was ablaze with concern about England's future.[47] In February, Peter Wentworth, a prominent Puritan voice in Parliament, planned to call on the queen to resolve the issue. He went to Westminster, as J. E. Neale describes, "equipped with speech, bill, objections and answers, a thanksgiving to the queen in the event of success, a rebuke in case of failure."[48] He also wrote an inflammatory booklet that remained in manuscript until 1598: *A Pithie exhortation to Her Majestie for establishing Her Successor to the Crowne.*[49] Persons, in a short pamphlet that amounts to a preview of the *Conference*, tried to exploit the tempestuous climate. He emphasized that Wentworth's efforts served as an impetus for a Netherlandish soirée during which a group of learned men discussed the succession.[50] They did so out of disappointment: "It was presumed . . . something would be determined thereof [concerning the succession] in Parliament . . . but when news that nothing at all had been done therein, but rather that one or two had been checked or committed for speaking the same," they decided to examine the issue themselves.

Succession wrangles always involve issues beyond genealogy. Uncertainty about England's future inspired many to consider the nature of monarchical institutions and the relationship between subject and monarch. As recent scholarship has emphasized, in England, such issues were often sorted out in the guise of reconstituted French polemics.[51] Individuals at the Elizabethan court understood the value of translating and appropriating anti-League polemics supporting Henry IV because they rejected rebellion against legitimate monarchs. By promoting works in Henry's favor, the Elizabethan regime defended both its ally and the queen against radical Catholics.

English Catholics were aware of this tactic. Englefield, in a paper presented to the pope justifying the *Conference*, suggested the book was a response to the nefarious work of Pierre de Belloy, whose *Apologie Catholique* had been translated to English in 1586. The *Apologie* argued against those who undermined Henry IV's succession to the French throne while maintaining firm loyalty to the regnant king, Henry III, and by extension, the proper rules of monarchical succession.[52] Belloy emphasized the primacy of consanguinity for maintaining the crown's integrity and emphasized the king's God-given authority. Subjects are, he claimed, "obliged to obey . . . kings, whether good or bad, because they have been elected, and they have been given to us by the hand of God."[53] The book also provided ancillary arguments that would have appealed to the queen and her polemicists: it ranted against Spain, insisted on the subjection of the Church to a monarch, and tried to minimize the divisions among different sorts of Christians. The *Conference* tried to fight back by appropriating elements of League polemics in England.

De iusta reipublicae christiana in reges impios et hereticos authoritate (On the just authority of Christian republics over impious and heretical kings) was the most extensive and pungent response to Belloy published in France (1590 and 1592).[54] The attribution to Guilelmo Rossaeo in the 1592 edition is false; recently, scholar François Valérian has settled on the English exile William Gifford as its author.[55] Despite the English pedigree, the book was a central piece of League propaganda.[56] It also served as at least a partial source for the *Conference*; since the sixteenth century, some have accused Persons of stealing it wholesale. More recently, José M. Ruiz has argued that a copy of *De iusta authoritate* at the English college in Valladolid bears evidence that parts of the *Conference* were indeed taken directly from it.[57] Persons was fully engaged in the shadowboxing dynamic where English problems were debated along the lines of French polemics, but unlike anti-League polemics, which could be adopted in England, the same could not be done with League material. The similarities between the *Conference* and its French counterpart are real, but they are limited to broad theoretical frameworks. Here the differences are just as telling as the similarities. Though Persons might have agreed with much of Gifford's book, he rejected key elements for the sake of his broader objectives.

Both books argue that polities are human creations. As Gifford explained it, "Natural law and God as creator of that nature and that law have given all people the full and free faculty to govern themselves."[58] Different forms of government are evidence that "particular people" can choose this or that form of "republic."[59] Persons argued that the magistrate's authority is "a human creature or a thing created by man, for by man's free choice this particular form of government . . . is appointed."[60] Thus "neither God nor nature prescribeth any . . . particular forms [of government], but concurreth with any that the commonwealth itself appointeth."[61] Both writers suggested that monarchy was the best form of government but that putative subjects, as purveyors of positive law, could choose their fate.

Especially within a monarchical context, Gifford and Persons argued that terms of reciprocity between subject and ruler are contractually set. The French tract suggests that royal authority is "transmitted" by the estates of the realm (bishops, nobles, and the people) through coronation oaths where subjects promise obedience in exchange for just rule and protection of the Church.[62] Persons argued that "the more orderly and organized the Prince commeth to his crown and dignity, the more express and certain these conditions and agreements between him and his people."[63] In commonwealths, "where matters pass by reason, conscience, wisdom and consultation . . . mutual and reciprocal oaths between Princes and subjects, at the day of their coronation of admission . . . have been much more established, made clear and put in use." This is particularly true in Christian realms where these ceremonies and relationships "hath been reduced to a more sacred and religious kind of union and concord."[64] Persons insisted on the strength of "this agreement, bargain and contract between the king and his common wealth, at his first admission" and argued that it was as binding and strong as any marriage contract.[65]

Subjects can remove the king who has broken his promises. While Gifford insisted that "popular tumults" should be avoided and that forces should be raised to defend the king when under (unjust) attack, subjects are not bound to *impious* monarchs who want to destroy the republic.[66] Because kings do not exist outside of the law or the promises they have made to their

subjects, subjects have the right and duty to resist, especially against heretics. In the 1590 edition, Gifford even suggested that a "private person" can
independently kill a tyrant so long as he carried out "the will of the republic."[67] Persons was wary of emphasizing individual rights to commit tyran-
nicide, so he followed the more prudent tone of Gifford's second edition by
merely pointing out the thorny issue before the interlocutors' conversation
is cut short by lunch.[68] Otherwise, the *Conference* also argues that monarchical
authority is not absolute but "delegated" and as such can be taken away.[69]
Persons insisted that subjects should be supportive of the good ruler, but "as
the whole body is of more authority then the only head, and may cure the
head if it be out of tune, so may the wealpublique cure or cutt of their heades
if they infest the rest."[70]

These arguments serve a double purpose in the *Conference* and *De iusta
authoritate*. They provide a logic for denying the claims of dangerous royal
claimants and justifications for the removal of a tyrant. In practical terms,
both books gave French and English Catholics the intellectual weapons to
either resist their monarch or work to ensure that a good Catholic took the
throne from the start.

Despite these similarities, Persons and Gifford treated confessional allegiances differently. *De iusta authoritate* was written in the heat of religious
conflict on the side of a politically powerful Catholic League and thus had
no reason to soft-pedal its arguments. The book mixes political theory with
anti-Protestant invective and powerful arguments in favor of Catholic institutions. For an English audience, absent active religious warfare and in the
context of persecution, Persons wrote in a more neutral tone. The *Conference*
is perhaps most remarkable for its calculated restraint.

The authors used different religious arguments to support the overturning of any "natural" succession. Gifford contended that spiritual concerns
are sufficient grounds to remove a king. The good monarch can only be he
who seeks to satisfy two ends, that of "nature and that of grace, of honesty
and of faith, of present life and of the future, temporal and eternal, and more
specifically to the most sacred end of divine grace, of the future life, and
of eternal happiness."[71] Unlike Gifford, who assaulted Henry and his faith,
Persons chose not to attack Elizabeth or the evils of Calvinism. Instead, he
discussed the importance of religious unity within the logic of, as he put it,
"reason of state." Because natural law dictates that political stability requires
religious peace, monarch and subjects must (in a fully functional state) share
the same faith. Persons insisted that if St. Paul "pronounced so absolutely
and plainly . . . that even in eating of a piece of meat, it is damnable for a

man to discern and yet to eat," how much worse it would be "for a man to dissemble or do against his own conscience, & judgment, that is to say, to discern and judge that he is an infidel, or heretic, or wicked man, or Atheist or erroneous in religion, and yet further his advancement and government over Christians."[72] This argument gestures toward the literature of the early 1580s, which forbade Catholics from consorting with the confessional enemy. Here, however, the religious equation has no defined variables. Persons offered a more general critique of the multireligious state: it would be "but great folly & oversight for a man of what religion soever he be, to promote to a kingdom in which [he] himself must live, one of contrary religion; for let the bargains and agreements be what they will . . . yet seeing the prince once made and settled, must needs proceed according to the principles of his own religion." Persons suspected it might be "impossible for two of different religions to love sincerely" and suggested that the animosity between those of and outside of the king's religion would result in open conflict. Moreover, those not sharing the monarch's religion would be subject to oppression.[73]

This realpolitik tack coheres with Persons's decision to avoid confessional diatribes. Though conspiracy theories and slander, which had become common during the previous two decades, could be read between the lines, the *Conference* never propels them. In it, Persons forsook the polemical for the analytical and assessed the possible leanings of various religious groups in England, including different shades of Protestants and Catholics.[74]

Persons and Gifford also diverged in their accounts of ecclesiastical authority. Gifford explained that there are separate spheres of activity between secular and religious institutions. While Christ gave "kings palaces, he gave bishops churches: to one the body, to the others souls; to one external matters of the civil republic; to the other interior affairs of the republic and of the holy church."[75] Because the Church was instituted by God and because it tends to superior things, it is superior to secular governance. He insisted that the Church does not exist within the state but the state within the Church. Though heretics might resist such logic, even Muslims understood it and supported the punishment of those who failed to protect ecclesiastical institutions.[76] Gifford repeatedly showed how secular governance depends on ecclesiastical assistance. Taxation, for example, depends on the will of high clergymen within the Estates-General. More broadly, laws (to which the prince is bound) must conform to ecclesiastical diktat. The Church does not make them, but they should emerge under the tutelage "of bishops and the instruction of synods."[77]

By contrast, Persons merely implied ecclesiastical power through historical examples of how bishops instituted political authority. Since the earliest
days of Christianity, monarchs had promised "ecclesiastical Prelates, at their
first admission" to uphold the true faith.[78] This went for all modern European
monarchies, including England, where the archbishop of Canterbury "doth
ordinarily do these ceremonies . . . as the Archbishop of Rheims doth in
France . . . with the same solemnity and honor according to the condition and
state of our country."[79] Consequently, bishops facilitated proper dethronement
in the name of the people, but Persons's emphasis is on the Church's supportive role to the commonwealth.

Gifford and Persons dealt with the pope differently too. Gifford provided
a substantial defense of papal authority as the successor to Peter. God had
created a perfect ecclesiastical hierarchy, and any effort to undermine the
leaders of the Church rejected God's power.[80] While he insisted on ample
episcopal authority, he also underlined the role popes traditionally played in
punishing monarchs who turned their back on the Church and how their
decisions had been acclaimed by good Christians.[81]

Persons did not discuss papal powers explicitly. When individual popes
appear in his book, they do not initiate or encourage political maneuvers, but
only (as with other bishops) confirm the people's will. For example, when
the Portuguese king, Don Sancho, was deposed, Persons argued that it was
with "the universal consent of all Portugal," approved by a Church council
and ultimately Pope Innocent IV "at the petition and instance of the whole
realm."[82] This distancing from papal politics is striking considering that the
Conference came shortly after the *Responsio*, which, as mentioned above, argues
for the papacy as adjudicator of succession quandaries and was thought by
contemporary Catholic readers to be a high papalist text.[83]

Persons clearly did not want to follow all arguments espoused by the
French League. His book thus departs radically from predictable talking
points in the battle against Henry IV. In fact, the *Conference* accepted his
succession. Consistent with its principal contention on the free will of the
commonwealth, the Salic Law (which barred a female succession) was not
a negotiable invention, as the Spanish and the League would have it, but
accepted as fact: "The world knoweth, how women are not admitted to succeed in the crown be they never so near in blood." Though the Spanish
monarchy and its allies would dismiss this aspect of French law as spurious, the *Conference*'s interlocutor needed to accept it because laws, like kings,
were created by the people. Once justly instituted, laws were legitimate.
Thus while there might be many arguments for female succession, all such

arguments "prevailed not, with the French as it doth not also at this day for the admission of Doña Isabella Clara Eugenia . . . unto the said crown of France, though by descent of blood there be no question of her next propinquity."[84] Persons claimed to "doubt not greatly of his [Henry IV's] title by propinquity of blood according to the law Salic."[85]

I suspect this sort of argument—together with a laundry list of Iberian depositions and elections—led to a certain coyness about the *Conference* in Spain. When Persons presented the *Raçonamiento* to the king and his advisors, his summary of part I was extremely thin on detail, except for the suggestion that the book countered Belloy and provided justification for monarchical selection. Surely knowing that Persons's book fundamentally undermined Philip's efforts to delegitimize Henry would not have pleased the king. Persons's decision to break with the Spanish line further suggests that he wanted to redirect focus from France to England.

Still, the book was generally congenial to Spanish interests; it was encoded so that a "good" Catholic could see a pro-Spanish reading. Persons struck a balance between publicizing Spanish claims (thus trying to nudge the regime to act on them) while leaving space for other interpretations.

Moreover, Persons wanted to write a book that would raise eyebrows and irritate the sensitive political situation in England. In the tradition of sophisticated propaganda, the book tried to deepen discord that would weaken the state. If Persons wanted to poison the well, he was successful.

Troublemaker

Persons dedicated the *Conference* to the earl of Essex, who had then emerged as an anti-Cecilian pole of authority at court. The book repaid Essex himself for having helped many of "Doleman's" friends in France and lauded him because there was no one, Persons said, "in more high & eminent place or dignity at this day in our realm, then your self, whether we respect your nobility or calling, or favor with your prince, or high liking of the people & consequently no man like to have a greater part of sway in deciding of this great affair [the succession] (when time shall come for that determination)."[86] Far from a genuine kindness to Essex, Persons wanted the book to be a kiss of death: linking Essex to the succession debate would compromise his role at court. To twist the knife a little, Persons purposefully used language that gestured at Essex's efforts to promote his noble credentials and his gestures at "popularity" that some at court deemed dangerous. If many of Persons's efforts in 1592 and 1593 centered on attacking Cecil, now he aimed to hurt the chancellor's nemesis.[87] On cue, Elizabeth fumed. Essex left court "wan and pale, being exceedingly troubled at this great Piece of Villainy done unto him."[88] Thereafter he undertook an aggressive campaign to rehabilitate his standing.[89]

Peter Lake has rightly suggested that the *Conference* sank deep roots in late-Elizabethan political culture. Evidence for this is exhaustive. To begin, Persons undoubtedly heightened anxieties in late Elizabethan England. The queen became more suspicious of potential claimants to the throne. Thus, for example, the regime soon arrested the earl of Hertford, whose claims Persons discussed in the *Conference* and who had not been shy about promoting his noble authority.[90] Cecil and others at court recognized that the book could be used as key evidence of Catholic hispanism and rebellious instincts. He sent it to James VI in hopes that it would convince the young king of the threat posed by Spain and Catholics more generally. Upon reading it, James was horrified. The crystallization of his famed "absolutist" political claims emerged in response to what he considered Personian challenges to his rightful succession.[91] In a broader public sphere, existing disquiet about England's future was only exacerbated. Challenges to the *Conference* sprouted in England and Scotland in pamphlet literature while preachers took to their pulpits against Personian ideas. Further, as Lake has shown, the succession question (again, through the prism of the *Conference*) was hashed out on the London stage, especially (but not exclusively) in Shakespeare's history plays.[92] Thus even as critics saw through Persons's rhetorical pose of neutrality, there was no way to ignore his book or avoid it.

From the start, some Catholics feared the project. Jesuit general Claudio Acquaviva did not appreciate the book's publication and wanted to stop it. Once again, he did not want the Society involved in politics. By the time Persons received word of the general's displeasure, the *Conference* had already been sent to Belgium for publication. Persons tried to excuse his rashness and explained that he had not anticipated the general's negativity. He would have otherwise slowed things down. But it was not all up to him anyway. Three or four other people helped write the book, and they seemed perfectly happy with its contents. He insisted that the first, more broadly theoretical part was extremely important to ensure that Catholics not accept "anyone who pretends to be successor by blood without any other condition being met as has occurred in England after Mary's death and then in France." The *Conference* reminded (Catholic) readers that they were still bound by conscience. On the genealogical discussion of part 2, he insisted that the book took no sides and that its main purpose was to challenge Elizabethan efforts to silence debate in order to "keep everyone blind in those matters [the succession]." Publicity would expose heretical infighting and Catholics would then see that they had "cloth to cut without scruples of conscience."[93]

Persons probably rolled his eyes at Acquaviva's complaints but was likely much more concerned about negative reactions after the book's publication. As one sympathetic contemporary put it, critics found in the *Conference* an excuse to say "a thousand bad things . . . without having yet seen it or read it."[94] Even among those sympathetic to anti-Elizabethan aggression, it seemed to do more harm than good. The Scottish Jesuit William Crichton, increasingly supportive of James's succession, reminded Persons of an old French proverb: "You don't catch a hare by a drum."[95] These were mild words compared to the kind of bickering the *Conference* helped kindle among members of various colleges. In Rome, the rector alleged, "[Students] speak mordantly against the book on the Succession to the Crown of England, and against its author."[96] As Persons and his allies would have it, seminarians took their cues from Flanders under the influence of exiled rabble-rousers Charles Paget, William Gifford, and some Scottish troublemakers.[97] Richard Barrett, rector at the college in Rheims, complained that students fell under the spell of "the selfsame faction at Bruxelles . . . against the Spaniards and such as take that way."[98]

The *Conference* had thus succeeded in consolidating turmoil among English priests of various types. Since Allen had died in 1594, dissension had followed; as Persons put it, troubles had "incredibly redoubled and grown." Catholics (lay and clerical) disagreed about the necessary course to achieve eventual liberation or toleration—they even disagreed on which of the two should be sought. The fissures were apparent in the tumults at the English college in Rome, in the constant backbiting in Flanders, in the secular-Jesuit stirs at Wisbech, and more generally, among those who favored accommodation to Elizabethan laws and advocated strict recusancy. Moreover, the *Conference* became exhibit A in the case against Persons as a rebellious Hispanophile whose only interest was promoting international Jesuit tyranny.[99] Enemies cawed about how Persons and Jesuits generally only wanted to destabilize governments and seize power.[100] William Watson (a secular priest) would promote anti-Jesuit bunk when he accused Persons of ecclesiastical innovations in order "to stop the discovery of his treacherous mind towards his country probatur for it came in . . . at that time when both in Spain Italy & the low countries his dealings began to be odious for his tyranny against all priests & lay Parsons it consented not to his Japan kingdom & in England his books & all their dealings being by cathol[ics] generally disliked & by Seminarists condemned and rejected as full of ambition, bloodshed, infamy & crime intended to or whole contrey."[101] These kinds of attacks accumulated like thick plaque, clogging any viable paths of communication between secular priests and Jesuits in England and across Europe.

The Succession Revisited

Apart from criticisms of the *Conference*, English Catholics had to face several uncomfortable realities in 1596. Perhaps most importantly, a growing rift between Philip and the pope posed dangers for any hope of concerted action against Elizabeth. Creswell, who by then was in Madrid, tried to mend the relationship. In April, he wrote Clement VIII, imploring him to intervene. He reminded the pope that discord might have terrible consequences, as it had in England. Though Henry VIII's break with the Church was sparked by lust, the king would not have followed through had previous altercations with Rome not caused him "to lose love and respect for the Apostolic See."[102] Creswell wanted to convince the Curia that despite everything, Philip was ultimately England's great hope. Yet he also wanted to leave the door open for papal assistance on other fronts; thus his insistence on the open-endedness of the *Conference*. He assured the pope that Catholics sought Philip's aid "because no one else could do it." Still, he wrote, "neither he nor they [other English Catholics] intend to make the king of Spain king of England." Philip simply wanted to match the infanta with England's future monarch—perhaps the duke of Parma.[103]

Papal politics aside, English Catholics also had to deal with Scottish intrigue. In 1595, Scottish rebels arrived in Madrid hoping to gain support from Philip. Although their interests did not wholly align with English Catholic ones, those like Creswell were willing to offer partial support, if only to interest Philip in British affairs again and to encourage an anti-James strategy as a counterweight to Catholic Stuart supporters. Nevertheless, citing the letdown experienced with the Catholic League in France, Creswell warned the Curia that all hopes should not be placed on fractious Scotsmen. Spanish Elizabethans advocated a wait-and-see strategy. They wanted to nurture Scottish schemes and encourage Philip II to act while they monitored how things developed before lending open support to anyone. As Stefania Tutino has argued, in uncertain times and ambiguous political circumstances, Persons wrote a Latin translation of the *Conference* to keep "options for the succession open, to give Rome a preeminent leadership in the affair."[104]

De regiae successionis apud Anglos iure (On the English law of royal succession) was completed in 1596 (in Spain) and was presented to the pope on bended knee in 1597.[105] It faithfully rendered part 2 of the *Conference*, with one additional chapter. Persons wanted to set the record straight amid all the trouble the book caused. In response to criticisms for its supposedly bold pro-Spanish stance, Persons emphasized the text's equanimity. For a Roman audience, however, something more than bland objectivity was necessary. Whereas in England, discussing papal rights seemed extraneous, the opposite was true in and around the Curia. Talk of papal powers had been omitted intentionally from the English text to avoid ill will and to prevent scaring off potential readers.[106] In its Latin form, however, a chapter would be devoted to the subject. Some (especially Protestants) in England would reject the legitimacy of papal authority because it failed to represent everyone equally, but Persons was not worried. Papal laws stood and were just. Indeed, there was no more important occasion for papal involvement and arbitration than the looming succession struggle.[107]

Spanish Elizabethan approaches to papal politics and its underpinning ideologies were complex.[108] Though the early modern period is often seen as the site of the (re)ascendance of a potent papacy, its power was always up for grabs. Various shades of the conciliar ideas that had marked the Middle Ages were alive and well,[109] but in the years covered by this book, dissension within Catholic ranks deepened due to several books by Jesuit scholar Robert Bellarmine, which, at least from Sixtus V's imperious vantage point, seemed to shackle papal powers. Bellarmine, who would grow close to English exiles and become a spokesperson for the English against James I in the early seventeenth century, already showed clear affinities with them by the late sixteenth.[110] Allen would take Bellarmine's side during the 1580s when Sixtus tried to suppress his *Controversiae*, especially his *De Romano Pontifice* (On the Roman pontiff). The English cardinal had seen theological merit in Bellarmine's work, as well as its political expediency for anti-Elizabethan efforts.[111] As Tutino has pointed out, Persons, through the Latin *Conference*, also gave his learned opinion on the Bellarmine controversy.

The crux of the debate between Bellarmine and papal forces was not about whether the pope could intervene in secular matters but how to justify intervention and its limits. Bellarmine argued that papal action depended not on direct secular powers but on the pope's spiritual authority. Persons argued much the same—that all commonwealths have two sets of powers and laws, one religious and the other secular. From the beginning, these were both instituted for more than procuring "political goods" (*bona politica*) and temporal happiness. The goal was more than the "comfort of the body and the senses, but also, and much more importantly, for the eternal well-being of the soul."[112] Labor should be divided: secular government should mind things of this world, and ecclesiastical government should tend to the hereafter. The Church should help man avoid a corrupt existence and punish the errant when necessary.[113] Ideally, both secular and spiritual realms would be godly, as both played a mutually supportive role on this earthly journey. But in the end, the ecclesiastical realm trumped the secular because affairs of the soul matter more than those of the flesh. The pope, as inheritor of Peter's universal spiritual jurisdiction, had the right to "direct, moderate, repress, and even correct and punish the civil magistrate" who failed to live up to the holy requisites of the commonwealth.[114] The pope did not wield imperial force invested through his ecclesiastical office, but he should tend to spiritual matters and conserve the true faith.[115] His power was thus not immediate but indirect and oblique.[116] The pope could and should call for and justify the deposition of heretics, but his command required secular assistance. Even if the pope's power was not direct, however, he could (and must) get involved.

Persons used historical evidence at variance with the English *Conference* to make his point. For example, the Latin and English versions both mention the Portuguese king Don Sancho, who was deposed by Innocent IV at a council in Rheims. In the English version, this was done at the request of the Portuguese commonwealth, represented by the archbishop of Braga. *De regiae successionis iure*, on the other hand, suggests a more active role by the pope and diminishes the role of the commonwealth: whereas in English, the emphasis is placed squarely on "the people," for Roman audiences, the deposition is carried out by the pope himself.

England's relationship with Rome received special attention. Again, Persons argued that the pope should not claim universal rights to intervene; however, he added that because Rome and London had long-established, close, "feudal" links, the English were the pope's vassals.[117] To prove this, Persons cited French lawyer and theorist Jean Bodin, who said that during the thirteenth century, King John had declared himself a papal tributary. Even before John, going back to the days of Ine of Wessex and Offa of Mercia in the eighth century, English kings had paid taxes to Rome. Moreover, the English traditionally sought papal assistance when confronted with tyrants. For Latinate audiences, the story of Richard II's deposition was told as a joint effort by ecclesiastical and secular forces;

the archbishop of Canterbury, together with other ecclesiastical authorities and the nobility, asked Boniface IX to censure the king.[118] When the *Conference* described this same episode, the role of ecclesiastical powers was given short shrift, with emphasis placed on the commonwealth's role in both institution and deposition.[119]

With the flick of a few words, the *Conference* took on new meanings. The pope came off as the ablest arbiter of European dissension, and it affirmed the legitimacy of the Catholic Church in a way that no previous iteration, Spanish or English, had. Meanwhile, it retained its aura of impartiality. The pro-Spanish arguments that were embedded in this (and every other) version of the text remained, but they could be rejected or embraced by the pope.

Apart from a papal audience, the Latin book was also read in Spain and worked there too. Roman authority was emphasized, but not at the expense of regal authority, which someone like Philip always sought to preserve. The indirect papal powers described might be controversial in Rome but would have been applauded in Spain, where the regime tried to minimize papal pretensions. Indeed, the Latin manuscript could be seen as a compromise, perhaps a theoretical path forward between Rome and Madrid.

Allen Resurrected

At the time the Latin *Conference* was written, another book gesturing at the Spanish succession circulated in manuscript. In part because of the king's age and because of the negative reaction to the *Conference*, some English Catholics turned their attention to the infanta's claims. By the fall of 1596, Englefield and other prominent exiles pleaded with Philip to support his daughter's rights.[120] Sometime that same year, Persons suggested that someone write a book to appease critics of an Anglo-Spanish union. He said "a little tract" should be composed "by some person of credit of the same [English] nation," who "as a friend of the common good of the nation" would write on the infanta's behalf. The book's author would show, Persons argued, that "it is a certain and well-known thing that your majesty has never pretended nor pretends having this kingdom for himself."[121] Persons suggested Englefield might be chosen to write it. Englefield did write a broadly disseminated defense, but Person's plan also resembles a short text written during the spring of 1596 by Allen's onetime secretary, Roger Baynes: *The Censure of C.A. Touching the Succession of England.*[122]

The Censure was framed as a response to a correspondent desperate to sort out the succession. The author claimed to have had access to the cardinal's "most secret affairs" and "knew his meaning fully in the cause." Allen, he said, supported the *Conference*. In fact, he had collected materials for such a project himself, which he sent to "FF.P"—presumably Persons. Allen had been concerned about the succession since Mary's reign. Back then, it had become a point of contention among putative Catholics, and Allen had blamed a small coterie of dubious advisors for convincing the queen not to select a legitimate Catholic heir. History should not repeat itself. Allen, Baynes wrote, "after reading of this Book [the *Conference*] . . . fell into hope that upon the sight thereof all such of our Nation as are wise and truly Catholic" would recognize "the liberty they have on the one side to make a good choice and the obligation of conscience on the other to favor no corrupted or suspected pretender."

Allen agreed with the *Conference*'s most important claims. Bloodlines were important, but religion was the main determinant of kingship. Many seemingly legitimate royal inheritors "have been justly barred . . . in all realms Christian and also deprived . . . for these [religious] and far lesser defects, and . . . this was allowed and ratified by God himself and by all good men, and . . . all Christian commonwealths had authority (yea obligation) to do and follow the same." While the *Conference* had argued for the benefits of religious uniformity and the importance of a shared faith between king and subject, it did so (as we have seen) in general terms. It favored no particular confession, as *The Censure* notes, so as "not to exasperate any party pretendant." In "private," however, Allen had no qualms. No one should be admitted to the English throne who was an enemy of the Catholic Church "or doubtfully affected towards the same." Whoever accepted or invited a heretic "ought not to be accompted for a true and zealous Catholic."

The infanta seemed the most prudent choice. Being the daughter of a great king and sister of a future one, "she could not be but very indifferent and amiable to all men neither could she want any sufficient forces either for her establishment in the Crown or for her defense and maintenance." Many would be wary of a foreigner, but soon she would marry someone amenable to both Philip and the English, *The Censure* explains, and the new monarchs "would be strangers to us for a time, yet would that quickly pass away, and their children would be English born, and themselves entering not by force but by love and composition would hold peace and be in fear and jealousy of none." Contrary to other pretenders, the infanta would not have to pander to her subjects, nor would she need strangers' help to maintain authority.

She would help avoid internecine English battles and protect against foreign aggression.

Not only would renewed amity with Spain be ensured, but the infanta would also end Spain's Lancastrian pretensions. As the *Conference* showed, the Lancastrian claim was potent, and there was no better way to "end that title" than to convince Philip "to pass the same over to his daughter." The infanta's succession was an antidote to Spanish Habsburg imperial aspirations! Some would still worry that the Spanish and English crown could one day be united, but Allen believed "in such a case, the second child or next of her [the infanta's] blood might remain with the Crown of England and so avoid that conjunction or subordination."

If we read *The Censure* together with the Latin *Conference*, we can easily see the sneaky qualities of Spanish Elizabethan polemics. Even as English Catholics wanted to allow room for flexible action with papal support, they were quick to promote an imposing voice (Allen's) to gloss the *Conference* in favor of the infanta and against James's claim. Persons and his supporters felt able to promote this sort of doublespeak because Allen's assessment did not fully resolve the *Conference*'s ambiguities. Instead, it offered a reading by a leading authority. As such, the book nudged Catholic readers toward the king's daughter, and it tried to shut out (English) Catholic critics. Allen's years as head of the exile community were viewed as halcyon days. Persons's enemies looked back to the cardinal's tenure longingly: those were the days, they thought, when our cause was in good standing, watched over by a man of wisdom and integrity.[123] These same men could not reject Allen's considered opinion, could they? To do so was to reject the man whose memory they supposedly cherished.

Conclusion

Efforts to manipulate political circumstances and create a context for a plausible Spanish succession took place when hopes for action seemed possible but far from certain. All the versions of the *Conference* and accompanying glosses wanted to rekindle the conversation either to disrupt political life (as it did in England) or to nudge allies (in Madrid and Rome) in certain directions. The books also aimed to provide material to be used in case of anti-Elizabethan action—a series of justifications for regime change and genealogical arguments that could easily be glossed in favor of Philip or his daughter.

These books allow us to understand how Spanish Elizabethans approached their polemical campaigns. We can observe the plasticity of their efforts, how they tried to shape various situations, how they adjusted to different audiences, and the breakneck speed at which they responded to negative feedback.

By the summer of 1596, circumstances would change and require renewed textual activities amid the salvos of war. During a time of anti-Spanish and anti-Jesuit animus, Persons needed to produce a text that would pave the path to England's salvation under Spanish guidance while ensuring that intra-English Catholic conflict was not exacerbated so that it would not interfere with the enterprise at hand.

8

PRACTICAL POLITICS AND CHRISTIAN REASON OF STATE

In 1596, as English and Dutch soldiers plundered Cádiz, shouts of "Down with the Pope!" were heard in the streets. Invaders broke into the town's Jesuit college and forced a quivering priest to stomp on a painting of Sixtus V that had been torn down from the wall.[1] They even desecrated a statue of the Virgin and Child in the city's cathedral. They dragged Holy Mother and Son, stripped of crucifix and orb, to the town square where the spectacle continued. They smashed her face and cut her arms. Baby Jesus tumbled onto the ground. Mary was left massacred, covered in mud. A tearful sight for many, but one of promise too. The heretic's sword did not destroy the saintly image altogether. The *Vulnerata*, as the abused sculpture would be known, survived as a memento of heretical evils and a reminder of martyrdom's virtues. English Catholics heard of the desecration and were eager to make amends for their compatriots' evils. They wanted to care for the effigy and hoped, as they put it, the "reverence which we shall do to the blessed virgin in this image shall exceed all the trespasses and disloyalties which heresy hath been able to invent."[2] When the splintered virgin arrived at the English college in Valladolid early in Philip III's reign, amid pomp and rejoicing, some thought it augured the rebirth and reflourishing of the English Church.[3] Now with a new Spanish king, the failures of the past might be overcome. But some revelers' smiles eventually tightened, especially among those who remembered that similar hopes had risen and fallen not too long ago.

Some had expected great things for English Catholicism in 1596, when they thought heretical violence would be met by the king's sword. The attack on Cádiz cut Spaniards to the core; it was a shame upon the nation, requiring vengeance. As the Elizabethan campaign's leaders—the earl of Essex and Lord Admiral Howard—puffed their feathers back home, Spanish Elizabethans renewed their calls for war.[4] The time for sleep was over and maybe now—given the lessons of past failures—God would forgive his flock and exterminate the enemy.

Robert Persons was in Seville when the English attacked. As always, his attentions were divided between high-level politicking and efforts to keep the English mission alive. In Seville, he quelled turf battles between the still-fledgling English college of St. Gregory and local ecclesiastical institutions.[5] The integrity of the English mission faced further challenges, partly because the fallout after the *Conference* exacerbated division within the English Catholic community. And so chafing amid the demands of possible Anglo-Spanish war, the tedium of his efforts to fortify the English colleges in Spain, and the internecine battles among English Catholics, Persons wrote *A Memorial for the Reformation of England*. The book offered his vision of how English renewal would be accomplished. It was the product of several contextual realities and concomitant polemical concerns and should be read through all the lenses that reveal its multivalence. There is more than a little reverie and cockeyed optimism in it, but the book was intended to affect real policy as well. To accomplish the latter, Persons needed to temper the wistful with the politic. The book was a white paper for a presumed Spanish invasion of England, pitched in such a way that it would be palatable to other English Catholics. As always, Persons was sensitive to several audiences, even if he never managed, or never quite cared, to please them all.

Making Amends?

In later years, Persons would claim that he wrote the *Memorial* at the behest of intimate companions and that it was meant "for the author and his nearest friends only."[6] Unlike some of his previous works, he wrote the book exclusively for a Catholic audience, and his decision to circulate it in manuscript suggests a measure of discretion. A version of the book circulated at the Spanish court in the summer or early fall of 1596, at the same time that its English version reached Catholic allies and enemies abroad.[7] Persons aimed to write a book anticipating England's Catholic renewal while trying to create a space for détente between feuding factions. He also wanted to win some people over to his side. The *Memorial* tried to promote English renewal without feeding polemical flames, to discuss fundamentally restructuring England in a Catholic way without embracing the many kinds of Jesuitical tyrannies that loomed large in the popular imagination. He felt compelled to do this not because he feared enemies among putative coreligionists—they were a lost cause—but because he understood and took seriously the misgivings of those who remained, haltingly and cautiously, his allies.[8] Perhaps he also had in mind, as he would in other circumstances, those "discontented Brethren" who have been induced "either by art, evil information, or oversight to yield or concur in some one thing, or other."[9]

Persons's "moderate" stance might be better understood in relation to Thomas Wright. Wright belonged to the Society of Jesus, and as late as 1594, he had a close relationship with Persons. They were as united by their deep piety as their willingness to skirt decorum for the sake of England's salvation. Such was their kinship that Persons defended Wright in the face of somewhat mysterious criticisms from Claudio Acquaviva in Rome. The Jesuit general complained about Wright's "little observation of rules and religious discipline and his liberality [*libertà*] in speaking very prejudicially."[10] Having been removed from Louvain, Wright went to Valladolid where he became an instructor at the English college (at Persons's side).

And then things got strange. Tiring of academic life, Wright wanted to go back to England and was released from the Society of Jesus. Persons became wary. He may have rued the day he had come to Wright's defense. And yet though they disagreed on certain key points, Persons never hated him the way he hated others. In fact, Persons seems to have received updates about Wright's whereabouts from Henry Garnet, who was then stationed as Jesuit superior in England. Such updates were made not in the spirit of snippy tattling but in temperate tones, suggesting Wright remained on respectful terms with English Jesuits. Moreover, Persons ended up showing Wright courtesy and even empathy amid disagreements much later in life—a kindness not ensured for his critics. Could Persons have known and even accepted Wright's plans as they developed in Valladolid? Though Persons's enemies would suggest they were in cahoots, it is hard to tell.[11] Still, Persons would have understood the logic motivating Wright's decision to go back to England and throw himself in the arms of Essex and his circle.

Wright tried to achieve what many on his side thought improbable: toleration. But this was only a means to an end. He hoped to facilitate the resurgence of Catholicism when God deemed it convenient. Though he would argue in defense of the political conformance Persons often rejected, he himself traveled to England under no pretense. Soon after arriving, he went north to visit Catholic kin and likely partook in some rabble-rousing that authorities complained veered into seditious talk. He touched on the "absurd and dangerous opinion of the killing of a tyrant," huffed Archbishop Hutton.[12] Even as Wright came under increased scrutiny and the Essex link became more hindrance than help, he refused to keep a low profile. He was, for example, involved in the notorious conversions of the poet William Alabaster and (perhaps) Ben Jonson, the playwright.[13]

Though Wright was a man of action, he did not neglect the printed word. The same year the *Memorial* was written, he poignantly described the situation of his fellow countrymen: they lived in the depth of winter, "when light lacketh, heat faylethe, Rivers are congealed, a hoary frost covereth the face of the earth." He described how the "light of true faith and religion is banished out of England, the heat of Charitie exiled, the floods of alms and hospitality . . . are frozen with imputative justice, and solifidian error."[14] He also wrote a punchy attack on various facets of Protestant theology and, perhaps more interestingly, an appeal to "Catholic-like Protestants" whom he compared to "straying sheep erring in the desert mountains, exposed to pray of all ravening woods."[15] He implored them, "Abandon for Christ Jesus sake their external conversation in religion, whose company internally you detest."[16] While he was sympathetic toward waverers—and would assume a gentler stance toward Protestants—he was very much in line with a Personian project in his basic ends (a Catholic England) and in wearing prominently his badge of true faith.[17] Moreover, he did not join the Jesuit-hater camp. In fact, as Garnet reported, he even canvassed the idea of returning to the order.[18] Despite his links to members of the Elizabethan regime, then, from the perspective of Persons and his allies, he never crossed to the dark side.

And yet Wright knew that to inspire the trust of the regime, to make the best of the opportunities provided by Essex, who was then establishing credibility as an irenic savior of England and an important pole of power at the Elizabethan court, he could not be a Jesuit. There were surely many reasons he chose to leave the order, but among them, he must have realized that the success of his mission depended on shedding his Jesuit identity.[19] This dramatic move was not only a private decision but a tactical one that rendered all his attestations of loyalty more feasible.

Wright also needed to remove the stench of treason by wedging some space between him, Rome, and Spain. To accomplish this, he wrote a brief tract read by Essex circles, Cecil, and possibly the queen herself: "An licitum sit catholicis in Anglia sumere, et aliis modis, reginam et regnum defendere contra Hispanos" (On whether Catholics in England may use arms and other means in defense of the queen and kingdom against the Spanish).[20] Wright cautiously constructed his advice to confused Catholics in a way that embraced anti-Catholic polemics of previous years. The text was as mordant a response to the Philopater tracts discussed above as might be expected from within the regime itself.

Some English Catholics, he said, were unsure of what to do because they feared resisting Spain meant resisting the pope, "which is a sin of disobedience."[21] They thought the king might have a just claim for aggression, given the queen's affronts. Should this be the case, some felt that they could not participate in favor of the wrongful party in warfare (Elizabeth). Moreover, how could Catholics resist a king (Philip II) "who endeavors to restore and amplify the Catholic faith?"[22] This is just the kind of hemming and hawing that typified Catholic treason and that inspired the Elizabethan regime's rage by statute, and this is precisely the kind of logic Wright wanted to reject. He insisted that the king of Spain had continually offended the queen and that his aggression was based not on religion but on expansionist aspirations.

Bad-mouthing a secular ruler was easy enough, but allowing disobedience to the pope proved ticklish. Although Wright did not reject the idea of papal intervention altogether, he suggested that the pope "may err in sending the Spaniard to England."[23] Wright admitted that it is "difficult business" to figure out when the pope may intervene but allowed for the possibility when "the subjects of one king, by an unanimous consent, (that is, the whole community, or the chief heads) have informed the pope of their state, and affirm the safety of souls are in extreme jeopardy."[24] Annoying as the Elizabethan regime might find this sliver of papalism, Wright rendered the pope's power against Elizabeth null, as no unanimous group of Englishmen would be calling the pope anytime soon. Such clawless papal authority (in political matters) created a space where Catholics could protest loyalty to the queen and legitimize the regime's actions against those who refused to let go of their Hispano-papal allegiances.

Wright's political intervention as described here is relevant to the *Memorial* because it takes us to an important discursive realm within the Catholic community. His book was sandwiched between more familiar maximalist positions taken by those who rejected the Elizabethan regime tout court and were waging an ongoing battle against conformity, on the one hand, and on the other, those who promoted anti-Jesuit attacks or saw the wisdom of lobbying for tolerance.[25] Though Persons understood the dangers of his Spanish alliance, he saw no other practical option and would not embrace Wright's anti-Spanish argument publicly. Persons would not hesitate to take a public Hispanophilic stance, perhaps most strikingly as he stood stone-faced before squabbling students at the English college and defended Spanish allegiances knowing that many in the audience could not stand the idea. And yet as we have seen, Persons could make a range of "loyalist" arguments on paper. As suggested by his ongoing civility (perhaps amity) with Wright, he also tolerated forms of loyalism so long as the endgame did not deviate from the goal of bludgeoning heresy.

The *Memorial* starts in medias res after the rise of a Catholic ruler and thus avoids any toxic talk of succession issues. Heretics, Persons explained, had "confounded" matters of succession and rendered them "uncertain." Consequently, whatever Catholic prince took the throne had to "assure"—by what means remains uncertain—"the succession of the crown by good provision of Laws . . . and in such a manner must he link the state of Catholic Religion and Succession together, as the one may depend, and be the assurance of the other." Perhaps the presumed legalism of the transition could have evoked memories of the *Conference*, but it was an issue that Persons thought best left unexamined. He avoided all talk of successors. Strikingly, though written in the (possible) wake of another Armada, Philip II was never mentioned.

The loudest silence, the most obvious omission, involved the Society of Jesus. Persons argued for the reinstitution of religious orders in England and insisted that they formed the lifeblood of the Christian commonwealth. At first, he imagined an initial reformation moment, when all orders would come together in London. This would be a "privilege above all other Kingdoms of the World, where religious orders are not seen together, and much less in the perfection of their first institute and observance." To ensure the ease and effectiveness of transition, only those orders that had been internally reformed and purified would be allowed into this idyll "to the end that the greater Glory of God be procured in all things." Because Persons believed religious men would facilitate Catholic renewal, he emphasized the promotion of those orders that "apply their labors to action, and to the help also of others." He tended to deemphasize contemplative orders, although he noted their importance and "the perfection of their first Institution."[26] It does not take much to see winks and nudges aimed at fellow Jesuits, but it is notable that Persons was so indirect.

Persons tried to be nimble about the papacy. The book does not question papal supremacy—and indeed points it out—but it is tellingly difficult to discern the nature of his authority. No doubt Rome would have a central role in Catholic England, but just what this role might be is ambiguous.[27] Remarkably, when Persons discussed Christ's first establishment of the Church, he did not mention Peter. "Christ, at his beginning upon earth," he explained, "framed unto himself a new order of clergy . . . choosing first Apostles, and giving them authority, to ordain others for their successors by imposition of hands, by the name of bishops."[28] The papacy hovers over the text as an external, disembodied force, confirming here, reaffirming there, but never having absolute control. In fact, local authorities could overrule the pope. For example, on the all-important issue of Church property, Persons argued that thorough reform must be carried out at all costs, in spite of the pope's possible tepidity.[29] At times, papal supremacy is posed as an open question: Parliament, in the wake of Catholic reconversion, should debate whether Elizabeth had ascended legally or "at the leastwise, whether she were true and lawful Queen, since the declarations and depositions published by Pius Quintus."[30] No doubt Persons thought that a good Catholic parliament would deem Elizabeth illegitimate, but here we see him soft-pedaling the issue, presumably for the readers' benefit.

Framed in this way, a discussion of what happens to England under a Catholic monarch is not at odds with Wright's basic impulses mentioned above and, by association, many who were not anti-Elizabethan hard-liners like Persons. This version of Catholic renewal came (relatively free) of the thorns—Hispanophilia, papal supremacy, overt Jesuitism—that made life difficult for many English Catholics.

The Deplorables

The *Memorial* did not aim to heal wounds among all Catholics; it tried to provide a context for moving away from those false brethren Persons deemed deplorable. Amid the many internal crises plaguing English Catholics, Persons (and his enemies) ultimately identified a stark difference between Catholics who had strayed but might yet be saved and the utterly hopeless. Despite Persons's criticisms of waverers and appeasers, his writings often show a level of empathy rooted in his own early experiences of submission to the Elizabethan regime. Weakness and lack of foresight were human qualities that could be compensated for by a regime change and proper education. If those who had a real spark of true faith erred because of cowardice and worldliness, others had no spark but tried to pass themselves off as true

Catholics.[31] Intra-Catholic polemics could only reach the fever pitch they did if the combatants identified in each other unbridgeable dissimilarities. Just as Persons and his ilk were deemed Machiavels with tyrannical intentions, Persons thought his enemies irredeemably corrupt—indeed, they were no different and likely worse than heretics.

Persons spoke from a position of moral superiority. He spent much time congratulating fellow exiles and emphasizing the virtues of English seminaries, but he also wanted to admonish those who did not meet the high expectations of those venerable institutions. That seminarians were given such fine instruction "should be a spur unto them to be answerable to the same in their lives and works, and to fear the most terrible sentence of St. Paul to the Hebrews, about the hard and miserable case of such as after much special grace received, slide back again to their everlasting and most intolerable Damnation." Persons said he hoped "that our Clergy in every degree from the highest to the lowest will endeavor . . . to conform themselves to all rules of Piety and Religion, and to hearken gladly to any good Counsel or remembrance of Order and Discipline that shall be offered." In general, he claimed to be optimistic about England's future because recusants—real Catholics—on whom future reform depended were free of the many corruptions afflicting (Catholic) Christendom. He insisted that England's reform should be like the purification of gold "when it cometh out of the fiery furnace, to wit, pure, simple, perfect, without corruptions, dregs or rust." Persons then imagined England as a garden overgrown with thistle and weeds to which the owner sets fire "and when all is consumed, then beginneth he to plant chosen and sweet herbs at his pleasure."[32]

This reforming imagery cuts two ways. On the one hand, Persons certainly had heretics in mind. More importantly, this language could be—and probably was—used to criticize nominal Catholics too. Indeed, in later conflicts, Persons would draw on his trove of purifying imagery with reference to secular-Jesuit tensions. The battles between the two were providential and should be seen as a means by which God would "boil out by fire all thy rust even to the quick, and will take from thee all the pewter thereby to leave thee pure silver" (Isa. i).[33] Persons's reformist plan was a kind of warning to those who remained recalcitrant: they would be the targets of those charged with cleaning England's impurities.

England would embrace Tridentine reforms but would also seek to surpass them in order to achieve "the perfect restitution of ecclesiastical Discipline that [was] in use in the ancient Christian Church." This would be possible because, as mentioned before, the incoming regime would carry out root-and-branch efforts "to begin of new and to build from the very foundation the external face of our Catholic Church, and to follow the Model which themselves will choose." Many would play a role in this change, but the probity of the chosen model would be ensured by a council of reformation made up of men selected by prince, Parliament, and the pope. They would be in charge of screening priests, none of whom would "enter the Realm without presenting himself before the Council within so many days after the entrance . . . for if this be not done . . . many scandalous, light, and inconstant people, partly upon novelty, partly upon hope to gain, will repair presently to England." Importantly, Persons said that only those who had remained true recusants "should be used and employed by the commonwealth in all Principal charges." Persons's message was one of (initial) exclusion in acknowledgment of pervasive sin (in England and the Continent), where things had gone afoul and where it had become hard to discern between good and bad.

The maintenance of a reconstituted visible Church depended on bishops. Persons called for a benevolent episcopal governance that encouraged a culture of temperance and sanctity. To this end, he advocated increasing the number of bishops to deal with the immensity of the task. A good bishop was, of course, only as good as his intentions, and so he must steer clear of worldly corruptions, unnecessary wealth, bawdy pleasures, and women. He also had to ensure that those of his household led circumspect lives. Through personal piety, the bishop would set the standard; through assiduous pastoral work, he was to bring the word of God to his diocese; and through vigilance, he would weed out corruption. Importantly, he would distribute ecclesiastical rewards and promotions. The selection process for these should result from regular visitations and subsequent acknowledgment of real virtues. The bishop should identify and support the promotion of good men, thus preempting social climbers.[34]

Persons imagined a Big Brother state. The laity would be watched by censors who "would look that no Man lived idly, nor brought up his children without some Exercise and means to live. . . . And this man might call to account also such men as lived suspiciously or scandalously, as by Carding and Dicing or spent riotously any way his own goods or his Wives."[35] Just as checks should be in place for the laity, clergy also needed them. Benefices should be given only after the most detailed examination of clerical worthiness, and such benefices could be removed based on demerits. The onus of this fell on the bishop, but episcopal authorities should come under scrutiny too. Princes and archbishops might licitly request visitors from the pope, and those who committed infractions would be demoted or moved to another office when necessary. The specter of real punishment should serve as "a continual Bridle and Spur to them, when they know they have no certainty, or perpetuity."[36] This, it should be noted, was an extreme proposition, undercutting episcopal authority, even as the ideal bishop became the linchpin for ecclesiastical probity.

Punishments would be useful, but they would not offer spiritual security, and they would take tolls on the punisher.[37] Consequently, Persons insisted waverers and Church enemies should be treated kindly. Their errors should even be tolerated for a time to ensure a "true and sincere conversion," which could only be achieved by a combination of "Deliberation, Recollection, Meditation, Instruction."[38] Such love could only be instilled through proper education. A combination of open debates between Protestant and Catholic theologians, public readings of books of theological controversy, sermons, and private conversations would draw people away from error toward Catholic truth.

Persons's plan envisioned the restitution of a scholastic curriculum at universities run by worthy Christians, properly overseen by their superiors. Those superiors would be watched carefully by bishops. As prescribed by Trent, seminaries would also be instituted, many of them attached directly to universities. So long as these were maintained properly, Persons insisted that they would produce England's ecclesiastical hierarchy.

Here we have a vision of gradual reform that likely conformed to Persons's ideals but also emphasized an empathetic approach at odds with emerging discourses against sanctimonious Jesuits intent on passing off draconianism for good faith to hide their Machiavellian schemes of domination.

Surveillance, good exemplars, and a solid education would take England a long way, but Persons believed all this impossible without the proper support of the state. Thus while finding ways to deal with heretics and Catholic wafflers was important, establishing the right political structures to make his vision viable was just as important. His discussion on the relationship between secular and spiritual realms was surely meant to entice English Catholic readers, but Persons hoped it would also appeal to, or at least influence, the one who might (hopefully) soon take hold of the English throne: Philip II.

On Spanish Reform

Persons looked forward to England's Catholic future by looking back at its miseries. As we have seen, *De schismate Anglicano* documented key errors committed by the Marian regime. Persons picked up—and amplified—this line of criticism ten years later in the *Memorial*, where he emphasized the superficiality of Marian reforms in which only the "external part was plastered without remedying the Root, the renewing of the Spirit which should have been the ground of all."[39] The regime embraced enemies as friends, and so reform proceeded as "a stage-play, where Men do change their Parsons and Parts, without changing their minds or affection." Dissimulators abounded, and they made use of papal as much as royal leniency. The most unscrupulous of those false Catholics would "send for a Bull of Toleration to Rome upon false Information, in the end that he might not be troubled; and with this he thought himself safe in conscience, and bound to no one." Through his chicanery, a false convert would be taken "for a great Catholic."[40] Mary's inability to ensure the true reformation of her subjects amounted to a "pernicious" error. Any plan for reform had to account for this first.[41]

Perhaps the most egregious Marian failure had to do with real estate. A sincere return to the Church required sinners claiming ecclesiastical properties to clear their consciences. Persons invoked Scripture: "Cleanse yourself thoroughly of the old Leaven" (1 Cor. 5:7). He argued, "The most principal old Leaven that distained and distempered the other actions of our Catholic Realm at the last change, and offended the eyes of our Just God most highly . . . took no sound order at all for the reasonable satisfaction, in this great affair of Restitution to be made to God and his Church."[42] Toleration exhibited by Mary and the pope had been the result of necessity: they took what they could get instead of losing it all.[43] But how could a man's conscience be soothed if he held on to property that was not his and used it in inappropriate ways? Lands being used against the wishes of institutional founders or donors could not "in any Reason or Law of Justice be wholly taken from those uses."[44] Proper restitution would ensure that "God's Justice in part may be satisfied, Men's Consciences quieted, their Estates at home for the time to come, assured, the world abroad edified and the Church of God, in some portion of equity, satisfied."[45]

Persons understood that wholesale restitution was unlikely. Given realities, "it seemeth not possible, or at leastwise not expedient, that any rigorous or exact satisfaction should be required in these affairs."[46] To mitigate potential problems, Persons argued that the Church might collect rents on ecclesiastical lands. By doing this, it "might be said in effect, that the whole were restored and thereby a certain proportion of equity in Restitution observed."[47] Landowners would stand to benefit from this arrangement because they would be paying out only a small part of the rents they collected from their tenants. Some, however, might be "overmuch impoverished." Should these be men of "special merit," authorities could easily find remedy in providing "some Office or some Lease of fee Farm of other Lands, that shall return wholly to the Church, or the like." Such largesse and compassion should be directed only at the faithful. Lands belonging to enemies of the Church should be taken from them completely.[48]

Persons's critique of Mary intended to hit Philip II directly. Though the *Memorial* does not point fingers at Philip, Persons tried to connect the dots elsewhere. In a letter he wrote encouraging a new Armada in 1596 and in which he told the king about the *Memorial*, he urged him, "considering the importance and difficulty of the business," to proceed with godly zeal.[49] Victories were only ensured by God's hand and so, he advised, it might be wise to "make some sort of offering to Our Lord." Philip might promise "to reinstate the Church of England to that freedom and to those privileges that it had when King Henry VIII departed from the union with the apostolic see." Most importantly, he suggested that the king vow to restore the "ecclesiastical properties that were taken away to placate the wrath of Our Lord." This should be done with some moderation and might be limited to the confiscation of rents as opposed to outright seizures (as he argued in the *Memorial*). Failure to deal with the property question, he warned, would likely lead to failure. Some said that Queen Mary's inability to deal with "this gravest sacrilege" ensured that "religion was quickly lost." Many people said that if the king were to make some "vow or promise" regarding Church lands, there would be great hope for future success. In mentioning Mary's failures, of course, Persons tried to ensure that Philip did not repeat them.

The plot thickens when we consider that Philip faced serious criticisms for his handling of Church affairs.[50] Enemies latched on to anti-Machiavellian tropes harping on the king's religiosity as a veil for his imperial desires. Some of these critiques underlined the king's abuse of the Catholic Church he claimed to defend. One anti-Philip tract that was meant to intervene in Portuguese affairs—but was used by other enemies as well—lamented the state of "the poor Church that suffers things that one scarcely dares say." If the dead could speak, they would talk of how the king had defiled and profaned those things "left for the satisfaction of their souls." The pamphlet also decried how the king stripped the clergy of their livelihoods.[51] This was a dynamic not lost on his subjects, so it is unsurprising that this tract was written not by "naturally" hostile parties—English or French Protestants, for example—but by "natural" allies. The critiques described were culled from correspondence exchanged by two prominent clerics, Philip's own subjects: Francisco Dávila and Luis de Granada.

Though full analysis is beyond the scope of this discussion, the critical discourse extant in Spain was no doubt familiar to Persons. One of the most forceful attacks on the king came from the pen of Sancho Busto de Villegas, sometime governor of the archbishopric of Toledo, who in 1574 eviscerated Philip's efforts to reap profits from "temporal" Church lands. Shocked by his plans to sell properties that had long belonged to the Church, Villegas had to protest. It was a matter, he said, "important to the conscience, authority and reputation of Your Majesty, and to religion and the Christian Republic." He reminded the king of Charles V's promise never to take things away from the Church that he had given to it. Speaking of Toledan properties, Villegas insisted they had been gifts from past monarchs—divinely consecrated gifts that should not be misappropriated by royal force. There were also practical reasons for maintaining the integrity of ecclesiastical holdings. He underscored that "prelates should have vassals and fortresses and authority to resist heretics." He menacingly reminded Philip of Lothair, a medieval king of France who stopped encroaching on the Church at the advice of one prelate who warned that "God would soon take away his kingdom."[52]

The same arguments would be revived in a later position paper from the 1590s amid debates about whether the archbishopric of Toledo might be lawfully divided by the king.[53] Here the anonymous author tried to establish the basic principle that secular authorities should be the Church's supporters and not its enemies. The author reminded readers of Constantine's wisdom at giving the Church many "kingdoms, states, and lands" so that it might be properly revered and respected.[54] He warned that God had shown his judgment "by taking away the lives of those who had done anything that might redound against the holy church and its peace."[55]

The sensitive situation in Spain is important because it framed and influenced how Persons developed his argument for politico-ecclesiastical reform. Criticisms of Philip II troubled Persons because should such instincts prevail in England, the country would be doomed. To counteract these tendencies, Persons embraced a reformist plan in line with a vision articulated by other Spanish Jesuit writers with whom he was close. The *Memorial* is a Spanish Elizabethan document par excellence; it has English objectives and audiences in mind, while being both influenced by Spanish ideas and meant to intervene in a set of Spanish debates.

Church and State

In Spain, discomfort with the tentacles of monarchical power elicited concrete plans for a kind of reform that fundamentally recalibrated church-state relations. Indeed, Persons's ideas resemble those of his most (in)famous Jesuit contemporary, Juan de Mariana.

During the 1590s, Mariana was, in his bookish way, politically active. The decade began with the printing of his magisterial history of Spain, *Historia de rebus Hispaniae* (History of Spain) and ended with the printing of what became his most inflammatory book, a book blamed for the murder of kings: *De rege et regis institutione* (On kingship and the education of the king). Mariana's *Historia* was nearly as controversial as *De rege*. It was a secular history dealing with hot-button political issues of the past and, implicitly, the present. Mariana knew—and expected—his book would be mined for the lessons it had to teach readers about their own times and places. *De rege* was conceived of as an epitome of the *Historia*'s lessons, and so it too must be read as an "active" book within a very particular set of contexts. It was commissioned in the early 1590s by García de Loaysa, then the tutor of young prince Philip (future Philip III), and it was read to him during the mid-1590s.[56] We can surmise, then, that the book was more than a philosophical project during a longed-for transformational reign after the bitter disappointments of Philip II's final years.

Though Mariana was a somewhat less vocal critic of Philip II than Pedro de Ribadeneyra, he too was perturbed. Recalling the Armada debacle, he explained failure as "retribution exacted for the grave delinquencies in our nation, and unless memory fails, it was the vile lusts of a certain prince which enraged the Divinity. The prince had forgotten the sacred personage he was . . . and the rumor spread abroad that he had dissipated himself beyond reason in licentiousness."[57]

Contemporaries understood the polemical value of Mariana's work. When Mariana sought Loaysa's assistance in printing *De rege* in 1599, the latter helped in hopes that the book would "make minds in Madrid more inclined to the problems of the Church" and more specifically, that it might serve as a way to redress royal attempts to undercut local ecclesiastical control of the "pueblos."[58]

Mariana thought there were boundaries between church and state, but the limits were ambiguous. Largely because he believed monarchs were constrained in their actions by laws, and ultimately by popular will, they could not have absolute coercive rights over the Church and its doctrines. Nor could "the people" have a say in Church governance, and much less theological matters. "If each prince in his kingdom could establish what should be felt and thought regarding religious matters, according to his judgment or that of his subjects," Mariana believed there would be no hope for "unity and harmony among all nations."[59] Realizing this, long-dead ancestors decided, "in accordance with divine law," that spiritual things should be placed under the direction of one head. This had not always been so. There were plenty of examples of princes having both spiritual and temporal powers, but Moses had changed this when he delegated authority to Aaron, and Christ when he delegated authority to Peter. Still, both spheres should be united by ties of esteem and mutual respect.[60] Religion should not be separated from the "civil body," for church and state are "united like body and soul"; "two distinct bodies" should not emerge out of "those that are twin members of the same body."[61]

For all the unifying rhetoric, there was—as in nature among twin elements—an imbalance. Mariana did not want to diminish royal authority, and in fact, he often emphasized the "heroic" nature of kingship. Still, he criticized secular encroachment on ecclesiastical turf. The king should ensure that his subjects followed one faith, and he should help repel secular challenges to spiritual authority, but his involvement should be measured. Priests should not be subject to secular laws, and in cases of malfeasance, offenses should be reported to Rome. He emphatically argued that ecclesiastical property should remain untouched. Special care should be taken so the Church and its bishops would maintain control of towns and fortresses received through previous concessions. This should be done out of prudence and foresight. Suppose a heretical ruler should one day take the crown: how could a destitute Church defend itself? Church officials were, of course, corruptible, but less so than laymen. If Germany and France had not fallen altogether, it was largely due to "the forces and the power of bishops."[62] Ecclesiastical riches were necessary because where priests were poor, religion became more corruptible. Ideally, the Church would garner the respect of its congregants through saintly behavior alone, but this was unrealistic. Those who sought to diminish churchly wealth were moral posturers anyway.[63] He dismissed outright the notion that because church and state were distinct, priests should reject "civil goods and destinies." Only men of "malicious intention" argued thus. They failed to realize temporal dignities could be used to augment "the majesty of religion."[64]

Mariana encouraged political activism. While scholars have often emphasized his constitutionalist bent, Harald Braun has shown that the most radical element in Mariana's *De rege* was his argument for "royal-ecclesiastical co-rulership" in which "bishops are to suffuse the whole of secular government with their benevolent authority."[65] Maintaining episcopal properties, indeed their rights over whole towns, would allow and encourage bishops to uphold their status as "ministers and guardians of the public good, as required by patriotism and the sacred orders that they have received."[66] Indeed, bishops were not only religious leaders but "also like princes and great lords of the political community."[67]

More than episcopal *independence*, bishops should be part of secular government. Mariana lamented the disuse into which Spanish *cortes* had fallen. The institution was created so that no important business could be decided on "without the consent of nobles and the people": "Oh, that our princes would re-establish [this custom]!" Why, he asked, have traditional *cortes* been ruined by "the exclusion of nobles and bishops, making impossible that common consent on which the common good is based, only so that private and public matters be resolved by the king's will and the whim of the few?"[68] Here Mariana called for the establishment of a truly representative body infused with good men, including the best of them all: priests.

Priests would help ensure local justice in Mariana's Spain. Ecclesiastical matters should come under ecclesiastical purview, and where bishops held primary secular authority, they would oversee secular justice as well. Moreover, Mariana reminded readers that Charlemagne had appointed "bishops and distinguished people" to inspect the conduct and integrity of civil magistrates.[69] Thus the king's men, and presumably civic authorities more generally, would be subject to occasional ecclesiastical review.

Mariana suggested ways the Church might gain lay sympathies. As part of a larger plan to lower war costs, he argued for greater restraint in the distribution of royal patronage among soldiers. Retired soldiers might be awarded various forms of employment or, with proper papal approbation, be given ecclesiastical "rents and benefices." These rewards, however, should only be granted to those warriors "notable for their integrity."[70] More broadly, Mariana insisted that just as clergymen should be given political power, "princes and magistrates of recognized probity and prudence should be allowed to participate in ecclesiastical honors and riches." Moved by hopes of such advancement, laymen "would feel more love toward clergymen and would defend with more zeal the rights and property of the Church." Otherwise, alienated from ecclesiastical riches, they would convince the king that the wealth of lazy priests should be used to "alleviate the state's misery and cover the expenses of war." This was a very real fear during Mariana's own time, when, as he put it, royal coffers were empty and the king's subjects were burdened with heavy tributes.[71] Mariana envisioned the Church as a source of lay patronage. By acting as such, he hoped bonds of mutual support would be enhanced.

The impulse to delineate separate spheres of action and to argue for fundamental interdependence between church and state created tensions that were not resolved. Still, Mariana tried. His solution centered on the belief that secular objectives should be tied to salvation; every individual action should be based on Christian morality. To this end, Mariana wanted to secure the Church's maximum control over spiritual matters *and* augment ecclesiastical influence in temporal affairs. The Church would serve as the king's ally or, seen from another perspective, would greatly influence governance.

Though the *Memorial* is not a carbon copy of Mariana's vision, Persons's basic understanding of problems and general solutions to those problems were similar. Given Philip's questionable reputation in some circles—and given that he was thought to be a key player in England's reform—Persons explained there were fundamental differences between temporality and spirituality, between laity and clergymen. This had been established "since the very beginning of the Christian religion and the primitive church." To argue otherwise was to fall into the heretical error of mixing, collapsing, and confusing both estates.[72] Just as man is made up of body and soul, so society is made up of the temporal and the spiritual. Just as the soul is superior to the body, so the spiritual realm supersedes the temporal. Because men of the cloth attend to the soul, "so much excelleth the state and vocation of clergymen, the state of temporal men." This remained true, according to Church fathers, "notwithstanding that in their particular lives layman may be better than clergyman, and be preferred before him in matters of salvation."[73] Far from hindering secular rule, however, temporal authority was "confirmed and established" by spiritual leaders so long as it tended toward virtue. Thus when "Princes began to be Christians, and subject themselves also to this spiritual government and jurisdiction of souls, and to be sheep of these spiritual pastors, among the rest, they were admitted without detriment . . . of their temporal state and government, so far forth as it concerned the temporal good of the commonwealth, which is peace, wealth, justice, and the like."[74]

At its core, however, the relationship was unequal. If earthly powers were forbidden from intruding in Church affairs, Persons suggested that clergymen choose to disengage from worldly matters.[75] The example par excellence of secular disinterest was Christ, who while the "most lawful king . . . of this world," insisted his kingdom was not of it (John 18:36). Terrestrial things were inferior to celestial ones. Good rulers understood this and, like Constantine, willingly humbled themselves "unto their pastors and governors of Christ's Church, showing thereby to be the true nurses and foster-fathers of Christ's Church."[76]

Persons, like Mariana, proposed a recalibration of church-state relations. Despite a theoretical asymmetry, both powers would, in a properly run commonwealth, remain mutually supportive, and would work toward the same salvific goals. Persons's plan did not call for the destruction of parliamentary or royal powers, but it did call for the suffusion of clerical power in those governmental organs.

Persons envisioned a rekindled episcopate playing crucial political roles. Importantly, bishops would help select knights and burgesses for Parliament. They would "judge their virtue and forwardness in religion, and . . . confirm their election, or have a negative voice."[77]

Bishops would lessen traditional animosities between center and periphery, between monarch and uppity grandees. Persons advised the king to create more nobles, thereby diminishing individual powers. Instability because of overmighty magnates would be diminished because if "any one should go about to be insolent, the other would be able to repress him."[78] Furthermore, assurances should be made that "dignities, prerogatives, public emoluments, offices and preferments, as are to be in the countries, where these great men dwell should depend on the prince immediately and not of them." The prince should also make sure "that some other men, also of dignity . . . [who] depend only on him [the prince], as namely bishops, should have sway with them [nobles], and commissions in all matters belonging to the public." To circumvent the overweening powers of landed magnates, bishops would see to it that "when any poor man were injured by a great he might be heard easily, and remedied, and so taken into the prince's peculiar protection, as he durst complain, and not fear afterwards the others power and violence." All this, he continued, would be done so "that the people would only depend on the prince, and great men would come into less suspicion and danger, and the commonwealth and prince stand more assured from troubles."[79] Details are sparse, but the point is clear. All roads should lead to London via the local cathedral. Bishops would settle local disputes to diminish the authority of lords and ensure general peace; it would be through them that royal benevolence/justice would reach the countryside. The episcopate would be the local face of monarchical power. Put differently, bishops would assert their own princely authority.

Nobles need not worry. Increased episcopal powers would create a more equitable landscape for grandees themselves. The powerful, Persons explained, would be "preserved by our catholic prince, in their ancient honors, dignities, and privileges; and whatsoever injury, or dis-estimation hath been laid upon them, these later years . . . it is to be removed."[80] Moreover, a renewed England would provide a productive outlet for their virile energies. Persons envisioned gentry and nobility as vigorous defenders of the faith. He suggested many of them might be co-opted by the Church. Among the aforementioned council of reformation's efforts to reestablish a potent ecclesiastical hierarchy, Persons advised the creation of a new military order (with appropriate marriage dispensations from the pope) to "fight heretics in whatsoever country they should be employed." Far from plain heretic-hunting, Persons said, they might also play a role in protecting "our seas of England from pirates, and our land from public theft." This new order would spawn lay confraternities, not unlike the *hermandades* in Spain, to carry out local police work.[81]

Clergymen would act as firewalls. A key to good governance was good counsel, and who better to counsel the king than priests? Aside from secular royal advisors, Persons called for the establishment of a "Table of Conscience." Inspired by Portuguese precedent, it would be made up of learned men "notorious for their Piety and good conscience whether they were of religious orders or no, and the head or chief of these, commonly the king's own confessor, who might with more security, by council and assistance of these able men, direct the king's mind." Not only would king and kingdom benefit from decisions properly and piously made, but subjecting royal acts to the scrutiny of such counsel would have other perks: "As for the world abroad," Persons insisted, "it must needs be a singular great justification of all his acts, intentions, and attempts, in the eyes and tongues of all men, seeing he doth them by the direction to so irrepressible a consultation."[82] The king's soul and the king's policies should both be under the same director(s).

Priests should serve as the king's alter egos. The king would distribute rewards and punishments, but Persons suggested this duty be shared with "some special good man, . . . his confessor or the like."[83] To ensure proper vigilance, the king should order regular visitations and have reports written to him "touching all subjects in every country, province, university, cathedral churches, houses of law, and particular law."[84] The king should review these, but in cases of negative reports concerning "principal men," his appointed aid (again, preferably his confessor) should be given license to "as of himself by way of friendship admonish the said party of the opinion and report that is of him, to the end he might look about him, and amend that which were amiss before the prince should be forced to take knowledge thereof." This semi-informal process was Persons's way of insisting that governance be imbued with charity in hope of an ever-elusive Pax Christiana. Just as this approach would give clergymen more de facto clout, it would also "remedy more evils" and would procure the prince "more hearty good will."[85] In protecting the king from backlash after punishments rendered, in avoiding predictable elite paroxysms, the confessor would become a key player in distributing justice and royal patronage.

Much as the crown would be helped and guided by spiritual leaders, so too Parliament should be infused with ecclesiastical blood. In the past, the House of Lords had been home to regular clergy, specifically abbots. Since a newly reformed England would have few men of such dignity, Persons asked if "it were not reason to make some recompence by admitting some other principal men of these orders that had interest in times past, as for example some provincials, or visitors of St. Benet's order?" Bishops would take their place among lords as well. In the lower house, aside from suggesting that, initially, only greater towns be represented (presumably because these would be re-Catholicized first), he also argued for the inclusion of "some mixture of ecclesiastical and religious [men] . . . as namely of some deans, or archdeacons, or of some heads of colleges or universities, and some provincials, or visitors, or special men to be chosen of some religious orders to be intermixt amongst the burgesses and knights of the shires."[86] Carefully chosen clerics, Persons insisted, "may be presumed to be able to give as good advice in all points, belonging to the good laws and ordinations for manners and government as burgesses and knights of the shire . . . and in particular they would have a special eye to the assurance and preservation of Catholic religion, which is a principal consideration."[87]

Despite ecclesiastical involvement, secular institutions would not be wholly undermined. Parliament would continue to be the "fountain, as it were, of all public laws, and settled orders within the land."[88] From its very (re)inception, it had to adjudicate the legality of statutes made under heretical monarchs and under past parliaments. Moreover, it had a decisive voice in ascertaining the legality of Elizabeth's reign. It would also decide the validity of titles distributed during her rule and, perhaps most importantly, would initiate the devolution of Church property. Parliamentary subcommittees would oversee ambitious legal and university reforms, the establishment of seminaries, and more, all aimed to put "our common wealth in joint again." By supporting such ample parliamentary powers, Persons may have been setting up a clash between secular and ecclesiastical institutions. Such possible dissension, however, was mitigated by the presence of priests in the heart of Parliament. Moreover, Persons insisted that many of Parliament's initial reforms be delegated to the council of reformation.[89] Just as internal probity would be upheld by clergy, so Parliament would delegate authority to outside ecclesiastical authorities capable of overseeing the commonwealth's good course.

The solution to present problems as described by Persons was thus similar to Mariana's. Royal power was maintained, and the stability of the state was propped up by various forms of ecclesiastical influence, especially episcopal authority and priestly participation in the existing structures of secular rule. Moreover, secular impulses would find a controlled valve within the Church by incorporating them in different kinds of ecclesiastical institutions. The monarchy would undoubtedly play a key role in upholding and defending the Church, but this relationship was premised on the ultimately supportive nature of royal intervention.

Much of this might seem pat, but that it required saying by both Mariana and Persons reminds us that—in both Spanish and English circles—it was not.

As further evidence that Persons wrote in tandem with a broader Spanish and Jesuit program, we should take note of a glaring reference made in the *Memorial*. Lest he lose focus and linger on ideal princely qualities—this was not a mirror of princes—Persons endorsed Ribadeneyra's *Tratado de la religion y virtudes del principe christiano* (Treatise on the religion and virtues of a Christian prince). He recommended it to better understand many "particulars" left out of the *Memorial*. The *Tratado* was "worthy to be read by all good princes, for it will put them in mind of many rare and necessary points." Further, "whatsoever prince would read it diligently, or appoint every day, at his best leisure, but some little part thereof to be read unto him, with attention, and he would continue this exercise with desire to please God, to discharge his conscience, and to govern well his commonwealth, he would hardly do amiss . . . and should have need of little other counsel for taking the right way in all his occasions."[90] This was more than a mere plug. It allowed Persons to clue his reader into the underlying logic of his plan *and* to join Ribadeneyra's efforts to influence Philip II's behavior.

When Ribadeneyra published the *Tratado* in 1595, he offered an antidote for pervasive corruption. His text was a screed against Machiavellians and *politiques* who, in their devilish atheism, treated matters of state and matters of faith separately. No doubt, a secular ruler should ensure his subjects' "temporal happiness": Ribadeneyra did not underplay royal powers as they pertained to secular justice, war, and commerce.[91] But he argued that success on these fronts must not be divorced from religion. Indeed, he wanted to replace preposterous notions of a *secular* reason of state with a *Christian* one. The *Tratado* argued that because the soul is superior to the body, both secular and religious authorities needed to work toward the maintenance of true faith. The prince's primary duty was to "seek God out, to keep his Holy Faith, and to ensure all his subjects keep it."[92] All his decisions should be based on a Christian logic: kings needed "no other teacher, nor any other guide than the Christian religion."[93] Consequently, they should always consult God, through the mediation of priests, before acting.[94] In return, of course, the Church would ensure loyalty to the crown in those things "not contrary to divine law."[95]

While royal authorities should ensure the good behavior of clerics and should even, if papal allowances existed, select bishops (technically "present" them), Ribadeneyra held a firm stance on Church independence.[96] The king should beware of infringing on spiritual matters; monarchs were, he warned, "guards of divine law, but not interpreters: they are ministers of the Church, but not judges, they are armed to punish heretics, the rebel, the sacrilegious, and those who persecute or disturb the Church, but they are not legislators."[97] He asked, "If justice is a virtue which gives each what is rightfully his, Caesar what is of Caesar, and God what is of God, how can a prince maintain justice who takes from God what is his?"[98] Elsewhere he focused on priestly authority. Citing Plutarch, he claimed that in ancient Greece, priests were viewed with the same respect as kings. In Christian times, he reminded readers, many wise men had concluded that priestly powers stood *above* monarchical ones, and in a related point, Ribadeneyra discussed how clergymen *instituted* kings.[99]

By way of stern warning, the *Tratado* described the divine punishment of bad kings. Undoubtedly kingdoms that lacked "true religion" would fail. The prince who cared more for a "false reason of state" than God's law would necessarily lose "the state, prudence, and power."[100] Ribadeneyra used biblical and more recent historical precedents to make the point. The strategy employed by "Pharisees and Jewish princes" against Jesus exemplified the effects of inherently faulty secular logic. Pharisees and Jews hoped that by killing Christ, the wrath of jealous Roman authorities would be avoided. Instead, after the crucifixion, God ordained that Rome savagely attack Jerusalem, thereby inflicting "one of the gravest and most horrible punishments the world has ever seen."[101] Ribadeneyra also explicitly endorsed regicide. Summarizing recent French events, he informed readers that by God's "just judgment" Henry III had recently been killed by "a poor, young, simple, honest monk."[102]

If Ribadeneyra discussed the limits of monarchical rule, he was vague on the kinds of church-state interactions so matter-of-factly described by his English confrere (or Mariana). Ribadeneyra never intended to offer a concrete strategy; he provided a general Christian logic meant to pervade all aspects of (political) life. To be sure, he emphasized the role of clergy as counselors but offered relatively few specifics. Similarly, he implied the coercive powers of priests, but only from the safe distance of historical exempla. Still, history meant something. He relied on an idealized monarch, Constantine, to hint at the political role of the episcopate. Not only had the emperor submitted himself to ecclesiastical authority, but he also insisted that bishops should be heeded in both ecclesiastical *and* secular matters.[103] This was a subtle expression of a theocratic inclination that appeared elsewhere in Ribadeneyra's oeuvre—in his history of the English schism, for example, he insisted that "churches and ecclesiastical prelates be rich, and that they have authority." He pointed approvingly to Germany, where Catholicism had been conserved in those parts "subject to Bishops and church prelates."[104]

Echoes

The resonances among Mariana's, Persons's, and Ribadeneyra's work are important. They speak to a shared stance and shared strategy, and they reveal the insistence with which these writers tried to shift the regime's thinking. Although there is no direct evidence that these texts were part of a concerted plan, they point to a multiregistered effort to get a set of reformist thoughts across. Ribadeneyra remained vague in particulars but reached a broad audience (in and out of court, and in and out of Spain) via print during the king's own lifetime. Mariana's book was apparently trickier, and so it remained in manuscript until 1599, though it entered court via Prince Philip's tutor to inform the thoughts of the future monarch. Persons brought the issues and solutions canvased by his Spanish confreres to the king's own desk in what he must have thought of as a culminating moment when theories could be turned into action.

Everything that Persons and his Spanish colleagues said about church-state reforms was perfectly plausible given early modern realities. Although there are some novel aspects in these texts—the movement of bad bishops willy-nilly in Persons's *Memorial* seems like one—the plans discussed here were all couched in a language of historical continuity. Moreover, despite contemporary polemics to the contrary, the basic assumptions about ecclesiastical-monarchical relations and the institutional translation of those ideals were far from dead even as these men wrote. The important place of bishops in the halls of policy, not to mention the key role of theologians and confessors in the directing of policy and political action in Spain, is undeniable.[105] The reach of these religious forces is perhaps most palpable in the workings of Portugal's Council of Conscience (a body that Persons imagined in England) where, as one recent historian suggests, it served as the moral compass of the Portuguese empire.[106] The English Catholic efforts discussed here are interesting not because they are innovative but because they reflect a set of assumed possibilities.

A broad concern for Christendom made Persons's message relevant to a range of (Catholic) audiences in England, Spain, and elsewhere. Persons framed the struggle against English heresy in universal terms. Proper English reforms would be a first step in efforts against heresies across Europe—England would be "made spectacle of all the world," an example for all to behold.[107] More than a mere example of piety, however, England would play a direct role in Europe's salvation. Its revamped universities would be home to pious scholars from abroad, and England's seminaries would produce missionaries for the darkest parts of the Continent. Not only would English seminarians fight the good fight across the Channel, but seminaries would welcome the persecuted—from Germany, Denmark, Poland, and Scotland—who would be, after proper English instruction, empowered to help their own countrymen. Thus would the "old glorious Piety and Zeal of our ancestors the Saxons . . . who after their own conversion were converters almost of all Nations round about them," be revived.[108]

CONCLUSION TO PART III

The preceding pages have shown the multiple purposes of the Personian project. The *Conference* and related books tried to create a set of arguments for a Spanish succession that would be promoted upon landfall. These books also had the more immediate purpose of publicizing a conversation in order to destabilize ongoing negotiations, to create sites of public argument that would inhibit any decisions deemed detrimental to the cause at hand. The *Memorial* reveals a similar dynamic. On the one hand, it was a text about how to proceed with England's Catholic renewal; on the other, it tried to provide a space for Catholics to imagine what the future would look like after Elizabeth, even amid intra-Catholic feuding. Both books attempted to cultivate a readership that would ultimately constitute a post-Elizabethan England all the while providing a road map for action.

The tensions and ambiguities of these projects are partly a result of their Spanish orientation. Persons had to figure out how to communicate to audiences in Madrid *and* abroad. English Catholics carried out a range of enabling activities for future Habsburg action in places and for audiences hostile to Philip's authority. Moreover, as we have seen throughout, communication with the king required flexibility. The *Conference* and the *Memorial* were as much tools to nudge and prod the king as they were to make his life easier.

This study also reveals Persons to be a promoter of "Spanish" ideas among English audiences. Just as the *Memorial* shares much with the work of Ribadeneyra and Mariana, scholars have also noticed connections between the *Conference* and Mariana's contractualist thought.[1] Indeed, one might argue that Persons's work was the first serious interaction in England with a line of Hispano-Jesuit writing that would be increasingly vilified in the seventeenth century.

While the *Conference* and the *Memorial* can be considered as emblems of ideological positioning or thought experiments, I have described them as artifacts of political action. At various points, these books reveal early modern ways of perceiving a commonwealth, a range of assumptions that informed antiheretical discourse, and most importantly, ideas about the relationship between church and state. But as should be clear by now, Persons and his allies could be flexible about how they discussed these issues given different political situations. Persons probably *believed* that for a state to thrive, it needed to be Catholic and that church-state relations needed recalibration to ensure protection for the Church, but my primary concern has not been to uncover what he believed. Instead, I have described contractualist elements at the core of the *Conference* and its reason-of-state arguments as postures taken to enable a set of discussions and debates that Persons and his allies thought immediately useful. Likewise, the *Memorial* and related Spanish texts can easily be seen as anti-Machiavellian tracts with important things to say about a *Christian* formulation of reason of state à la Ribadeneyra, but I show that neither Spanish nor English Jesuits were interested in pristine theories. Together, their books show that certain ideals were articulated to forge real change. The anti-Machiavellian animus touched on here—and that scholarship has explored for decades now—existed within the context of concrete strategic planning to ensure that the state could uphold holy aspirations.[2]

Conclusion

English Catholic plots did not end after Philip II's death in 1598, and yet the political landscape changed enough that the polemical tactics studied here shifted. Books, of course, remained important. Writing to Philip III in 1617, Joseph Creswell insisted that Christendom had been saved from total "perdition and ruin" only by well-inked presses. He claimed that only books could squeeze through confessionally divided regions where priests could not. Devotional works conserved the "well-intentioned," while other texts exposing "the artifice of heretics" helped save those who had strayed. Creswell said that this in the context of requests for royal subventions in future projects, emphasizing that English Catholics never wrote "anything that might offend anyone."[1] Maybe he meant "anyone at the Spanish court"; otherwise, he was telling a pious lie. Regardless, the very suggestion of inoffensiveness is a reminder that polemical stratagems underwent important changes in light of Philip III's quest for a Pax Hispanica.[2] The preceding pages have captured a Spanish Elizabethan moment that emerged specifically out of fin de siècle politico-religious strife.

English Catholics actively manipulated the texts they produced to meet the needs of varying circumstances. Gestures at ecumenicism could give way to violent lambast, the tyrant here could be the dupe there, the pope's power in one book could be mitigated by the commonwealth in another, and even a language of reason of state was negotiable depending on the needs of the time. The ability to produce adequate responses to the moment depended on deeply ingrained intellectual tools. The men studied here adhered to the humanist principles of rhetorical flexibility and textual manipulation at the heart of persuasive activities. They also embraced a range of casuistical practices, grappling ticklish questions of conscience that allowed for equivocation. Authors employed these techniques to appeal and adequately speak to different audiences.

Spanish Elizabethans inhabited a strange liminal realm between the center and periphery of power. They had the ear of Philip II's regime, and yet they remained outsiders. Elizabeth deemed them unnatural subjects, and they never became "naturales" of Castile or the king's other domains. Should their mission be successful, they had to exploit this paradox. This dynamic is clearest in efforts to offer both critique and compliment amid Philip's inconstancy. It is also implied by the various strategies of publicity we have seen here. Archives are filled with memorials from English Catholic exiles to the Habsburg regime, but this period sees a turn toward the publication of state matters, and to do this effectively, authors embraced ambiguity. Especially in books meant for Continental audiences, they did not need to restrain anti-Elizabethan animus, but they did have to be careful about how they pitched their ideas to Catholics. They had to pose probing questions and offer cutting advice while allowing, rhetorically at least, for the notion of free interpretation, albeit with enough direction to elicit the right one. History was a perfect vehicle for this; so were fake conferences.

Throughout, I have dwelt on Spanish Elizabethan activities not as "discursive practices" or "linguistic games" (which they surely were) but as evidence of political engagement and action. This book has discussed three *kinds* of textual interventions, which are imbricated while still maintaining distinct qualities. Part 1, on Nicholas Sander's history, showed how texts were used to affect behavior; part 2, on the Philopater tracts and related books, revealed efforts to shape perceptions; and part 3, on the succession and renewed plans for conquest, described texts that tried to provide the intellectual infrastructure for political action. These activities were ultimately of a piece, because all the books studied here were weaponized. During the French Wars of Religion, Franciscans paraded with muskets ready to fight the enemy; Jesuits may have shot cannon against the infidel at Lepanto in 1571; and English priests smuggled books into England and wrote pungent books.

Efforts by English Catholic exiles were successful to the extent that they became embedded in Spanish political culture. This book has underlined a reality that is only now starting to receive proper attention: the extent to which

Spanish Elizabethan narratives profoundly affected the Spanish mind-set.[3] Throughout, we have seen their work appropriated in Spain and witnessed the adoption of an English voice as a prominent thread in Spanish polemics. These absorptions often reconstituted and redeployed the ambiguities of English Catholic books to speak to tensions within a Spanish political sphere. That this could happen with relative ease, as in Pedro de Ribadeneyra's work, shows us just how much Spanish Elizabethan polemics drew on and promoted broadly applicable techniques to discuss themes about Catholic insufficiencies that also worked well in Spain. Moreover, that the regime was sensitive to the positives and negatives of some Spanish Elizabethan polemics and their Spanish iterations shows how Philip could not help but play by the rules of public discourse.

If there is an ideological undercurrent to this book, it concerns the relationship between church and state. Every section has dealt with works that try to define the mutual duties of secular rulers and spiritual authority. There has not been a coherent line on the topic since, as the *Conference* shows in high relief; reason of state could be employed by the same authors who claimed such earthly logic would lead to damnation. As a result, these texts caution us against an impulse to assume that early modern secular and spiritual matters were hopelessly intertwined. This notion is often the facile conclusion of modern scholarship. While there is no doubt that the boundaries were hazy, and impulses theocratic, the authors discussed here could and indeed did draw lines between worldly and spiritual authority, even if their ultimate goals coincided. Both realms could be involved in each other's activities but only insofar as they helped each other achieve godly aims within their jurisdictions. Because Spanish Elizabethans saw salvation as a universal goal, sometimes the Church won out, but the more salient concern had to do with secular trespasses that had destroyed proper, indeed traditional, delineations of activity. Because resetting boundaries was at the core of their efforts, the authors discussed here understood that their arguments were fundamentally political, if only because they lived in a political world gone awry.

Spanish Elizabethan efforts remind us that the Counter-Reformation—understood as an aggressive stance against heresy and its abettors—was as much a phenomenon of spiritual regeneration as one of raw politics and polemic. An older historiography undoubtedly understood this, but of late this factor seems to have been minimized or neglected amid a focus on ecclesiology and missionizing.[4] Spanish Elizabethan activities were not unique, as evinced by the fact that they were embedded within broader spheres of Catholic activity in Spain and across Europe. Moreover, their efforts were not singular in trying to speak to, and thereby constitute, various publics. That this should be so is not surprising, considering that many of the figures studied here belonged to the Society of Jesus, who were master publicists.[5] English Catholics carried out their efforts with missionary zeal. They tried to direct the attention of readers toward political and earthly habits that kept salvation as a central goal. This was done within a sphere of publicity that hinged on cultivating the right kind of political culture with pen and paper in hand.

Notes

Introduction

1. Pissurno, "O Casamento do Cardeal."
2. [Belloy], *Declaration du droit*; James, "French Armada?"
3. Cristóbal de Moura to Antonio Pérez, Lisbon, September 8, 1578, in BNE, Mss. 1930, 74r–v.
4. Valladares, *Conquista de Lisboa*.
5. Velázquez, *Entrada que en el reyno*, 121v; Fernández-González, "Negotiation Terms."
6. Parker, *World Is Not Enough*, 10–11.
7. Santa Cruz to Philip II, Terceira, May 1583, in Duro, *Armada invencible*, 241.
8. Escalante, *Discursos*, 112.
9. Ibid., 117.
10. Carroll, *Martyrs and Murderers*.
11. Parker, *Grand Strategy*.
12. Rodríguez-Salgado, "Paz ruidosa."
13. Robert Persons et al., "Memorial for King Philip II and Pope Gregory XIII," May 1582, in Persons, *Correspondence*, 331.
14. Ibid., 340.
15. "Memorial Contained in a letter from Ludovico Taverna, nuncio in Spain, to Tolomeo Galli, cardinal of Como," Madrid, October 10, 1582, in Persons, *Correspondence*, 345.
16. Parker, *Success Is Never Final*, 21.
17. Hammer, *Elizabeth's Wars*, 2.
18. Doran, *Monarchy and Matrimony*.
19. Collinson, "Elizabethan Exclusion Crisis."
20. Doran and Kewes, *Doubtful and Dangerous*.
21. Lake, "Anti-popery."
22. Walsham, *Church Papists*.
23. Bossy, "Heart of Robert Persons."
24. Francis Englefield to the Privy Council, August 18, 1563, in Harrison, "Sir Francis Englefield," 40; Lechat, *Réfugiés Anglais*, 36.
25. Loomie, *Spanish Elizabethans*.
26. Speech by Cromwell on September 17, 1656, in Carlyle, *Oliver Cromwell's Letters and Speeches*, 3:72.
27. Highley, *Catholics Writing the Nation*, 151–87.
28. Clancy, *Papist Pamphleteers*.
29. Haile, *Elizabethan Cardinal*; Duffy, "William, Cardinal Allen"; Williams, "William Allen."

30. Edwards, *Robert Persons*; Eguiluz, *Robert Persons*.
31. Loomie, *Spanish Elizabethans*, 14–51.
32. Peck, *Leicester's Commonwealth*, 12.
33. Highley, *Catholics Writing the Nation*.
34. Starn, *Contrary Commonwealth*, 1.
35. Ibid.; Jordan, *From England to France*.
36. Terpstra, *Religious Refugees*, 7.
37. Kaplan, *Early Modern Ethnic*; Spohnholz and Waite, *Exile and Religious Identity*.
38. Trevor-Roper, *Europe's Physician*, 12.
39. Descimon and Ruiz Ibáñez, *Ligueurs de l'exil*; Janssen, *Dutch Revolt*.
40. Namely, *"Our Way of Proceeding?"*; *Building the Faith*; and *Lest Our Lamp*.
41. Bossy, "Elizabethan Catholicism"; Loomie, "Spain and English Catholic Exiles."
42. Gibbons, *English Catholic Exiles*; Bela, Calma, and Rzegocka, *Publishing Subversive Texts*.
43. Corens, *Confessional Mobility and English Catholics*.
44. Pirillo, *Refugee-Diplomat*.
45. Burke, *Exiles and Expatriate*, 2–3.
46. Said, "Reflections on Exile," 144–45.
47. Ibid., 148.
48. Grafton, *Worlds Made by Words*, 9.
49. Pettegree, *Brand Luther*.
50. Lake and Pincus, "Rethinking the Public Sphere," 6.
51. Bouza, *Papeles y opinión*.
52. Olivari, *Avisos, pasquines, y rumores*, 24.
53. Elliott, *History in the Making*, 160.
54. Lake and Questier, "Agency, Appropriation and Rhetoric"; Lake and Questier, "Puritans, Papists, and 'Public Sphere.'"
55. Pérez, *Rebelión de las palabras*.
56. Lake, *Bad Queen Bess?*; Lake and Questier, *Antichrist's Lewd Hat*; Bellany and Cogswell, *Murder of King James I*.
57. Bouza, *Palabra e imagen*.

Introduction to Part I
1. Heylin, *Ecclesia restaurata*, 294 (emphasis mine).

2. Burnet, preface to *History of the Reformation*, n.f.
3. Lewis, *Rise and Growth*, xiii.
4. Pollen, *English Catholics*, 306.
5. Burnet, preface to *History of the Reformation*, n.f.
6. Kinsela, *Rise and Progress*.
7. "Noticia de la vida y escritos del P. Ribadeneira," in Ribadeneyra, *Historia del cisma de Inglaterra*, xi.
8. Milward, *Religious Controversies of Elizabethan Age*, 71; Duffy, *Reformation Divided*, 287.
9. Highley, "Pestilent and Seditious Book," 148.
10. Lake, *Bad Queen Bess?*, 257–81; Houliston, "Missionary Position."

Chapter 1
1. Veech, *Dr. Nicholas Sanders*.
2. Sander to William Maitland, Leuven, January 16, 1572, in *Catholic Record Society: Miscellanea XIII*, 8.
3. Cecil, *Execution of Justice*, 30; Smith, *Ancient and Present State*, 164; Hore, "Woods and Fastnesses," 156.
4. Beare, *Historiae Catholicae Iberniae compendium*, 100v.
5. Bayne, *Anglo-Roman Relations*, 169–70; Sander, *De visibili monarchia libri octo*, sig. *iiij; Sander to John Rastell, Rome, 1562[?], in Wainwright, "Some Letters and Papers," 5–6. Description of "penetrating gaze" borrowed from Teresa of Ávila, quoted in Parker, *Grand Strategy*, 15.
6. Sander to Bishop Sega, October 19, 1580, in Wainwright, "Some Letters and Papers," 54.
7. O'Donovan, "Irish Correspondence," 354–69.
8. Cecil, *Execution of Justice*, 13.
9. *Nicolai Sanderi Lib. 3 de Origine ac Progressu Schismatis Anglicani Opus Manuscriptum*, in AVCAU, Liber 1388.
10. *Treatise of Treasons*; Lake, *Bad Queen Bess?*, 69–96.
11. AVCAU, Liber 1388, fols. 153r–v, 160r–61r.

12. "Sandero sobre lo de Inglaterra" (1577), in AHN, Órdenes Militares, Legajo 3511, no. 12.

13. Illescas, *Historia pontifical y Catholica*.

14. Philip II to Guerau de Espés, El Escorial, June 28, 1568, in Gross et al., *Batalla del mar océano*, 2.

15. Gacto, "Censura política e Inquisición," 23–40.

16. Allen, *Defense*, 122.

17. Peck, *Leicester's Commonwealth*, 67–68, 70.

18. Sander, *De iustificatione*.

19. "Religione et doctrina conspicuis sacerdotibus, coeterisque sanctissime D. N. Gregorij XIII Pont. Max. Alumnis, qui in Collegijs Angliscanis Romae ac Duaci, divino amore accensi studia sua, animas, atque corpora Dei Opt. Maximi gloriae, & charisismae saluti consecrarunt," in Sander, *De iustificatione*, n.f.

20. "De vita et scriptis Nicolai Sanderi huius operis auctoris," in Sander, *De iustificatione*, n.f.

21. Persons to Agazzari, Rouen, December 13, 1984, in Persons, *Letters and Memorials*, 266.

22. Houliston, "Persons's Displeasure," 155–66; Peck, *Leicester's Commonwealth*, 1–62; Hicks, "Growth of a Myth."

23. Holmes, *Resistance and Compromise*, 131.

24. Persons to Agazzari, Rouen, December 13, 1984, in Persons, *Letters and Memorials*, 268.

25. Lake, "From *Leceister His Commonwealth*," 143.

26. Leslie, *Treatise Towching*.

27. Peck, *Leicester's Commonwealth*, 183.

28. Ibid., 64.

29. Ibid., 65–66, 70.

30. Ibid., 72.

31. Allen, *Defense*, 129–30.

32. Ibid., 56.

33. Ibid., 141.

34. Ibid., 68.

35. Ibid., 133.

36. Ibid., 131.

37. McGoldrick, "Rishton, Edward."

38. "Commission for Banishing Jesuits and Seminary Priests," in Petti, *Recusant Documents*, 20.

39. Sander, *De origine*, sig. āij(v)–āiij(r). Throughout, translations from Latin to English are taken from Lewis, *Rise and Growth*, with my occasional amendments to Lewis's translation noted as needed.

40. Lewis, *Rise and Growth*, cxlii; Sander, *De schismate Anglicano* (1585), āij(v).

41. Knox, *First and Second Diaries*, 206.

42. "Un estratto delli tre Libri del cominciamento et progreso dello scisma et heresia en Inglaterra," in BNE, Mss. 2058, 130v–35r.

43. Pollen, "Dr. Nicholas Sander"; Gasquet, "Treasure of the Archives"; Persons, *Certamen ecclesiae Anglicanae*, 300–305. Persons's hand can be seen on the margins throughout and specific mention of Allen's intervention ("C:A" in the text) is sporadic. AVCAU, Liber 1388, fol. 50r.

44. Sander, *De schismate Anglicano* (1585), sig. āiij.

45. Allison and Rogers, *Contemporary Printed Literature*, 1:135–36, entry 972.

46. Thanks to Dr. Aaron Pratt, curator of early modern books at the Harry Ransom Center (Austin, Tex.), for pointing this out.

47. Janssen, *Dutch Revolt*, 104–28.

48. McCoog, "Construing Martyrdom," 95–127.

49. *De iustitia Britanica*.

50. [Gibbons], *Concertatio Ecclesiae Catholicae*, 7.

51. Persons, *De persecutione Anglicana commentariolus*, 2.

52. Siebert, "Zwischen Kaiser und Papst"; Lockhart, *Frederick II*, 198–241; Ghering, *Anglo-German Relations*, 81–112.

53. Bonomi to Cardinal Ristucci, Aachen, September 12, 1585, in Ehses and Meister, eds. *Nuntiaturberichte*, 1:141.

54. *Crudelitatis Calvinianae*; Pettegree and Walsby, *Netherlandish Books*, 1037, entry 23749.

55. "Ad principes populosque catholicos," in *Crudelitatis Calvinianae*, n.f.

56. Sander, *De schismate Anglicano* (1585), 1r–v.

57. Ibid., 5r–7v.

58. McCoog, *"Our Way of Proceeding?,"* 175–76.

59. Bartoli, *Dell'istoria*, 227.

60. Allen to Agazzari, Rheims, June 12, 1585, in Renold, *Letters of Allen and Barrett*, 155.

61. AHN, Órdenes Militares, Legajo 3511, no. 27.

62. Pole, *Ad Henricum Octauum Britanniae Regem*, cxi ff.

63. Meyer, *England and the Catholic Church*, 35.

64. Sander to Allen, Madrid, November 6, 1577, in Allen, *Letters and Memorials*, 38.

65. Sander, "Copia del recuerdo que ha dado el Doctor Sandero, sobre el remedio de las cosas de Inglaterra," in AGS, Estado 830, fol. 167.

66. Sermon preached in Douai on October 15, 1585. "De haeresis recidiva in Belgio," in Stapleton, *Orationes academicae*, 2:101–37.

67. Ward, "Law of Treason," 64–65.

68. Persons's "De editione duorum voluminum pro *Historia ecclesiastica Anglicana*," in Persons, *Certamen ecclesiae Anglicanae*, 292–99; Verstegan to Persons, Antwerp, April 30, 1593, in Petti, *Letters and Despatches*, 134.

69. Sander, *De schismate Anglicano* (1585), sig. āij(v).

70. Possevino, *Bibliotheca selecta*, 138.

71. Kelley, *Versions of History*, 312.

72. Burke, "Tacitism."

73. Biegerum, *Flores*.

74. Humphrey, *Iesuitismi*; Biegerum, *Flores*, 3–5.

75. Biegerum, *Flores*, 6–7.

76. "Sandero sobre lo de Inglaterra" (1577), in AHN, Órdenes Militares, Legajo 3511, no. 12.

77. [Cope], *Antisanderus*.

78. Sander, *De schismate Anglicano* (1585), 14v–15r.

79. Ibid., 66v.

80. Ibid.

81. Ibid., 140r–v.

82. This is true of *Leicester's Commonwealth*. Leslie, *Treatise Towching*; Leslie, *Defence of the Honour*.

83. Pollen, *English Catholics*, 147–51.

84. Meyer, *England and the Catholic Church*, 85.

85. Cecil, *Execution of Justice*, 21.

86. "Ad consolationem et instructionem quorundam Catholicorum angustiis constitutorum questiones Aliquot." Crosignani, McCoog, and Questier, *Recusancy in Early Modern England*, 99.

87. *Facultates concesse PP. Personio et Edmundo Campiano pro Anglia die 14 Aprilis 1580*, in ARSI, Fondo Gesuitico 720 A-II/2.

88. Allen, *Defense*, 122.

89. Quoted in Sander, *De schismate Anglicano* (1585), 182r–85r.

90. Lewis, *Rise and Growth*, 38; Sander, *De schismate Anglicano* (1585), 142v–43v.

91. Lewis, *Rise and Growth*, 238; Sander, *De schismate Anglicano* (1585), 143v.

92. Lewis, *Rise and Growth*, 238; Sander, *De schismate Anglicano* (1585), 143v.

93. Lewis, *Rise and Growth*, 240; Sander, *De schismate Anglicano* (1585), 145r.

94. Sander, *De schismate Anglicano* (1585), 147r.

95. Ibid., 146v.

96. Ibid., 154v.

97. Lewis, *Rise and Growth*, 287; Sander, *De schismate Anglicano* (1585), 173r. In his translation, Lewis translates *solio* as "closet." I have chosen to amend his translation to have it read "throne."

98. Lewis, *Rise and Growth*, 283; Sander, *De schismate Anglicano* (1585), 170v.

99. Lewis, *Rise and Growth*, 269; Sander, *De schismate Anglicano* (1585), 162r.

100. Lewis, *Rise and Growth*, 288; Sander, *De schismate Anglicano* (1585), 174r.

101. Lewis, *Rise and Growth*, 290; Sander, *De schismate Anglicano* (1585), 175r.

102. Calderón de la Barca, *Schism in England*; Schuster, *Henry VIII*; Murphy, *St. Gregory's College*, 19–20.

103. Rankin, Highley, and King, *Henry VIII*;
Betteridge and Freeman, *Henry VIII and History*.
104. Sander, *De schismate Anglicano* (1585), 70v–71r.
105. Ibid., 103r.
106. Lewis, *Rise and Growth*, 162; Sander, *De schismate Anglicano* (1585), 103v.
107. Sander, *De schismate Anglicano* (1585), 105r.
108. Ibid.
109. Ibid., 105v.
110. Lewis, *Rise and Growth*, 19; Sander, *De schismate Anglicano* (1585), 105v.
111. Lewis, *Rise and Growth*, 19; Sander, *De schismate Anglicano* (1585), 105v.
112. Lewis, *Rise and Growth*, 19; Sander, *De schismate Anglicano* (1585), 105v.
113. Sander, *De schismate Anglicano* (1585), 8r.
114. Ibid., 9r.
115. Ibid., 56v.
116. Ibid., 27r–v.
117. Ibid., 27v.
118. Ibid., 175v.
119. Ibid., 177r.
120. Ibid., 185v.
121. Ibid., 159v–60r.
122. Ibid., 205r–7r.

Chapter 2

1. Essen, *Alexandre Farnèse*, 5:159.
2. For an example of this sort of bombast, see the portrait (with accompanying poem) of Alexander by Otto van Veen at the Los Angeles County Museum of Art (http://collections.lacma.org/node/207209). Lattuada, *Alessandro Farnese*.
3. Wernham, *Making of Elizabethan Foreign Policy*; Rodríguez-Salgado, "Paz ruidosa," 63–119.
4. Sander to Gregory XIII, June 1573, in ARSI, Anglia 30.I, fols. 74r–77r; "Discorso per la ricuperatione del regno d'Inghilterra alla Chiesa," in ASV, AA Arm I–XVIII, 3082, fols. 34r–42v.
5. Sander, *De schismate Anglicano*.
6. Persons to Idiáquez, Rome, May 20, 1586, in Persons, *Letters and Memorials*, 280.

7. [Cecil], *Declaration*; Gross et al., *Batalla del mar océano*, 1:512–16.
8. [Cecil], *Declaration*, 4.
9. Ibid., 5.
10. Ibid., 6.
11. Ibid., 18.
12. Sander, *De schismate Anglicano* (1586), 489.
13. Ibid., 491.
14. Ibid., 494–96.
15. Ibid., 495–97.
16. Ibid., 494.
17. Ibid., 491–92.
18. Mears, "Counsel, Public Debate, and Queenship," 629–50.
19. Ibid., 172.
20. Ibid., 174.
21. Note, for example, that phrases such as these were deleted: "Sed frustrà sane oculos in Caesarem, aut hominem quempiam coniectos habebant." Sander, *De schismate Anglicano* (1585), 76r.
22. Sander, *De schismate Anglicano* (1586), 157–62.
23. Dillon, *Construction of Martyrdom*, 81.
24. Sander, *De schismate Anglicano* (1586), 203.
25. Pole, *Ad Henricum Octauum Britanniae Regem*; Galloni, *De ss. martyrum cruciatibus*, 199.
26. Sander, *De schismate Anglicano* (1586), 133.
27. Ibid., 132–37.
28. Ibid., 124–25, 351–52.
29. Ibid., 107, 78; Mayer, "Sticking-Plaster Saint?," 205–22.
30. Simpson, *Edmund Campion*, 21, 112.
31. Sander, *De schismate Anglicano* (1586), 282.
32. Ibid., 283–84.
33. Persons, "Storie of Domesticall Difficulties"; Persons, "Certaine Notes."
34. Sander, *De schismate Anglicano* (1586), 334, 350.
35. Ibid., 349, 350.
36. Ibid., 263.
37. Ibid., 264, 265.
38. Ibid., 265.
39. Ibid., 267–68.
40. Ibid., 302–4.

41. Ibid., 382.
42. Stapleton to Johannes Moretus, Louvain, July 25, 1591, in Landtsheer, "Correspondence of Stapleton and Moretus," 463.
43. Lake and Questier, *Trials of Margaret Clitherow.*

Chapter 3

1. Ribadeneyra to Catarina de Villalobos, London, December 23, 1558, in Ribadeneyra, *Monumenta Historica,* 1:307, hereafter cited as *MHSI Ribadeneira.*
2. Ribadeneyra, "Confessiones," in *MHSI Ribadeneira,* 1:71.
3. Ribadeneyra to Jacobo Laínez, London, January 20, 1559, in *MHSI Ribadeneira,* 1:311.
4. Ibid.; McCoog, *"Our Way of Proceeding?,"* 34–38.
5. Persons to Ribadeneyra, Paris, September 10, 1584, in Persons, *Letters and Memorials,* 227–35.
6. Ribadeneyra, *Scisma* (1588), iv.
7. Weinreich, *Ribadeneyra's "Ecclesiastical History"*; Domínguez, "History in Action"; Ribadeneyra, *Historias de la contrarreforma,* 887–88; Gómez-Centurión, "New Crusade"; Burguillo, "Pedro de Ribadeneyra."
8. See Ribadeneyra's copy of the 1586 *De schismate Anglicano* at the Biblioteca Histórica, Universidad Complutense, shelfmark: FLL 16.258.
9. Ribadeneyra to Deza, August 17, 1587, in *MHSI Ribadeneira,* 2:77.
10. Höpfl, *Jesuit Political Thought,* 101.
11. AHN, Legajo 3712/1, fol. 19.
12. Kagan, *Lucrecia's Dreams,* 80.
13. Ibid., 95–101.
14. Kagan and Dyer, *Inquisitorial Inquiries,* 73; Kagan, *Lucrecia's Dreams,* 96.
15. Huerga, "Vida seudomística"; Domínguez, "From Saint to Sinner."
16. Memorial by Joseph Creswell, written on August 2, 1602, in RAH, Ms. 9–2320, 5v.

17. Ribadeneyra to Quiroga, Toledo, February 16, 1580, in *MHSI Ribadeneira,* 2:23.
18. Ibid., 24.
19. Domínguez, "History in Action."
20. Ribadeneyra to count of Feria, Rome, September 4, 1557, in Sebastiá, *Confesiones,* 157.
21. Rodríguez-Salgado, *Felipe II.*
22. Fernández Collado, *Gregorio XIII y Felipe II.*
23. Ribadeneyra to Guzmán, Madrid, May 1588, in *MHSI Ribadeneira,* 2:94.
24. Domínguez, "History in Action."
25. Acquaviva to Porres, Rome, September 8, 1587, in ARSI, Tolet. 3, fol. 111r; Olds, *Forging the Past.*
26. Acquaviva to Porres, Rome, October 6, 1587, in ARSI, Tolet. 3, fol. 115r.
27. Acquaviva to Porres, Rome, March 22, 1588, in ARSI, Tolet. 3, fols. 134v–35r.
28. "Carta para un privado [de] su Magestad," in BNE, Mss. 6525, 147v–50v at 147v.
29. Ribadeneyra to Guzmán, Madrid, May 1588, in *MHSI Ribadeneira,* 2:93; Weinreich, *Ribadeneyra's "Ecclesiastical History,"* 739; Ribadeneyra, *Historias de la contrarreforma,* 1332.
30. Ribadeneyra to Guzmán, Madrid, May 1588, in *MHSI Ribadeneira,* 2:93.
31. "Exhortación para los soldados y capitanes que van a esta jornada de Inglaterra en nombre de su capitán general," in *MHSI Ribadeneira,* 2:347–70.
32. Ibid., 358.
33. Ibid., 354.
34. Ibid., 358.
35. Ibid., 359.
36. Ibid., 363.
37. Ibid., 366–67.
38. There appear to have been two runs; only one carries the engraving.
39. Nadal, *Adnotationes et meditationes,* 455–57.
40. Ribadeneyra, *Scisma* (1588), 374r.
41. Ibid., 329r–v.
42. Ibid., 372r–v.
43. Ibid., 9r.
44. Ribadeneyra, *Flos sanctorum,* sig. ¶¶2v.

45. Ribadeneyra, *Scisma* (1588), 294v–95r.
46. Ibid., 171v.
47. Ribadeneyra to count of Feria, Rome, September 4, 1557, in Sebastiá, *Confesiones*, 157.
48. Ribadeneyra, *Scisma* (1588), 173v.
49. Ibid., 9v–11r.
50. Ibid., 143r–44v.
51. "Carta dos meses Maio e junho desta casa de Sao Roq da Comp.a de Jesus," in BA, Lisbon, Ms. 54-XI-38, 3d, fol. 10v; Brockey, "Jesuit Pastoral," 3–4.
52. McCoog, "*Our Way of Proceeding?,*" 250.
53. Note, however, that not all editions were published before the Armada's launch.
54. Christophe Plantin to François Costerus, Antwerp, August 10, 1588, in Denucé, *Correspondance de Christophe Plantin*, 8/9:415.
55. See Pedro López de Montoya's "Aprobación," in Ribadeneyra, *Scisma* (1588), sig. +4r–v.
56. Levy, *Propaganda and the Jesuit Baroque*, 122–27.
57. "Discurso de abertura de Felipe II às Cortes de 1588, e resposta do representatne dos procuradores," April 4, 1588, in Ribeiro da Silva, *Felipe II de Espanha*, 178–79.
58. Gómez-Centurión, *Invencible*, 59.
59. Ibid., 59–60.
60. Hoffman, *Raised to Rule*, 73. For the book in question, see BNE, Mss. 1451.
61. Córdoba, *De historia*, 7r.
62. Ribadeneyra, *Scisma* (1588), 367v.
63. Ibid., 368r.
64. Ibid.
65. Ribadeneyra, *Obras*, 447.
66. "The Constitutions of the Society of Jesus and Their Declarations," in Ganss, *Constitutions*, 275.
67. "Al Principe don Felipe nuestro Señor," in Ribadeneyra, *Scisma* (1588), sig. +5r. After this first page the dedicatory is not paginated.
68. Ribadeneyra, *Scisma* (1588), 9r.
69. Weinreich, *Ribadeneyra's "Ecclesiastical History,"* 79–80.
70. Ribadeneyra, *Scisma* (1588), 236r.
71. Ibid., 240r.
72. Ibid., 239v.
73. Ibid., 332r.
74. Ibid., 336v.
75. Ibid., 350v.
76. Ibid., 351r.
77. Hoffman, *Raised to Rule*, 74–75, 76–77; "Epílogo breve," in Philip IV, *Historia de Italia*, xi.
78. Bomba, "Caesar's Conscience," 16.
79. Mexia, *Historia imperial*, sig. a2r–v.
80. Maravall, "La oposición político-religiosa a mediados del siglo XVI: El Erasmismo tardío de Felipe de la Torre," in *Oposición política*, 53–92; Truman, "Felipe de la Torre," 83–93.
81. Feros, *Kingship and Favoritisms*, chap. 3.
82. Ribadeneyra, *Vida*, 165r.
83. Iñurritegui Rodríguez, *Gracia y la república*, 304.
84. Ribadeneyra, *Scisma* (1588), n.f.
85. Peralta, *Relacion*, sig. A11r–v.
86. Ribadeneyra, *Scisma* (1588), 76r–v.
87. Ibid., 210v.
88. Ibid., 146v.
89. Ibid., 84r.
90. Ibid., 65r.
91. Ibid., 162r.
92. Approbation by Alonso Gregorio on October 15, 1588, in Ribadeneyra, *Scisma* (1588).
93. Granada to Ribadeneyra, Lisbon, August 13, 1588, in Ribadeneyra, *Obras*, 447.
94. Florian Anisson to count of Villaumbosa, Madrid, August 16, 1674, in Ribadeneyra, *Historia ecclesiastica* (1674), sig. ¶4v.
95. Ibid., n.f.
96. Ribadeneyra, *Scisma* (1588), 374r.
97. Nuncio (Cesare Spacciani) to Cardinal Montalto, Madrid, July 6, 1588, in ASV, Segretaria di Stato, Spagna 34.
98. Granada to Ribadeneyra, Lisbon, August 13, 1588, in Ribadeneyra, *Obras*, 447.
99. Pedro de Ribadeneyra, *Hystoria ecclesiastica del scisma del reyno de Inglaterra* (Lisbon: Monoel de Lyra, 1589), in Mansueto Library, Chicago, Special Collections, BR375.R6 (v.1).

The prayer is the "Deus qui per immaculatam virginis conceptione."

100. Gómez-Centurión, *Invencible*, 77.
101. [Persons], *Copie of a Letter*, 3–4.
102. "Carta para un privado [de] su Magestad," in BNE, Mss. 6525, 147v–50v.
103. Ibid., 147v.
104. Ibid., 148v–49r.
105. Ibid., 150r.
106. Ibid., 149r.
107. Ribadeneyra, *Tratado de tribulación*, 23v.

Conclusion to Part I

1. Howard, *Reception of Machiavelli*.
2. Granada, *Memoriall*; Loarte, *Excercise of a Christian Life*; Persons, *Christian directorie*.
3. Persons, *Christian Directory*, ed. Houliston, 9.
4. Granada, *Memoriall*, 1–3.
5. Persons, *Christian directorie*, 9r.
6. Granada, *Juan de Avila*, 4 fn. 5.
7. Roldán-Figueroa, *Ascetic Spirituality*.
8. Granada, *Obras completas*, 16:38.
9. Ávila, *Obras*.
10. Lake and Questier, *Trials of Margaret Clitherow*, 68–76.
11. Crouzet, *Guerriers de Dieu*, 2:443–44.
12. Sander, "Copia del recuerdo que ha dado el Doctor Sandero, sobre el remedio de las cosas de Inglaterra," in AGS, Estado 830, fol. 167.
13. Forteza, "Monsters and Saints."
14. Martínez, *Repertorio*, 245; Gruzinski, *What Time Is It There?*, 82–84; Leonard, "On the Lima Book Trade," 511–25.
15. Rowe, *Saint and Nation*, 114–15.
16. Mariana, "Treatise on Alteration of Money," 286–87.

Introduction to Part II

1. Brockey, *Journey to the East*, 36.
2. Ollé Rodríguez, "Estrategias filipinas respecto a China."
3. Ibid., 549.
4. Ibid., 556.
5. Parker, "Place of Tudor England."

6. Don Juan de Silva to Esteban Ibarra, Coimbra, August 13, 1589, in Biblioteca Casanatense, Rome, Ms. 2417, 37v.
7. Juan de Garnica, *De hispanarum monarchia*, in Mansueto Library, Chicago, Ms. 1130, 117; Marino, "Anti-Campanellan Vision."
8. Campanella, *Monarchia di Spagna*, 25–27.
9. Zerner, *Juan de Herrera*, 108–15; Kagan, *Lucrecia's Dreams*, 124.

Chapter 4

1. "Capítulo de una Carta de Londres escrita a los 23 de junio de 1591," in ACSA, Series 2, Legajo 6, no. 2.
2. Chacón, *De signis sanctissimae crucis*.
3. Bossy, "Rome and Elizabethan Catholics," 135–42.
4. ANTT, Inquisiçao de Lisboa, Proceso 2028, fol. 6r.
5. O'Connor, *Irish Voices*.
6. Blackfan, *Annales*, 13–14.
7. Ibid., 5.
8. Anonymous letter dated June 12, 1587, in BL, Additional Ms. 28, 374, fol. 88.
9. Persons to Idiáquez, March 3, 1591, in ABSI, Collectanea P I, 246e.
10. Nuncio to cardinal of Como, Madrid, October 20, 1582, in Persons, *Letters and Memorials*, 169.
11. Olivares to Philip II, Rome, January 27, 1587, in Allen, *Letters and Memorials*, 268.
12. Philip II to Parma, September 1, 1586, in Gross et al., *Batalla del mar océano*, 1:333.
13. Yepes, *Historia particular*, sig. ¶4v.
14. Mendoza, *Theorica y practica*, 20–21.
15. Olivares to Philip II, Rome, January 27, 1587, in Allen, *Letters and Memorials*, 268.
16. Allen, *Admonition*.
17. Williams, *St. Alban's College Valladolid*; Burrieza and Harris, *Misión de Robert Persons*.
18. Blackfan, *Annales*, 13–14.
19. Burrieza Sánchez, *Valladolid, tierras y caminos*, 218.

20. AGS, Estado 166, fol. 136.
21. *Informacion que da el padre Roberto Personio, de nacion ingles* [. . .], reprinted in Persons, *Relacion de algunos martyrios*, 62r–76r.
22. Ibid., 62r–63v.
23. Ibid., 67r.
24. Ibid., 71v–72v.
25. Ibid., 73r–v.
26. Ibid., 74r–v.
27. Ibid., 75v.
28. Ibid., 76r.
29. Hicks, "Robert Persons, S.J.," 197.
30. Before the Armada, a Jesuit in the Americas would send Philip his poetic account of Edmund Campion's death. Elsewhere, the archbishop of Peru rejoiced in his tears at the latest news about holy Englishmen. On the first, see Herrera Alemán, *Mártires*; on the second, see Yepes to Persons, Madrid, October 29, 1596, in AAW, Series 1, vol. 5, 306r.
31. Yepes, *Historia particular*.
32. *Breve catalogo de los martyres que han sido de los colegios y seminarios ingleses que residen en Roma y en la ciudad de Rhemis* (Valladolid, Spain: Diego de Córdova, 1590), in ABSI, Anglia A I, fol. 53.
33. Persons, *Relacion de algunos martyrios*.
34. Ibid., 1r.
35. Ibid., 2v–2r.
36. "A la señora Infante de España Doña Ysabel," in Persons, *Relacion de algunos martyrios*, n.f.
37. Persons, *Relacion de algunos martyrios*, 9v–10r.
38. Ibid., 72r–v.
39. Ibid., 56r–57r.
40. "Real Provisión para que se pueda pedir limosnas," July 22, 1589, in ACSA, Series 2, Legajo 1, doc. 2.
41. Transcript of letter from Allen to Philip II, Rome, July 10, 1591, in ACSA, Series 2, Legajo 1, doc. 8.
42. *Algunos motivos y razones, que ay para favorecer los seminarios ingleses* (n.p., n.d.), fol. 1, in ACSA, Series 2, Legajo 1.
43. Yepes, *Historia particular*, sig. ¶5v.
44. Ruiz, *King Travels*, 146–93.
45. Acosta to Gil González, Valladolid, August 5, 1592, in ARSI, Hispania 143, 304r–5v.
46. Ortiz, *Relation of the Solemnitie*, 43.
47. Ruelens, *Passetemps de Jehan Lhermite*, 148; Cock, *Jornada de Tarazona*, 32; Leturia, "Abrazo de Felipe II," 287–98.
48. Cano Echevarría, "'Comfort Without Offence'?," 32.
49. Persons, *Relation*; Creswell, *Relacion de un sacerdote*.
50. Creswell, *Relacion de un sacerdote*, 40r.
51. Ibid., 55v.
52. Ibid., 28r.
53. Ibid., 29v.
54. Ibid.
55. Ibid., 39r.
56. Ibid., 55r.
57. Giesey, *If Not, Not*; Gascón Pérez, *Alzar banderas contra su rey*.
58. Pérez, *Pedaço de Historia*, 44.
59. Creswell, *Relacion de un sacerdote*, 37v–38r.
60. *Holie Bible*, 1:569.
61. Ibid.
62. Creswell, *Relacion de un sacerdote*, 38v.
63. Cuadra Blanco, "King Philip of Spain."
64. Highley, *Catholics Writing the Nation*, 176–77.
65. Persons, *Relation*, 39.
66. Creswell, *Relacion de un sacerdote*, 47v (emphasis added).
67. Persons quotes the verse in Latin; this English translation is from the Douay-Rheims Bible.
68. Persons, *Relation*, 43.
69. Ibid., 32–33.
70. Creswell, *Relacion de un sacerdote*, 42r.
71. Beaver, "Holy Land."
72. Arande, *Beggars, Iconoclasts, Civic Patriots*, 172.
73. Cock, *Jornada de Tarazona*, 32.
74. Ribadeneyra, *Tratado del príncipe Cristiano*, in *Obras escogidas*, 467.
75. *Epigrammata sereniss.o exellentissimoq Hispaniarum Principi Philippo 3*, in BNE, Mss. 2492.
76. Herrera, *Advertencias*.
77. Guzmán, *Advertencias*.
78. Penzi, "Loys Dorléans."

79. "A don Francisco de Tejada, don Felix de Guzmán su hermano," in Guzmán, *Advertencias*, n.f.
80. Herrera, *Advertencias*, sig. 3r.
81. "A don Francisco de Tejada, don Felix de Guzmán su hermano," in Guzmán, *Advertencias*, n.f.
82. Gibbons, *English Catholic Exiles*, 105; [Dorléans], *Advertissement*.
83. Herrera, *Advertencias*, sig. ¶5r.
84. Don Juan de Velázquez to Philip II (Summary), January 19, 1592, and Don Juan de Velázquez to Philip II (Extract), June 5, 1592, in Ungerer, *Spaniard in Elizabethan England*, 1:51–53 at 52, 55–58 at 56.
85. Monter, *Frontiers of Heresy*, 93–103.
86. Herrera, *Advertencias*, 24v–25r, 64r–65v, 40v.
87. Ibid., 50v–51r, 69r–v, 3r–v.
88. Ibid., 9r–v.
89. Ibid., 9r–10r, 11r–12v, 20r.

Chapter 5
1. Figueiro, *Spaniards monarchie*, n.f.
2. Read, *Lord Burghley and Queen Elizabeth*, 468.
3. Houliston, "Lord Treasurer and the Jesuit," 384–85; Astruther, *Seminary Priests*, 1:63–68.
4. Jones, *Governing by Virtue*, 210.
5. *A declaration of great troubles pretended against the Realme by a number of Seminarie Priests and Iesuites* [. . .] (London: Christopher Barker, 1591), quoted in Strype, *Annals*, 78–85, hereafter cited as *Proclamation*; Lake, *Bad Queen Bess?*, 330–33.
6. *Proclamation*, 78–79.
7. Cecil, *Copy of a Letter*.
8. *Proclamation*, 79.
9. Ibid., 80.
10. Ibid., 79.
11. Kamen, *Philip of Spain*, xi.
12. Kagan, *Clio*, 99–104.
13. Ibid., 129; Kagan, *Rey recatado*.
14. Kagan, *Clio*, 130.
15. Loomie, *English Polemics*, 19.
16. Persons, *Elizabethae Angliae Reginae*, hereafter cited as *Responsio ad edictum*, following conventional abbreviation; Loomie, "Authorship of 'An Advertisement'"; Persons to Acquaviva, Valladolid, August 11, 1592, in ARSI, Fondo Gesuitico 651, no. 640; AGS, Estado K. 1630, fol. 7.
17. Loomie, "Authorship of 'An Advertisement,'" 205.
18. Ibid., 204.
19. Duke, "William of Orange's *Apology*, 1580."
20. Verstegan, *Advertisement*, 7.
21. Sander, *De schismate Anglicano* (1585), 207r; Sander, *De schismate Anglicano* (1586), 500.
22. Persons, preface to *Responsio ad edictum*, n.f.
23. Persons, *Responsio ad edictum*, 64.
24. Ibid., 67–69.
25. Ibid., 72.
26. Ibid., 71.
27. Ibid., 78.
28. Ibid., 78–79.
29. Ibid., 117.
30. Ibid.
31. Ibid., 104–5.
32. Ibid., 107.
33. Ibid., 108–9.
34. Ibid., 106.
35. Ibid., 103.
36. [Persons], *Responce a l'iniuste*.
37. Persons, *Responsio ad edictum*, 55.
38. Machielsen, "Lion, Witch, and King."
39. Persons, *Responsio ad edictum*, 248–49.
40. Ibid., 207–8, 236.
41. Ibid., 52–53, 59–60.
42. Ibid., 34.
43. Ibid., 85–86.
44. Ibid., 97.
45. Persons, preface to *Responsio ad edictum*, n.f. (paragraph 11).
46. Persons, *Responsio ad edictum*, 60.
47. Stapleton to Persons, Louvain, April 16, 1597, in Knox, *First and Second Diaries*, 391.
48. [Stapleton], *Apologia*.
49. Machielsen, "Lion, Witch, and King."
50. [Persons], *Newes from Spayne and Holland*.
51. Ibid., 14v–19r.

52. [Stapleton], *Apologia*, 11, 16.
53. Ibid., 89–89 (foliation error).
54. Ibid., 87–88, 89 (foliation error).
55. Brotton, *Sultan and the Queen*.
56. Terpstra, *Religious Refugees*, 39–45.
57. Duke, "William of Orange's *Apology*, 1580," 53, 58, 75.
58. Machielsen, "Lion, Witch, and King," 36–37.
59. [Stapleton], *Apologia*, 113–16.
60. Southwell to Verstegan, December 1591, in Petti, *Letters and Despatches*, 1–33.
61. Ibid., 11.
62. Ibid., 12.
63. Ibid., 15.
64. Ibid.
65. Southwell, *Humble Supplication*.
66. Ibid., 45.
67. Ibid., 2.
68. Ibid., 1.
69. Ibid., 45.
70. Ibid., 23.
71. Ibid., 35.
72. Ibid., 14.
73. Ibid., 13.
74. Ibid., 29.
75. Ibid.
76. Ibid., 39.
77. Arblaster, *Antwerp and the World*; Rombauts, *Richard Verstegen*.
78. Arblaster, *Antwerp and the World*, 55–60.
79. Verstegan, *Advertisement*, 5.
80. Verstegan, *Declaration*, 3.
81. Ibid., 8.
82. Ibid.
83. Ibid., 9–11.
84. Verstegan, *Advertisement*, 30–31.
85. Ibid., 20–21, 48.
86. [Watson], *Sparing discoverie*, 54.
87. Ibid.

Chapter 6

1. Herrera, *Historia de lo sucedido*.
2. Ibid., sig. ¶5.
3. Ibid., 168v.
4. Ibid., 3v–4r.
5. Ostenfeld-Suske, "Official Historiography," 305.

6. Iñurritegui Rodríguez, "Antonio de Herrera y Tordesillas," 138–39.
7. Herrera, *Diez libros*.
8. Gil Pujol, "Fuerzas del Rey."
9. Herrera, *Diez libros*, sig. ¶3r.
10. Ibid., 4r–v.
11. Kagan, *Clio*, 138.
12. "Clausula de una carta muy discreta embiada en el año 1592 a Guillelmo Cecilio," in Yepes, *Historia particular*, n.f.
13. Creswell, *Exemplar literarum*.
14. Yepes, *Historia particular*, sig. ¶5r–v.
15. Ribadeneyra, *Segunda parte*.
16. Ibid., sig. ¶¶4r–v.
17. Persons to Idiáquez, Madrid, December 4, 1593, in ARSI, Hispania 136, fols. 169v–70r; Ribadeneyra, *Historias de la contrarreforma*, 886.
18. Weinreich, *Ribadeneyra's "Ecclesiastical History,"* 49; Ribadeneyra, *Historias de la contrarreforma*, 885.
19. AHN, Inquisición 4436, nos. 6, 57, 63.
20. Ribadeneyra, *Segunda parte*, 81r.
21. Vázquez de Prada, *Felipe II y Francia*, 394–410; Jensen, *Diplomacy and Dogmatism*, 216–18.
22. Iñurritegui Rodríguez, *Gracia y la república*, 199–269.
23. Ribadeneyra, *Tratado de tribulación*, 224r–v.
24. Ibid., 180r–v.
25. Ibid., 222r.
26. Ibid., 14v–15r.
27. Ibid., 178r.
28. Ibid., 177v.
29. Ibid., 243r.
30. Ibid.
31. Ibid., 59v.
32. Ibid., 177v.
33. Ibid., 161v–52r.
34. Ibid., 176r–v.
35. Ibid., 175r.
36. Sánchez-Molero, *Felipe II*, 315.

Conclusion to Part II

1. Pollini, *Storia ecclesiastica*, sig*4v.
2. Bozzio, *De signis ecclesiae Dei*.
3. *Mercurii Gallobelgici*, sig. +++2r, 326–33.

4. Darcy to Cecil, Venice, April 28, 1592, in TNA, S.P. 99-I, part 2, 199v.
5. Lake, *Bad Queen Bess?*, 417.
6. Domínguez, "The Politics of Destroying Books: The Case of Girolamo Pollini's *Ecclesiastical History of the English Revolution* and Its English Response" (forthcoming).
7. Bacon, "Aduertisement," 309.
8. Gajda, *Earl of Essex*.
9. Popper, *Ralegh's "History,"* 82–84.
10. Parker, "Place of Tudor England," 173, 177.

Introduction to Part III

1. O'Donell, "Refugiados ingleses."
2. Persons, *Conference*. Here I will use an accurate version of the *Memorial* printed (by anti-Catholics) in the seventeenth century: Gee, *Jesuit's Memorial*. I have also consulted the version at ABSI, Ms. 19/3/36: *A Memoriall for the reformation of Englande*.
3. García Hernán, *Irlanda y el Rey Prudente*, 2:196.

Chapter 7

1. "Memorias de las escripturas q se hallan en el Archivo de Simancas tocantes a Inglaterra," October 1567, in IVDJ, Envio 6, vol. 1, 2r.
2. Elder, *Copie of a letter*, sig. Ci(v)–Cii(v).
3. "Por la sucesion de Inglaterra y Escocia sacado de las escrituras que ay en los archivos reales & Simancas con el arbol Della," in BFZ, Madrid, Altamira 161, doc. 138.
4. Memorial dated March 18, 1587, in Persons, *Letters and Memorials*, 294.
5. Allen and Persons to Philip II, Rome, after March 24, 1587, in Persons, *Letters and Memorials*, 295.
6. Ibid., 298.
7. Ibid.
8. Knecht, *French Civil Wars*, 269.
9. Iñurritegui Rodríguez, *Gracia y la república*, 261.
10. [Dractan], *Relacion*.

11. Ibid., 31r–v, 34v.
12. Ibid., 11v.
13. BNE, Mss. 23199, hereafter cited as *Raçonamiento*.
14. Holmes, "Authorship and Early Reception"; Hicks, "Father Robert Persons"; Loomie, "Richard Stanyhurst."
15. Englefield to Clement VIII, Valladolid, September 2, 1596, in ASV, Borghese II, 448 A–B, fol. 392r.
16. Camillo Borghese to Cardinal Aldobrandino, Madrid, March 1594, in ASV, Borghese III, 94c, fol. 277v.
17. *Raçonamiento*, 33r.
18. Ibid., 33r–38r, 178r–80r.
19. Ibid., 184v.
20. Herrera, *Cinco libros*, 25.
21. *Raçonamiento*, 203v–6r.
22. Ibid., 210r; Bouza, *Imagen y propaganda*, chap. 5; Bouza, *Portugal no tempo dos Filipes*, chap. 1.
23. *Raçonamiento*, 213r.
24. Ibid., 213v.
25. Ibid., 215r.
26. Ibid., 186v–87r.
27. Rodríguez-Salgado, "Anglo-Spanish War," 1–44.
28. Garibay, *Ilustraciones geneologicas*.
29. Creswell to Aldobrandino, Madrid, March 25, 1595, in ASV, Borghese III, 124 g. 2, fol. 6r.
30. Creswell to Aldobrandino, Madrid, October 22, 1595, in ASV, Borghese III, 124 g. 2, fol. 77r.
31. "Memorial del Padre Personio al Rey Acerca de la planeada invasión de Inglaterra," in Eguiluz, *Robert Persons*, doc. 25, 423.
32. *Raçonamiento*, 17v–18r.
33. Ibid., 134r–38v.
34. Ibid., 136r.
35. Persons, *Conference*, pt. 2, 194–95.
36. Ibid., 196.
37. Ibid., 202.
38. Ibid., 203.
39. Ibid., 205.
40. Ibid., 207.
41. Ibid., 210.
42. Ibid., 211–12.
43. Ibid., 208–9.

44. Ibid., 214.

45. Ibid., 219–20.

46. Ibid., 221.

47. Collinson, "Elizabethan Exclusion Crisis"; Doran and Kewes, *Doubtful and Dangerous*; Questier, *Dynastic Politics.*

48. On Wentworth, see Neale, *Elizabeth and Her Parliaments*, 251–66; Neale, "Peter Wentworth."

49. Tyacke, "Puritan Politicians."

50. [Persons], *Newes from Spayne and Holland.*

51. Parmelee, *"Good Newes from Fraunce"*; Lake, *Bad Queen Bess?*, 231–56.

52. "Illustris viri francisci Ingelfildi Equitis aurato qui consillijs olim secretioribus Mariae Angliae Reginae fuerat, judicium ac censura de libro successionis," in BAV, Vat. Lat. 6227, 154v.

53. [Belloy], *Apologie Catholique*, 126.

54. *De iusta authoritate* (1590); Rossaeo, *De iusta authoritate* (1592). Unless otherwise noted, reference will be made to the 1592 edition, which Persons seems to have read.

55. Valérian, *Prête anglais contre Henri IV.*

56. Baumgartner, *Radical Reactionaries*, 145–60.

57. Ibid., 174; Ruiz, "Robert Persons, S.J."

58. Rossaeo, *De iusta authoritate*, 17.

59. Ibid.

60. Persons, *Conference*, pt. 1, 17.

61. Ibid., 13.

62. Rossaeo, *De iusta authoritate*, 67.

63. Persons, *Conference*, pt. 1, 83.

64. Ibid., 83–84.

65. Ibid., 219.

66. Rossaeo, *De iusta authoritate*, 104–5.

67. *De iusta authoritate* (1590), 394.

68. Persons, *Conference*, pt. 1, 81.

69. Ibid., 73.

70. Ibid., 38.

71. Rossaeo, *De iusta authoritate*, 139.

72. Persons, *Conference*, pt. 1, 216.

73. Ibid., 217.

74. Ibid., 2, 240–46.

75. Rossaeo, *De iusta authoritate*, 124–25.

76. Ibid., 138.

77. Ibid., 128–29.

78. Persons, *Conference*, pt. 1, 211.

79. Ibid., 114.

80. Rossaeo, *De iusta authoritate*, 519.

81. Ibid., 548.

82. Persons, *Conference*, pt. 1, 53.

83. "Denuncatio haec aliquos locos libri P. Personii," in ACDF, Rome, St St SS I-e, 1041r.

84. Persons, *Conference*, pt. 1, 31.

85. Ibid., 122.

86. Ibid., sig. *2r–v.

87. Gajda, *Earl of Essex*, 136.

88. Dickinson, *Court Politics*, 82.

89. Hammer, *Polarisation of Elizabethan Politics*, 145.

90. Ibid., 355; Breight, "Realpolitik and Elizabethan Ceremony."

91. Lake, "King (Queen) and Jesuit."

92. Lake, *How Shakespeare*; Hammer, "Shakespeare's Richard II."

93. Persons to Acquaviva, June 16, 1594, in ARSI, Hispania 136, fol. 162v.

94. "Relacion del principio, progresso y fin de la tribulacion del colegio ingles en Roma," in BL, Additional Ms. 21, 203, 7v.

95. Houliston, *Catholic Resistance*, 87; McCoog, "Harmony Disrupted"; Houliston, "Hare and the Drum."

96. Agazzari to Persons, August 27, 1596, in Tierney, *Dodd's Church History of England*, 3:lxxv; Gasquet, *History*, 97.

97. Creswell to Aldobrandino, Madrid, October 22, 1595, in ASV, Borghese III, 124 g. 2, fol. 76v.

98. Barrett to Persons, Rome, April 10, 1596, in Renold, *Letters of Allen and Barrett*, 250.

99. Lake and Questier, *Trials of Margaret Clitherow*, chaps. 7–9; Pritchard, *Catholic Loyalism.*

100. "Abstract of the Memorial and sundry Letters against the Jesuits. Sept.–Dec. 1597," in Law, *Archpriest Controversy*, 1:7–8.

101. "Watsons Thirty Reasons," in Law, *Archpriest Controversy*, 1:90–100 at 92.

102. Creswell to Clement VIII, Madrid, April 26, 1596, in ASV, Borghese III, 124 g. 2, fol. 93r.

103. Creswell to Aldobrandino, Madrid, October 22, 1595, in ASV, Borghese III, 124 g. 2, fol. 76r.

104. Tutino, "Political Thought," 56.

105. ASV, Borghese IV, 103, hereafter cited as *De regiae successionis iure*. Folio citations correspond with handwritten rather than printed pagination. Edwards, *Robert Persons*, 198.

106. *De regiae successionis iure*, 2r, 3r, 4v.

107. Ibid., 123v–24r, 128r.

108. Clancy, "English Catholics."

109. Oakley, *Conciliarist Tradition*.

110. Tutino, *Empire of Souls*.

111. Godman, *Saint as Censor*, 136.

112. *De regiae successionis iure*, 124v.

113. Ibid., 124v–25r.

114. Ibid., 126r–v.

115. Tutino, "Political Thought," 48–49; *De regiae successionis iure*, 124r–v.

116. *De regiae successionis iure*, 124v.

117. Ibid., 128v.

118. Ibid., 129r–30v, 131v.

119. Persons, *Conference*, pt. 1, 61.

120. "Address of the English Catholics in Spain to Philip II," in Hume, *Calendar of State Papers*, 4:636.

121. "Puntos principales para facilitar y assegurar la Empresa de Ynglaterra," in AGS, Estado 839, fol. 126.

122. ACSA, Series 2, Legajo 12, docs. 11–13. Reference is being made here to the English version, doc. 13. The document is unpaginated. Another English version is at AAW, Anglia A, vol. 9, 68r–70r.

123. ASV, Borghese IV, 252, fols. 1ff.

Chapter 8

1. Abreu, *Asalto de Cádiz*, 271.

2. Quoted in Redworth, *She-Apostle*, 83.

3. Burrieza Sánchez, "Reparando las heridas."

4. Hammer, "Myth-Making."

5. McCoog, *"And Touching Our Society,"* 261–81.

6. Persons, *Manifestation of the Great Folly*, 56r.

7. "Un estratto di certi Capi cavati da un libro inglese scritto a mano chiamato Memoriale pro Reformatione Anglie . . ." and "Abstracto d'un libro inglese scritto l'anno 1596 [. . .]," in AAW, vol. 5, 547r–61r. A full Latin version—presumably the one that circulated at court—can be found at ACSA, Libro 30.

8. Scarisbrick, "Robert Persons's Plans"; Carrafiello, *Robert Persons*, chaps. 4–5; Clancy, "Notes"; Bossy, *English Catholic Community*, 21–24; Houliston, *Catholic Resistance*, 87–92; Holmes, *Resistance and Compromise*, 161–65; McCoog, *Building the Faith*, 389–92.

9. [Persons], *Brief Apologie*, 203v.

10. Crosignani, "*De adeundis ecclesiis protestatium,*" 181.

11. Watson, *Decacordon*, 150.

12. Gajda, *Earl of Essex*, 130.

13. Stroud, "Ben Jonson and Father Wright."

14. Wright, *Disposition or Garnishement*, sig. A2.

15. Ibid., n.f.

16. Ibid., sig. Dv.

17. Wright, *Certaine articles or forcible reasons*.

18. McCoog, *Building the Faith*, 46.

19. Gajda, *Earl of Essex*, 108–41.

20. Stroud, "Father Thomas Wright"; Crosignani, "*De adeundis ecclesiis protestatium,*" 179–201; Pritchard, *Catholic Loyalism*, 61–67; Holmes, *Resistance and Compromise*, 199–200; Hammer, *Polarisation of Elizabethan Politics*, 177 n. 150.

21. Wright, "Licitum sit," 584.

22. Ibid., 584.

23. Ibid., 589.

24. Ibid., 590.

25. These distinctions are, of course, caricatures.

26. Persons, *Memorial*, 76–77, 185–90.

27. Cf. Scarisbrick, "Robert Persons's Plans," 39.

28. Persons, *Memorial*, 195.

29. Ibid., 66.

30. Ibid., 108.

31. Pollen, "Memoir I," 19–20.

32. Ibid., 12.

33. From "Epistle dedicatorie," in [Persons], *Treatise of three conversions*, 1:n.f.
34. Persons, *Memorial*, 91–92, 123–27, 131.
35. Ibid., 89–90.
36. Ibid., 134.
37. Ibid., 143.
38. Ibid., 25, 32.
39. Ibid., 20.
40. Ibid., 21.
41. Ibid., 26.
42. Ibid., 49–50.
43. Ibid., 51.
44. Ibid., 50.
45. Ibid., 52.
46. Ibid., 50.
47. Ibid., 53–54.
48. Ibid., 54.
49. "Puntos principales para facilitar y assignar la Empresa de Inglaterra," in AGS, Estado 839, fol. 120.
50. "Relazione di Vincenzo Gradenigo (1586)," in Alberí, *Relazioni*, 1:389.
51. *Declaration sommaire*.
52. "Papel que Don Sancho Busto de Villegas, Gobernador del Arzobispado de Toledo, en ausencia de Don Bartolome Carranza, escribiò al Rey Felipe II a 15 de agosto de 1574," in Valladares, *Seminario erudito*, 6:216–36.
53. "Sobre la division del Arcobispado de Toledo," in RAH, Salazar y Castro Ms. N-4 (9–1010), 244r–50r.
54. Ibid., 245v.
55. Ibid., 246r.
56. Braun, "Scholasticism and Humanism," 55.
57. Ibid., 124.
58. Ibid., 69; Cirot, *Mariana Historien*, 37.
59. Mariana, *Dignidad real*, 115. Translations here from this Spanish edition after comparison with Mariana, *De rege et regis institutione*.
60. Ibid., 116–17.
61. Ibid., 282.
62. Ibid., 120.
63. Ibid., 121–22.
64. Ibid., 117.
65. Braun, *Juan de Mariana*, 146–60.
66. Mariana, *Dignidad real*, 102.
67. Ibid., 102–3.
68. Ibid., 101.
69. Ibid., 277.
70. Ibid., 315.
71. Ibid., 285.
72. Persons, *Memorial*, 192–93.
73. Ibid., 195.
74. Ibid., 197.
75. Ibid., 76.
76. Ibid., 199–200.
77. Ibid., 104.
78. Ibid., 239.
79. Ibid., 238–40.
80. Ibid., 220.
81. Ibid., 79, 212.
82. Ibid., 206.
83. Ibid., 217.
84. Ibid., 215.
85. Ibid., 218.
86. Ibid., 102–3.
87. Ibid., 104.
88. Ibid., 102.
89. Ibid., 109–10.
90. Ibid., 219.
91. Ribadeneyra, *Tratado de la religion*, 5.
92. Ibid., 38.
93. Ibid., 33.
94. Ibid., 35–36.
95. Ibid., 180.
96. Ibid., 236.
97. Ibid., 116.
98. Ibid., 72.
99. Ibid., 230–32, 66.
100. Ibid., 76–77.
101. Ibid., 83.
102. Ibid., 90.
103. Ibid., 122.
104. Ribadeneyra, *Scisma* (1588), 84r.
105. Reinhardt, *Voices of Conscience*; Rurale, *Religiosi*.
106. Marocci, *Consciência*.
107. Persons, *Memorial*, sig. A4r.
108. Ibid., 150–51.

Conclusion to Part III
1. Salmon, "Catholic Resistance Theory."
2. Bireley, *Counter-Reformation Prince*; Fernández-Santamaria, *Natural Law, Constitutionalism*.

Conclusion

1. Creswell to Philip III, St. Omer, August 10, 1617, in RB, Madrid, Mss. II/2225, 77r; Bouza, "Contrarreforma y tipografía."
2. Allen, *Philip III*.
3. Guerrero and Fernández, *Image of Elizabeth I*.
4. Freddy Cristóbal Domínguez, "But a 'Stage-Play': A Counter-Reformation View of the Marian Church" (forthcoming).
5. Beltrán, *Compañía de Jesús*.

Bibliography

Archives Consulted and Manuscript Sources

Archives of the Archdiocese of Westminster, London [AAW]

Archivio della Congregazione per la Dottrina della Fede, Rome [ACDF]

Archivio Segreto Vaticano, Vatican City [ASV]

Archivium Britannicum Societatis Iesu, London [ABSI]

Archivium Romanum Societatis Iesu, Rome [ARSI]

Archivo Colegio San Albano, Valladolid [ACSA]

Archivo General de Simancas, Simancas [AGS]

Archivo Histórico Nacional de España, Madrid [AHN]

Archivum Venerabilis Collegii Anglorum de Urbe, Rome [AVCAU]

Arquivo Nacional Torre do Tombo, Lisbon [ANTT]

Biblioteca Apostolica Vaticana, Vatican City [BAV]

Biblioteca Casanatense, Rome

Biblioteca da Ajuda, Lisbon [BA]

Biblioteca Francisco de Zabálburu, Madrid [BFZ]

Biblioteca Nacional de España, Madrid [BNE]

British Library, London [BL]

Instituto Valencia de Don Juan, Madrid [IVDJ]

Mansueto Library, Chicago

National Archive, The, Kew [TNA]

Real Academia de la Historia, Madrid [RAH]

Real Biblioteca, Madrid [RB]

Printed Primary Sources

Abreu, Pedro de. *El asalto de Cádiz de 1596.* Edited by Manuel Bustos Rodríguez. Cádiz: Universidad de Cádiz, 1996.

Alberí, Eugenio, ed. *Le relazioni degli ambasciatori veneti al senato durante il secolo decimosestimo.* Florence: Alberí, 1861.

Allen, William. *An Admonition to the Christian Nobility.* N.p., 1588.

———. *The Letters and Memorials of William Cardinal Allen, 1532–1594.* Edited by Thomas Knox. London: David Nutt, 1882.

———. *A True, Sincere, and Modest Defense of English Catholics.* In The Execution of Justice in England by *William Cecil and A True, Sincere, and Modest Defense* of English Catholics *by William Allen*, edited by Robert Kingdon. Ithaca: Cornell University Press, 1965.

Ávila, Juan de. *Obras del Padre Maestro Iuan de Avila, predicador en el Andaluzia.* Madrid: Pedro de Madrigal, 1588.

Bacon, Francis. "An aduertisement touching seditious writing." In *The Oxford Francis Bacon: Early Writings, 1584–1596.* Edited by Alan Stewart with Harriet Knight. Oxford: Clarendon Press, 2012.

Bartoli, Daniello. *Dell'istoria della compagnia di gesú. L'Inghilterra parte dell'Europa.* Rome: Stamperia Varese, 1667.

Beare, Philip O'Sullivan. *Historiae Catholicae Iberniae compendium.* Lisbon: Petro Crasbeeckio, 1621.

Belloy, Pierre de. *Apologie Catholique [. . .].* N.p., 1586.

———. *Declaration du droit de legitime succession, sur le royaume de Portugal [. . .].* Antwerp: 1582.

Biegerum, Iulium. *Flores calvinistici.* Naples: Ioannem Baptistam Zangerum, 1585.

Blackfan, John. *Annales colegii anglorum vallesoletanum.* Edited by Peter E. B. Harris. Valladolid: Royal English College, 2008.

Botero, Giovanni. *Diez libros de la razon de estado.* Translated by Antonio de Herrera. Madrid: Luys Sanchez, 1593.

Bozzio, Tomasso. *De signis ecclesiae Dei.* Rome: Iacobi Tornerlj, 1591.

Burnet, Gilbert. *The History of the Reformation of the Church of England.* London: T. H., 1679.

Calderón de la Barca, Pedro. *The Schism in England (La cisma de Inglaterra).* Edited by Kenneth Muir and Ann L. Mackenzie. Warminster, U.K.: Aris & Phillips, 1990.

Campanella, Tommaso. *La monarchia di Spagna: Prima stesura giovanile.* Edited by Germana Ernst. Naples: Istituto Italiano per gli Studi Filosofici, 1989.

Carlyle, Thomas, ed. *Oliver Cromwell's Letters and Speeches.* Boston: Dana Estes and Charles E. Lauriat, 1884.

Catalogus und ordentliche Verzeichuß de Newgekrönten anderhalb hundert streitbarn Barfüsser Martyrer, Welche alle in Engellandt, Niderland, Flandern, Franckreich, Irland, Ungarn und Oesterreich [. . .] Ingolstadt, Germany: Wolfgang Eder, 1585.

Catholic Record Society: Miscellanea II. Edited by J. H. Pollen. London: Arden Press, 1906.

Catholic Record Society: Miscellanea XIII. London: Whitehead & Son, 1926.

Cecil, William. *The Copy of a Letter sent out of England to don Bernardino Mendoza.* London: Thomas Vautrollier for Richard Field, 1588.

———. *A Declaration of the Causes Moving England to Give Aid to the Defense of the People Afflicted and Oppressed in the Low Countries.* London: Christopher Barker, 1585.

———. *The Execution of Justice in England.* In *The Execution of Justice in England by William Cecil and A True, Sincere, and Modest Defense of English Catholics by William Allen,* edited by Robert Kingdon. Ithaca: Cornell University Press, 1965.

Chacón, Alfonso. *De signis sanctissimae crucis, Que diversis olim orbis regionibus, & nuper hoc anno 1591.* Rome: Ascansium & Hieronymum Donangelos, 1591.

Cock, Enrique. *Jornada de Tarazona hecha por Felipe II en 1592.* Edited by Alfredo Morel-Fatio and Antonio Rodríguez Villa. Madrid: M. Tello, 1879.

Conestaggio, Geronimo. *Dell'unione del regno di Portogallo alla corona di Castiglia.* Genoa: Girolamo Bartoli, 1585.

Cope, Anthony. *Antisanderus duos continens dialogos non ita pridem inter viros quosdam doctos Venetiis hábitos.* Cambridge, 1593.

Córdoba, Cabrera de. *De historia, para entenderla y escrivirla.* Madrid: Luis Sánchez, 1611.

Creswell, Joseph. *Exemplar literarum, missarum, e Germania, a D Gulielmum Cecilium, consiliarum Regium.* N.p., 1592.

———. *Relacion de un sacerdote ingles, escrita a Flandes, a un cavallero de su tierra, desterrado por ser Catolico.* Madrid: Pedro de Madrigal, 1592.

Crosignani, Ginevra, Thomas McCoog, and Michael Questier, with the assistance of Peter Holmes, eds. *Recusancy in Early Modern England: Manuscript and Printed Sources in Translation.* Toronto: PIMS, 2010.

Crudelitatis Calvinianae exempla duo recentissima ex Anglia. N.p., 1585.

De iusta reipub. Christianae in rrges [sic] impios et haereticos authoritate. Paris: Guilielmum Bichonium, 1590.

Declaration sommaire des ilegitimes usurpations des roiaumes de Portugal, Navarre at autres pays [. . .]. Antwerp, 1583.

De iustitia Britanica, sive Anglica, quae contra Christi martyres continenter exercetur. Ingolstadt, Germany: Davidis Sartorii, 1585.

Denucé, J., ed. *Correspondance de Christophe Plantin.* Antwerp: De Groote Boekhandel, 1918.

Dorléans, Louis. *Advertissement des Catholiques Anglais aux Francois Catholiques.* N.p., 1586.

Dractan, Thomas. *Relacion que embiaron las religiosas del monasterio de Sion de Inglaterra.* Madrid: Viuda de Pedro de Madrigal, 1594.

Duke, Alastair, ed. "William of Orange's Apology, 1580." *Dutch Crossing: Journal of Low Countries Studies* 22, no. 1 (1998): 3–96.

Duro, Cesáreo Fernández. *La armada invencible.* Madrid: Tipográfico de los Sucesores de Rivadeneyra, 1884.

Ehses, Stephan, and Aloys Meister, eds. *Nuntiaturberichte aus Deutschland Nebts Ergänzenden Aktenstücken (1585–1590).* Paderborn, Germany: Ferdinand Schöningh, 1885.

Elder, John. *The copie of a letter sent into Scotlande.* N.p., 1554.

Escalante, Bernardino de. *Discursos de Bernardino de Escalante al rey y sus ministros (1585–1605).* Edited by José Luis Casado Soto. Santander: Universidad de Cantabria, 1995.

Figueiro, Vasco. *The Spaniards monarchie and the leaguers Olygarchie.* London: Richard Field, 1592.

Galloni, Antonio. *De ss. martyrum cruciatibus.* Rome: Typographia Congregationis Oratorij apud S. Mariam in Vallicella, 1594.

Ganss, George E., ed. *The Constitutions of the Society of Jesus.* St. Louis: Institute of Jesuit Sources, 1970.

Garibay, Esteban de. *Ilustraciones geneologicas de los Catholicos reyes de las Españas.* Madrid: Luis Sánchez, 1596.

Gee, Edward, ed. *The Jesuit's Memorial for the Intended Reformation of England under their First Popish Prince.* London: Richard Chiswel, 1690.

Gibbons, John. *Concertatio Ecclesiae Catholicae in Anglia Adversus Calvinopapistas & Puritanos [. . .].* Trier, Germany: Edmundum Hatotum, 1583.

Granada, Luis de. *A memoriall of a Christian Life.* Rouen, France: George L'Oyselet, 1586.

———. *Obras completas.* Edited by Álvaro Huerga. Madrid: Fundación Universitaria Española Dominicos de Andalucía, 1997.

———. *Vidas del Padre Maestro Juan de Avila.* Edited by Luis Sala Balust. Barcelona: Juan Flors, 1964.

Gross, Jorge Calvar, José Ignacio González-Aller Hierro, Marcelino de Dueñas Fontán, and Maria del Campo Mérida Valverde, eds. *La batalla del mar océano entre España e Inglaterra (1568–1588).* Madrid: Turner, 1988.

Guerreiro, Affonso. *Das festas que se fizeram na cidade de Lisboa.* Lisbon: Francisco Correa, 1581.

Guzmán, Félix de. *Advertencias que dan los Catolicos ingleses, a los Catolicos de Francia del peligro que están de perder la Religion, si admiten a la Corona príncipe herege.* Madrid: Pedro Madrigal, 1592.

Harrison, Alfred Allen. "Sir Francis Englefield." *Dublin Review* 119 (July–October 1896): 34–76.

Herrera, Antonio de. *Advertencias que los Catolicos de Inglaterra escrivieron a los Catolicos de Francia*. Zaragoza: Lorenço de Robles, 1592.

———. *Cinco libros [. . .] de la historia de Portugal*. Madrid: Pedro de Madrigal, 1591.

———. *Diez libros de la razon de estado*. Madrid: Luys Sanchez, 1593.

———. *Historia de lo sucedido en Escocia e Inglaterra*. Madrid: Pedro de Madrigal, 1589.

Herrera Alemán, Francisco de. *Los mártires de la reforma en Inglaterra*. Edited by Eusebio Gómez and Honorio Muñoz. Manila: Librería de la Universidad de Sto. Thomas, 1938.

Heylin, Peter. *Ecclesia restaurata: The History of the Reformation of the Church of England*. London: R. B., 1674.

The Holie Bible Faithfully Translated into English out of the Authentical Latin. Vol. 1. Douai, Belgium: Lawrence Kellam, 1609.

Hume, Martin, ed. *Calendar of State Papers: Elizabeth, 1587–1603*. London: Eyre and Spottiswoode, 1899.

Humphrey, Laurence. *Iesuitismi pars secunda puritanopapismi, seu doctrinae Iesituicae rationibus ab Ed. Campiano comprehensaae [. . .]*. London: Thomas Middleton, 1584.

Illescas, Gonzalo de. *Historia pontifical y Catholica*. Salamanca, Spain: Domingo de Portonarijs, 1569.

Kagan, Richard L., and Abigail Dyer, eds. *Inquisitorial Inquiries: Brief Lives of Secret Jews and Other Heretics*. Baltimore: Johns Hopkins University Press, 2004.

Kinsela, M., ed. *The Rise and Progress of the English Reformation*. Dublin: J. Christie, 1827.

Knox, Thomas Francis, ed. *The First and Second Diaries of the English College, Douay*. London: David Nutt, 1878.

Landtsheer, Jeanine de. "The Correspondence of Thomas Stapleton and Johannes Moretus: A Critical and Annotated Edition." *Humanistica Lovaniensia* 45 (1996): 430–503.

Law, T. G., ed. *The Archpriest Controversy: Documents Relating to the Dissensions of the Roman Catholic Clergy, 1597–1602*. London: Camden Society, 1896.

Leslie, John. *A Defence of the Honour of the Right Highe, Mighty, and Noble Princesse Marie Queene of Scotlande*. London: Flete Strete, 1569.

———. *A Treatise Towching the Right, Title, and Interest of the Most excellent Princesse Marie Queene of Scotlande*. N.p., 1584.

Lewis, David, ed. *The Rise and Growth of the Anglican Schism*. London: Burns and Oates, 1877.

Loarte, Gaspar de. *The Excercise of a Christian Life*. N.p., 1584.

Loomie, Albert, ed. *English Polemics at the Spanish Court: Joseph Creswell's Letter to the Ambassador from England*. New York: Fordham University Pres, 1993.

Mariana, Juan de. *La dignidad real y la educacion del rey*. Edited by Luis Sanchez Agesta. Madrid: Centro de Estudios Constitucionales, 1981.

———. *De rege et regis institutione libri III*. Toledo, Spain: Pedro Rodríguez, 1599.

———. "A Treatise on the Alteration of Money, 1609." In *Sourcebook in Late-Scholastic Monetary Theory*, edited by Stephen J. Grabill, 241–304. Plymouth, U.K.: Lexington Books, 2007.

Martínez, Enrico. *Repertorio de los Tiempos y historia natural desta Nueva España*. Mexico City: Enrico Martinez, 1606.

Mendoza, Bernardino de. *Theorica y practica de guerra*. Antwerp: Plantin Press, 1596.

Mercurii Gallobelgici. Cologne, Germany: Viduam Godefredi Kempensis, 1598.

Mexia, Pedro. *Historia imperial y cesárea*. Basel, Switzerland: Ioan Oporino, 1547.

Murphy, Martin, ed. *St. Gregory's College, Seville, 1592–1767*. London: Catholic Record Society, 1992.

Nadal, Jerónimo. *Adnotationes et meditationes in Evangelia quae in sacrosancto missae sacrificio toto anno leguntur*. Antwerp: Martinus Nutius, 1595.

O'Donovan, John, ed. "The Irish Correspondence of James Fitz Maurice of Desmond." *Journal of the Kilkenny* and *South-East of Ireland Archaeological Society*, n.s., no. 2 (1859): 354–69.

Ortiz, Antonio. *A Relation of the Solemnitie wherewith the Catholike Princes K Phillip the III and Quene Margaret were receyved in the Inslilsh Colledge of Valadolid*. Translated by Francis Rivers. N.p, 1601.

Peck, D. C., ed. *Leicester's Commonwealth: The Copy of a Letter Written by a Master of Art of Cambridge (1584) and Related Documents*. Athens: Ohio University Press, 1985.

Peralta, Francisco de. *Relacion que el Padre Francisco de Peralta de la Compania de Iesus* [. . .]. Seville: Alonso Rodriguez Gamarra, 1616.

Pérez, Antonio. *Un pedaço de Historia de lo sucedido en Zaragoça de Aragon a 24 de setiembre del año de 1591*. Pau, France, 1591.

Pérez, Jesús Gascón, ed. *La rebelión de las palabras*. Zaragoza: Prensas Universitarias Universidad de Zaragoza, 2004.

Persons, Robert. *A Brief Apologie, or Defence of the Catholike Ecclesiastical Hieararchie* [. . .]. N.p., n.d.

———. "Certaine Notes of Memory Concerning the First Entrance of ye Soc. of Jesus into England." In *Catholic Record Society: Miscellanea II*, edited by J. H. Pollen. London: Arden Press, 1906.

———. *Certamen ecclesiae Anglicanae*. Edited by Joseph Simons. Assen, Netherlands: Van Gorcum, 1965.

———. *A Christian directorie guiding men to their salvation*. N.p., 1585.

———. *The Christian Directory: The First Booke of the Christian Exercise, Appertayning to Resolution*. Edited by Victor Houliston. Leiden: Brill, 1998.

———. *A Conference about the Next Succession to the Crowne of Ingland*. N.p., 1594.

———. *The Copie of a Letter Lately Written by a Spanishe Gentleman, to his Friend of Sundry Calumnies, There Falsely Bruited and Spred Amonge the People*. N.p., 1589.

———. *The Correspondence and Unpublished Papers of Robert Persons, SJ*. Vol. 1, *1574–1588*. Edited by Victor Houliston,

Ginevra Crosignani, and Thomas M. McCoog. Toronto: PIMS, 2017.

———. *Elizabethae Angliae Reginae haeresin calvinianam propugnatis, saevissimum in Catholicos sui regni Edictum*. Lyon: Pierre Roussin, 1592.

———. *The First Booke of the Christian Exercise*. N.p., 1582.

———. *Letters and Memorials of Father Robert Persons, S.J.* Edited by Leo Hicks. London: Catholic Record Society, 1942.

———. *A Manifestation of the Great Folly and Bad Spirit of Certayne in England Calling Themselves Secular Priests*. N.p., 1602.

———. *Newes from Spayne and Holland* [. . .]. N.p., 1593.

———. *De persecutione Anglicana commentariolus*. Ingolstadt, Germany: Wolfgang Ederus, 1592.

———. *Relacion de algunos martyrios, que de nuevo han hecho los hereges de Inglaterra*. Madrid: Pedro de Madrigal, 1590.

———. *A Relation of the King of Spaines Receiving in Valliodolid*. N.p., 1592.

———. *Responce a l'iniuste et sanguinaire edict d'Elizabeth Royne d'Angleterre* [. . .]. Lyon: Iean Pilehotte, 1593.

———. "A Storie of Domesticall Difficulties." In *Catholic Record Society: Miscellanea II*, edited by J. H. Pollen. London: Arden Press, 1906.

———. *A Treatise of three conversions of England from Paganisme to Christian Religion*. N.p., 1603.

Petti, Anthony G., ed. *The Letters and Despatches of Richard Verstegan*. London: Catholic Record Society, 1959.

———. *Recusant Documents from the Ellesmere Manuscripts*. London: Catholic Records Society, 1968.

Philip IV. *Historia de Italia donde se describen todas las cosas sucedidas desde el año de 1494 hasta el de 1532 por Francisco Guicciardini*. Madrid: Librería de la viuda de Hernando, 1889.

Pole, Reginald. *Ad Henricum Octauum Britanniae Regem, pro ecclesiasticae unitatis defensione, libri quatuor*. Rome: Antonium Bladum, ca. 1539.

Pollen, J.H., ed. "Memoir I: Father Persons' Autobiography." In *Catholic Record Society: Miscellanea II*, 12–47. London: Arden Press, 1906.

Pollini, Girolamo. *Storia ecclesiastica della rivoluzione d'Inghilterra, divisa in cinque libri*. Florence: Giunti Press, 1591.

Possevino, Antonio. *Bibliotheca selecta*. Rome: Vatican, 1593.

Reinolds, William. *Calvino-Turcismus id est, Calvinisticae perfidiae, cum Mahumetana collation*. Antwerp: Petri Belleri, 1597.

Renold, P., ed. *Letters of William Allen and Richard Barrett, 1572–1598*. Oxford: Oxonian Press, 1967.

Ribadeneyra, Pedro de. *Flos sanctorum de las vidas de los santos*. Barcelona: Juan Piferrer, 1734.

———. *Historia del cisma de Inglaterra*. Cádiz: Imprenta de la Revista Médica, 1863.

———. *Historia ecclesiastica del scisma de Inglaterra*. Madrid: Pedro de Madrigal, 1588.

———. *Historia ecclesiastical del scisma del reyno de Inglaterra*. Madrid: Imprenta Real, 1674.

———. *Historias de la contrarreforma*. Edited by Eusebio Rey. Madrid: Biblioteca de Autores Cristianos, 1955.

———. *Monumenta Historica Societatis Iesu: Patris Petri de Ribadeneira*. Madrid: Editorial Ibérica, 1920.

———. *Las obras del P Pedro de Ribadeneyra de la Compañia de Iesus, agora de nueuo revistas y acrecentadas*. Madrid: Viuda de Pedro Madrigal, 1595.

———. *Obras escogidas del Padre Pedro de Rivadeneira*. Edited by Don Vicente de la Fuente. Madrid: M. Rivadeneira, 1868.

———. *Segunda parte de la Historia Ecclesiastica de Inglaterra*. Alcalá, Spain: Juan Íñiguez de Lequerica, 1593.

———. *Tratado de la religion y virtudes que deve tener el Principe Christiano, para governar y conservar sus estados*. Madrid: Pedro de Madrigal, 1595.

———. *Tratado de tribulación*. Madrid: Pedro de Madrigal, 1589.

———. *Vida del P. Ignacio de Loyola, fundador de la religión de la Compañia de Iesus*. Madrid: Alonso Gómez, 1583.

Ribeiro da Silva, Francisco, ed. *Felipe II de Espanha, Rei de Portugal*. Zamora, Spain: Fundación Rei Afonso Henriques, 2011.

Roldán-Figueroa, Rady. *The Ascetic Spirituality of Juan de Avila, 1499–1569*. Leiden: Brill, 2010.

Rossaeo, Guilelmo. *De iusta reipub. Christianae in reges impios et haereticaos Authoritate*. Antwerp: Ionnem Keerbergium, 1592.

Ruelens, Ch., ed. *Le passetemps de Jehan Lhermite*. Antwerp: J.-E. Buschmann, 1890.

Sander, Nicholas. *De iustificatione contra colloquium Altenburgense*. Trier, Germany: Edmundus Hatotus, 1585.

———. *De origine ac progressu schismatic Anglicani, liber tres*. Cologne, Germany, 1585.

———. *De origine ac progressu schismatis Anglicani libri tres*. Rome: Bartholomaei Bonfadini, 1586.

———. *De visibili monarchia libri octo*. Louvain, Belgium: John Fowler, 1571.

Schuster, Louis A., ed. *Henry VIII: A Neo-Latin Drama by Nicolaus Vernulaeus*. Austin: University of Texas Press, 1964.

Sebastiá, Miguel Lope, ed. *Confesiones: Autobiografía documentada*. Bilbao, Spain: Ediciones Mensajero, 2009.

Southwell, Robert. *A Humble Supplication for her Majestie*. Edited by R. C. Bald. Cambridge: Cambridge University Press, 1953.

Stapleton, Thomas. *Apologia pro Rege Catholico Philippo II*. Constance, Germany: Theodorum Samium, 1592.

———. *Orationes academicae, Micelleneae triginat quatuor*. Antwerp: Ioannem Keerbergium, 1600.

Stewart, Alan, with Harriet Knight, eds. *The Oxford Francis Bacon: Early writings, 1584–1596*. Oxford: Clarendon Press, 2012.

Treatise of Treasons Against Q Elizabeth and the Croune of England. N.p., 1572.

Ungerer, Gustav, ed. *A Spaniard in Elizabethan England: The Correspondence of Antonio Pérez's Exile.* 2 vols. London: Tamesis, 1974.

Valladares, Antonio, ed. *Seminario erudito que comprehende varias obras ineditas, criticas, morales, instructivas, politicas, historicas y jocosas de nuestros mejores autores antiguos y modernos.* Madrid: Don Blas Roman, 1788.

Velázquez, Isidro. *La entrada que en el reyno de Portugal hizo la M. R. de Don Phillipe Invictissimo.* Lisbon: Manuel de Lyra and Symon Lopez, 1583.

Verstegan, Richard. *An advertisement written to a secretarie of my L. Treasurers of Ingland, by an Inglishe Intelligencer as he passed through Germanie towardes Italie.* N.p., n.d.

——. *A declaration of the true causes of the great troubles, presupposed to be intended against the realm of England.* N.p., 1592.

Watson, William. *A decacordon of ten quodlibetical questions.* N.p., 1602.

——. *A sparing discoverie of our English Iesuits, and of Fa. Parsons proceedings*

under pretence of promoting the Catholike Faith in England. N.p., 1601.

Weinreich, Spencer. *Pedro de Ribadeneyra's "Ecclesiastical History of the Schism of England": A Spanish Jesuit's history of the English Reformation.* Leiden: Brill, 2017.

Wright, Thomas. "An licitum sit catholicis in Anglia sumere, et aliis modis, reginam et regnum defendere contra Hispanos. Resolved by one Wryght, a priest as it seems, of the college of Doway." In *Annals of the Reformation and Establishment of Religion,* edited by John Strype, 3:583–97. Oxford: Clarendon Press, 1874.

——. *Certaine articles or forcible reasons. Discovering the palpable absurdities and most notorious and intricate errors of the Protestant religion.* London, 1600.

——. *The Disposition or Garnishement of the Soule To receive worthilie the blessed Sacrament, devyded into Three Discourses* [. . .]. Antwerp: Ioachim Trognesius, 1596.

Yepes, Diego de. *Historia particular de la persecución de Inglaterra.* Madrid: Luis Sánchez, 1599.

Secondary Sources

Allen, Paul C. *Philip III and the Pax Hispanica, 1598–1621: The Failure of Grand Strategy.* New Haven: Yale University Press, 2000.

Allison, A. F., and D. M. Rogers. *The Contemporary Printed Literature of the English Counter-Reformation.* Aldershot, U.K.: Scolar Press, 1989.

Arande, Peter. *Beggars, Iconoclasts, and Civic Patriots: The Political Culture of the Dutch Revolt.* Ithaca: Cornell University Press, 2008.

Arblaster, Paul. *Antwerp and the World: Richard Verstegan and the International Culture of Catholic Reformation.* Leuven: Leuven University Press, 2004.

Astruther, Godfrey. *The Seminary Priests: Elizabethan, 1558–1603.* Durham: Ushaw College, 1968.

Baumgartner, Frederic J. *Radical Reactionaries: The Political Thought of the French Catholic League.* Geneva: Droz, 1975.

Bayne, C. G. *Anglo-Roman Relations, 1558–1565.* Oxford: Clarendon Press, 1913.

Beaver, Adam. "A Holy Land for the Catholic Monarchy: Palestine in the Making of Modern Spain, 1469–1598." Ph.D. diss., Harvard University, 2008.

Bela, Teresa, Clarinda Calma, and Jolanta Rzegocka, eds. *Publishing Subversive Texts in Elizabethan England and the Polish-Lithuanian Commonwealth.* Leiden: Brill, 2016.

Bellany, Alastair, and Thomas Cogswell. *The Murder of King James I.* New Haven: Yale University Press, 2015.

Beltrán, José Luis. *La compañía de Jesús y su proyección mediática en el mundo hispánico durante la edad moderna.* Madrid: Silex, 2010.

Betteridge, Thomas, and Thomas Freeman, eds. *Henry VIII and History*. Farnham, U.K.: Ashgate, 2012.

Bireley, Robert. *The Counter-Reformation Prince: Anti-Machiavellianism or Catholic Statecraft in Early Modern Europe*. Chapel Hill: University of North Carolina Press, 1990.

Bomba, Nicholas. "Caesar's Conscience: Counsel and Crisis in the Hispanic World, 1500–1560." Ph.D. diss., Princeton University, 2010.

Bossy, John. "Elizabethan Catholicism: The Link with France." Ph.D. diss., Queen's College, University of Cambridge, 1960.

———. *The English Catholic Community*. London: Darton, Longmann & Todd, 1976.

———. "The Heart of Robert Persons." In *The Reckoned Expense: Edmund Campion and the Early English Jesuits*, edited by Thomas McCoog, 142–58. Rome: IHSI, 2007.

———. "Rome and Elizabethan Catholics: A Question of Geography." *Historical Journal* 7, no. 1 (1964): 135–42.

Bouza, Fernando. "Contrarreforma y tipografía. ¿Nada más que rosarios en sus manos?" *Cuadernos de historia moderna* 15 (1999): 73–88.

———. *Imagen y propaganda: Capítulos de historia cultural del reinado de Felipe II*. Madrid: Akal, 1998.

———. *Palabra e imagen en la Corte: Cultura oral y visual de la nobleza en el Siglo de Oro*. Madrid: Abada, 2003.

———. *Papeles y opinión: Políticas de publicación en el Siglo de Oro*. Madrid: CSIC, 2008.

———. "Portugal en la monarquía hispánica." 2 vols. Ph.D. diss., Universidad Complutense, 1987.

———. *Portugal no tempo dos Filipes*. Lisbon: Cosmos, 2000.

Braun, Harald E. *Juan de Mariana and Early Modern Spanish Political Thought*. Hampshire, U.K.: Ashgate, 2007.

———. "Scholasticism and Humanism in the Thought of Juan de Mariana." Ph.D. diss., University of Oxford, 2000.

Breight, Curt. "Realpolitik and Elizabethan Ceremony: The Earl of Herford's Entertainment of Elizabeth at Elvetham, 1591." *Renaissance Quarterly* 45, no. 1 (Spring 1992): 20–48.

Brockey, Liam. "Jesuit Pastoral, Theater on an Urban Stage: Lisbon, 1588–1593." *Journal of Early Modern History* 9, no. 1–2 (2005): 3–50.

———. *Journey to the East: The Jesuit Mission to China, 1579–1724*. Cambridge: Harvard University Press, 2007.

Brotton, Jerry. *The Sultan and the Queen: The Untold Story of Elizabeth and Islam*. New York: Penguin, 2017.

Burguillo, Javier. "Pedro de Ribadeneyra y la inestabilidad del discurso histórico-literario en torno a la Empresa de Inglaterra." In *Saberes inestables. Estudios sobre expurgación y censura en la España de los siglos XVI y XVII*, edited by Dámaris Montes, María José Vega, and Víctor Lillo Castañ, 173–200. Frankfurt am Main: Iberoamericana Vervuert, 2018.

Burke, Peter. *Exiles and Expatriate in the History of Knowledge, 1500–2000*. Waltham: Brandeis University Press, 2017.

———. "Tacitism." In *Tacitus*, edited by T. A. Dorey, 149–71. London: Routledge, 1969.

Burrieza Sánchez, Javier. "Reparando las heridas: El nacimiento de una devoción de 'contrarreforma.'" *BROCAR* 26 (2002): 107–50.

———. *Valladolid, tierras y caminos: Presencia de la Compañía de Jesús en la provincia de Valladolid, 1545–1767*. Valladolid, Spain: Diputación de Valladolid, 2007.

Burrieza Sánchez, Javier, and Peter Harris. *La misión de Robert Persons: Un Jesuita inglés en la antigua corte de Valladolid*. Valladolid: English College, 2010.

Cano Echevarría, Berta, Ana Sáez Hidalgo, Glyn Redworth, and Mark Hutchings. "'Comfort Without Offence'? The Performance and Transmission of Exile Literature at the English College, Valladolid, 1592–1600." *Renaissance and Reformation / Renaissance et Réforme* 31, no. 1 (2008): 31–67.

Carrafiello, Michael. *Robert Persons and English Catholicism, 1580–1610.* London: Associated University Presses, 1998.

Carroll, Stuart. *Martyrs and Murderers: The Guise Family and the Making of Europe.* Oxford: Oxford University Press, 2011.

Cirot, Georges. *Mariana Historien.* Bordeaux: Feret & Fils, 1904.

Clancy, Thomas H. "English Catholics and the Papal Deposing Power, 1570–1640." *Recusant History* 6, no. 3 (October 1961): 114–40.

———. "Notes on Persons's 'Memorial.'" *Recusant History* 5 (1959): 17–34.

———. *Papist Pamphleteers: The Allen-Persons Party and the Political Thought of the Counter-Reformation in England, 1572–1615.* Chicago: Loyola University Press, 1964.

Collinson, Patrick. "The Elizabethan Exclusion Crisis and the Elizabethan Polity." *Proceedings of the British Academy* 84 (1993): 51–92.

Corens, Liesbeth. *Confessional Mobility and English Catholics in Counter-Reformation Europe.* Oxford: Oxford University Press, 2019.

Crosignani, Ginevra. *"De adeundis ecclesiis protestatium": Thomas Wright, Robert Parsons, S.J., e il dibattito sul conformismo occasionale nell'Inghilterra dell'età moderna.* Rome: IHSI, 2004.

Crouzet, Denis. *Les guerriers de Dieu: La violence au temps des troubles de religion vers 1525–1610.* Paris: Champ Vallon, 1990.

Cuadra Blanco, Juan Rafael de la. "King Philip of Spain as Solomon the Second: The Origins of Solomonism of the Escorial in the Netherlands." In *The Seventh Window: The King's Window Donated by Philip II and Mary Tudor to Sint Janskerk in Gouda (1557),* edited by Wim de Groot, 69–180. Hilversum, Netherlands: Verloren, 2005.

Descimon, Robert, and José Javier Ruiz Ibáñez. *Les ligueurs de l'exil: Le refuge catholique français après 1594.* Paris: Champ Vallon, 2005.

Dickinson, Janet. *Court Politics and the Earl of Essex, 1589–1601.* New York: Routledge, 2015.

Dillon, Anne. *The Construction of Martyrdom in the English Catholic Community, 1535–1603.* Farnham, U.K.: Ashgate, 2002.

Domínguez, Freddy C. "From Saint to Sinner: Sixteenth-Century Perceptions of 'La Monja de Lisboa.'" In *A New Companion to Hispanic Mysticism,* edited by Hillaire Kallendorf, 297–322. Leiden: Brill, 2010.

———. "History in Action: The Case of Pedro de Ribadeneyra's *Historia ecclesiastica del scisma de Inglaterra.*" *Bulletin of Spanish Studies* 93, no. 1 (2016): 13–38.

Doran, Susan. *Monarchy and Matrimony: The Courtship of Elizabeth.* London: Routledge, 1996.

Doran, Susan, and Paulina Kewes, eds. *Doubtful and Dangerous: The Question of Succession in Late Elizabethan England.* Manchester: Manchester University Press, 2014.

Duffy, Eamon. *Reformation Divided: Catholics, Protestants and the Conversion of England.* London: Bloomsbury, 2017.

———. "William, Cardinal Allen, 1532–1594." *Recusant History* 22, no. 3 (1595): 265–90.

Edwards, Francis. *Robert Persons: The Biography of an Elizabethan Jesuit, 1546–1610.* St. Louis: Institute of Jesuit Resources, 1995.

Eguiluz, Federico. *Robert Persons: "El architraidor."* Madrid: Fundación Universitaria Española, 1990.

Elliott, J. H. *History in the Making.* New Haven: Yale University Press, 2012.

Essen, León van der. *Alexandre Farnèse prince de Parme gouverneur gènèral des Pays-Bas.* Brussels: Nouvelle sociètè d'èditions, 1937.

Fernández Collado, Ángel. *Gregorio XIII y Felipe II en la Nunciatura de Felipe Sega (1577–1581): Aspectos político, jurisdiccional y de reforma*. Toledo: Estudio Teológico de San Ildefonso, 1991.

Fernández-González, Laura. "Negotiation Terms: King Philip I of Portugal and the Ceremonial Entry of 1581 into Lisbon." In *Festival Culture in the World of the Spanish Habsburgs*, edited by Fernando Checa Cremades and Laura Fernández-González, 87–114. Farnham, U.K.: Ashgate, 2015.

Fernández-Santamaria, J. A. *Natural Law, Constitutionalism, Reason of State and War: Counter-Reformation Spanish Political Thought*. 2 vols. New York: Peter Lang, 2005.

Feros, Antonio. *Kingship and Favoritisms in the Spain of Philip III, 1598–1621*. Cambridge: Cambridge University Press, 2000.

Forteza, Deborah. "Monsters and Saints: Tudors, Stuarts and English Catholics in Early Modern Spanish Discourses." Ph.D. diss., Notre Dame, 2017.

Gacto, Enrique. "Censura política e Inquisición: La Historia Pontifical de Gonzalo de Illescas." *Revista de la Inquisición* 2 (1992): 23–40.

Gajda, Alexandra. *The Earl of Essex and Late Elizabethan Political Culture*. Oxford: Oxford University Press, 2012.

———. "Tacitus and Political Thought in Early Modern Europe." In *The Cambridge Companion to Tacitus*, edited by A. J. Woodman, 253–68. Cambridge: Cambridge University Press, 2009.

García Hernán, Enrique. *Irlanda y el Rey Prudente*. Madrid: Laberinto, 2003.

Gascón Pérez, Jesús. *Alzar banderas contra su rey: La rebelión aragonesa de 1591 contra Felipe II*. Zaragoza: Prensas Universitarias de Zaragoza, 2010.

Gasquet, A. *A History of the Venerable English College, Rome*. London: Longmans, Green, 1920.

———. "A Treasure of the Archives." *Venerabile* 3 (1927): 114–20.

Ghering, David. *Anglo-German Relations and the Protestant Cause: Elizabethan Foreign Policy and Pan-Protestantism*. New York: Routledge, 2013.

Gibbons, Katy. *English Catholic Exiles in Late Sixteenth-Century Paris*. Woodbridge, U.K.: Boydell, 2011.

Giesey, Ralph E. *If Not, Not: The Oath of the Aragonese and the Legendary Laws of Sobarbe*. Princeton: Princeton University Press, 1969.

Gil Pujol, Francisco Xavier. "Las fuerzas del Rey y la generación que leyó a Botero." In *Le forze del principe: Recursos, instrumentos y límites en la práctica del poder soberano en los territorios de la monarquía hispánica: actas del Seminario Internacional*, edited by José Javier Ruiz Ibáñez, Mario Rizzo, and Gaetano Sabatini, 969–1022. Murcia: Universidad de Murcia, 2004.

Godman, Peter. *The Saint as Censor: Robert Bellarmine Between Inquisition and Index*. Leiden: Brill, 2000.

Gómez-Centurión, Carlos. *La invencible y la Empresa de Inglaterra*. Madrid: NEREA, 1988.

———. "The New Crusade: Ideology and Religion in the Anglo-Spanish Conflict." In *England, Spain and the Gran Armada, 1585–1604*, edited by M. J. Rodríguez-Salgado and Simon Adams, 264–99. Maryland: Barnes and Noble Books, 1991.

Grafton, Anthony. *Worlds Made by Words: Scholarship and Community in the Modern West*. Cambridge: Harvard University Press, 2009.

Gruzinski, Serge. *What Time Is It There? America and Islam at the Dawn of Modern Times*. Cambridge, MA: Polity, 2010.

Guerrero, Eduardo Olid, and Esther Fernández, eds. *The Image of Elizabeth I in Early Modern Spain*. Lincoln: University of Nebraska Press, 2018.

Haile, Martin. *An Elizabethan Cardinal: William Allen*. London: Pitman & Sons, 1914.

Hammer, Paul E. J. *Elizabeth's Wars: War Government and Society in Tudor England, 1544–1604*. New York: Palgrave, 2003.

———. "Myth-Making: Politics, Propaganda and the Capture of Cadiz in 1596." *Historical Journal* 40, no. 3 (1997): 621–42.

———. *The Polarisation of Elizabethan Politics: The Political Career of Robert Devereux, 2nd Earl of Essex, 1585–1597*. Cambridge: Cambridge University Press, 1999.

———. "Shakespeare's Richard II, the Play of 7 February 1601, and the Essex Rising." *Shakespeare Quarterly* 59, no. 1 (Spring 2008): 1–35.

Hennes, J. H. *Der Kampf um das Erzstift Köln zur Zeit der Kurfürsten Gebhard Truchsess und Ernst von Baiern*. Cologne, Germany: M. DuMont Schauberg, 1878.

Hicks, Leo. "Father Robert Persons, S.J., and the Book of Succession." *Recusant History* 4 (1957–58): 104–37.

———. "The Growth of a Myth: Father Robert Persons, S.J., and Leicester's Commonwealth." *Studies: An Irish Quarterly Review* 46, no. 181 (Spring 1957): 93–105.

———. "Robert Persons, S.J., and the Seminaries in Spain." *Month* 157, no. 801 (March 1931): 193–204.

Highley, Christopher. *Catholics Writing the Nation in Early Modern Britain and Ireland*. Oxford: Oxford University Press, 2008.

———. "'A Pestilent and Seditious Book': Nicholas Sander's *Schismatis Anglicani* and Catholic Histories of the Reformation." In *The Uses of History in Early Modern England*, edited by Paulina Kewes, 151–71. San Marino, Calif.: Huntington Library, 2006.

Hoffman, Martha. *Raised to Rule: Educating Royalty at the Court of the Spanish Habsburgs, 1601–1634*. Baton Rouge: Louisiana State University Press, 2011.

Holmes, Peter. "The Authorship and Early Reception of *A Conference About the Next Succession of England*." *Historical Journal* 23, no. 2 (June 1980): 415–29.

———. *Resistance and Compromise: The Political Thought of the Elizabethan Catholics*. Cambridge: Cambridge University Press, 1982.

Höpfl, Harro. *Jesuit Political Thought: The Society of Jesus and the State, c. 1540–1630*. Cambridge: Cambridge University Press, 2004.

Hore, Herbert Francis. "Woods and Fastnesses in Ancient Ireland." *Journal of Archaeology* 6 (1858): 141–61.

Houliston, Victor. *Catholic Resistance in Elizabethan England: Robert Persons's Jesuit Polemic, 1580–1610*. Aldershot, U.K.: Ashgate, 2007.

———. "The Hare and the Drum: Robert Persons's Writing on the English Succession, 1593–6." *Renaissance Studies* 14, no. 2 (June 2000): 235–50.

———. "The Lord Treasurer and the Jesuit: Robert Persons's Satirical Response to the 1591 Proclamation." *Sixteenth Century Journal* 32, no. 2 (Summer 2001): 383–401.

———. "The Missionary Position: Catholics Writing the History of the English Reformation." *English Studies in Africa* 54, no. 2 (2011): 16–30.

———. "Persons's Displeasure: Collaboration and Design in Leicester's Commonwealth." In *Publishing Subversive Texts in Elizabethan England and the Polish-Lithuanian Commonwealth*, edited by Teresa Bela, Clarinda Calma, and Jolanta Rzegocka, 155–66. Leiden: Brill, 2016.

Howard, Keith David. *The Reception of Machiavelli in Early Modern Spain*. Woodbridge, U.K.: Tamesis, 2014.

Huerga, Álvaro. "La vida seudomística y el proceso inquisitorial de Sor María de la Visitiación." *Hispania sacra* 12 (1959): 35–130.

Iñurritegui Rodríguez, José María. "Antonio de Herrera y Tordesillas: Historia y discurso político en la monarquía Católica." In *Repubblica e Virtù: Pensiero politico e Monarchia Cattolica fra XVI e XVII secolo*, edited by Cesare Mozzarelli and Chiara Continisio, 121–50. Rome: Bulzoni, 1995.

———. *La Gracia y la república*. Madrid: UNED, 1998.

James, Alan. "The French Armada? The Azores Campaigns, 1580–1583." *Historical Journal* 55, no. 1 (2012):1–20.

Janssen, Geert. *The Dutch Revolt and Catholic Exile in Reformation Europe*. Cambridge: Cambridge University Press, 2014.

Jensen, De Lamar. *Diplomacy and Dogmatism: Bernardino de Mendoza and the French Catholic League*. Cambridge: Harvard University Press, 1964.

Jones, Norman. *Governing by Virtue: Lord Burghley and the Management of Elizabethan England*. Oxford: Oxford University Press, 2015.

Jordan, William. *From England to France: Felony and Exile in the High Middle Ages*. Princeton: Princeton University Press, 2015.

Kagan, Richard L. *Clio and the Crown: The Politics of History in Medieval and Modern Europe*. Baltimore: Johns Hopkins University Press, 2009.

———. *Lucrecia's Dreams: Politics and Prophecy in Sixteenth-Century Spain*. Berkeley: University of California Press, 1990.

———. *El rey recatado: Felipe II, la historia y los cronistas del rey*. Valladolid: Universidad de Valladolid, 2004.

Kamen, Henry. *Philip of Spain*. New Haven: Yale University Press, 1997.

Kaplan, Yosef, ed. *Early Modern Ethnic and Religious Communities in Exile*. Newcastle, U.K.: Cambridge Scholars, 2017.

Kelley, Donald, ed. *Versions of History from Antiquity to the Enlightenment*. New Haven: Yale University Press, 1990.

Knecht, R. J. *The French Civil Wars, 1562–1598*. New York: Longman, 2000.

Lake, Peter. "Anti-Popery: The Structure of a Prejudice." In *Conflict in Early Stuart England: Studies in Religion and Politics, 1603–1642*, edited by Richard Cust and Ann Hughes, 72–106. London: Longman, 1989.

———. *Bad Queen Bess? Libels, Secret Histories, and the Politics of Publicity in the Reign of Queen Elizabeth I*. Oxford: Oxford University Press, 2016.

———. "From *Leicester His Commonwealth* to *Sejanus His Fall*: Ben Jonson and the Politics of Roman (Catholic) Virtue." In *Catholics and the "Protestant Nation": Religious Politics and Identity in Early Modern England*, edited by Ethan Shagan, 128–61. Manchester: Manchester University Press, 2005.

———. *How Shakespeare Put Politics on the Stage: Power and Succession in the History Plays*. New Haven: Yale University Press, 2017.

———. "The King (the Queen) and the Jesuit: James Stuart's 'True Law of Free Monarchies' in Context/s." *Transactions of the Royal Historical Society* 14 (2004): 243–60.

Lake, Peter, and Steven Pincus. "Rethinking the Public Sphere in Early Modern England." In *The Politics of the Public Sphere in Early Modern England*, edited by Lake and Pincus, 1–31. Manchester: Manchester University Press, 2007.

Lake, Peter, and Michael Questier. "Agency, Appropriation and Rhetoric Under the Gallows: Puritans, Romanists and the State in Early Modern England." *Past and Present*, no. 153 (November 1996): 64–107.

———. *The Antichrist's Lewd Hat: Protestants, Papists and Players in Post-Reformation England*. New Haven: Yale University Press, 2002.

———. "Puritans, Papists, and the 'Public Sphere' in Early Modern England: The Edmund Campion Affair in Context." *Journal of Modern History* 72, no. 3 (September 2000): 587–627.

———. *The Trials of Margaret Clitherow: Persecution, Martyrdom and the Politics of Sanctity in Elizabethan England*. London: Continuum, 2011.

Lattuada, Riccardo. *Alessandro Farnese: Un grande condottiero in miniatura: Il Duca* di Parma e Piacenza ritratto da Jean de Saiva. Milan: Beffi Arte, 2016.

Lechat, Robert. *Les Réfugiés Anglais dans les Pays-Bas durant le règne d'Élisabeth, 1558–1603*. Roulers, Belgium: Jules de Meester, 1914.

Leonard, Irving A. "On the Lima Book Trade, 1591." *Hispanic American Historical Review* 33, no. 4 (November 1953): 511–25.

Leturia, Pedro de. "El abrazo de Felipe II a los seminaristas ingleses de Valladolid (1592)." *Razón y fe* 117 (1939): 282–98.

Levy, Evonne. *Propaganda and the Jesuit Baroque*. Berkeley: University of California Press, 2004.

Lockey, Brian. *Early Modern Catholics, Royalists, and Cosmopolitans: English Transnationalism and the Christian Commonwealth*. Burlington, Vt.: Ashgate, 2015.

Lockhart, Paul Douglas. *Frederick II and the Protestant Cause: Denmark's Role in the Wars of Religion, 1559–1596*. Leiden: Brill, 2004.

Loomie, Albert. "The Authorship of *An Advertisement Written to a Secretarie of M.L. Treasurer of England*." *Renaissance News* 15, no. 3 (Autumn 1962): 201–7.

———. "Philip III and the Stuart Succession in England." *Revue belge de philologie et d'histoire* 43, no. 2 (1965): 492–514.

———. "Richard Stanyhurst in Spain: Two Unknown Letters of August 1593." *Huntington Library Quarterly* 28, no. 2 (February 1965): 145–55.

———. "Spain and the English Catholic Exiles, 1580–1604." Ph.D. diss., University College London, 1957.

———. *The Spanish Elizabethans*. New York: Fordham University Press, 1963.

Machielsen, Jan. "The Lion, the Witch, and the King: Thomas Stapleton's *Apologia pro Rege Catholico Philippo II*, 1592." *English Historical Review* 129, no. 536 (February 2014): 19–46.

Maltby, William. *The Black Legend in England*. Durham: Duke University Press, 1971.

Maravall, J. A. *La oposición política bajo los Austrias*. Barcelona: Ariel, 1972.

Marino, John A. "An Anti-Campanellan Vision on the Spanish Monarchy and the Crisis of 1595." In *A Renaissance of Conflicts: Visions and Revisions of Law and Society in Italy and Spain*, edited by John A. Marino and Thomas Kuehn, 367–94. Toronto: Centre for Reformation and Renaissance Studies, 2004.

Marocci, Giuseppe. *A consciência de um império: Portugal e o seu mundo (sécs. XV–XVII)*. Coimbra: Coimbra University Press, 2012.

Mayer, Thomas. "A Sticking-Plaster Saint? Autobiography and Hagiography in the Making of Reginald Pole." In *The Rhetorics of Life Writing in Early Modern Europe: Forms of Biography from Cassandra Fedele to Louis XIV*, edited by Mayer and D. R. Woolf, 205–22. Ann Arbor: University of Michigan Press, 1995.

McCoog, Thomas. "Construing Martyrdom in the English Catholic Community, 1582–1602." In *Catholics and the "Protestant Nation,"* edited by Ethan Shagan, 95–127. Manchester: Manchester University Press, 2006.

———. "Harmony Disrupted: Robert Persons, S.J., William Crichton, S.J., and the Question of Queen Elizabeth's Successor, 1581–1603." *Archivum Historicum, S.I.* 73 (2004):149–220.

———. *The Society of Jesus in Ireland, Scotland, and England, 1541–1588: "Our Way of Proceeding?"* Leiden: Brill, 1996.

———. *The Society of Jesus in Ireland, Scotland, and England, 1589–1597: Building the Faith of Saint Peter upon the King of Spain's Monarchy*. New York: Routledge, 2016.

———. *The Society of Jesus in Ireland, Scotland, and England, 1598–1606: Lest Our Lamp Be Entirely Extinguished*. Leiden: Brill, 2017.

———. *"And Touching Our Society": Fashioning Jesuit Identity in Elizabethan England*. Toronto: PIMS, 2013.

McGoldrick, James Edward. "Rishton, Edward, 1550–1585." In *The Oxford*

Dictionary of National Biography. Oxford: Oxford University Press, 2004.

Mears, Natalie. "Counsel, Public Debate, and Queenship: John Stubbs's *The Discoverie of a Gaping Gulf, 1579.*" *Historical Journal* 44, no. 3 (September 2001): 629–50.

Meyer, Arnold Oskar. *England and the Catholic Church Under Queen Elizabeth.* Translated by J. R. McKee. New York: Barnes and Noble, 1969.

Milward, Peter. *Religious Controversies of the Elizabethan Age: A Survey of Printed Sources.* London: Scolar Press, 1977.

Monter, William. *Frontiers of Heresy: The Spanish Inquisition from the Basque Lands to Sicily.* Cambridge: Cambridge University Press, 1990.

Neale, J. E. *Elizabeth and Her Parliaments, 1584–1601.* London: Jonathan Cape, 1957.

———. "Peter Wentworth." *English Historical Review* 39, nos. 153, 154 (1924): 36–54, 175–205.

Oakley, Francis. *The Conciliarist Tradition: Constitutionalism in the Catholic Church, 1300–1870.* Oxford: Oxford University Press, 2003.

O'Connor, Thomas. *Irish Voices from the Spanish Inquisition: Migrants, Converts and Brokers in Early Modern Iberia.* New York: Palgrave, 2016.

O'Donell, Hugo. "Los refugiados ingleses, un proyecto inédito para invadir Inglaterra (1594–1596)." In *Después de la Gran Armada: La historia desconocida (1588–1604),* 7–28. Madrid: Cuadernos Monográficos del Instituto de Historia y Cultura Naval, 1993.

Olds, Katrina. *Forging the Past: Invented Histories in the Counter-Reformation.* New Haven: Yale University Press, 2015.

Olivari, Michele. *Avisos, pasquines, y rumores: Los comienzos de la opinión pública en la España del siglo XVII.* Madrid: Cátedra, 2014.

Ollé Rodríguez, Manel. "Estrategias filipinas respecto a China: Alonso Sánchez y Domingo Salazar en la empresa de China (1581–1593)." Ph.D. diss., University of Barcelona, 1998.

Ostenfeld-Suske, Kira Kalina von. "Official Historiography, Political Legitimacy, Historical Methodology, and Royal and Imperial Authority in Spain Under Philip II, 1580–99." Ph.D. diss., Columbia University, 2014.

Parker, Geoffrey. *The Grand Strategy of Philip II.* New Haven: Yale University Press, 1998.

———. "The Place of Tudor England in the Messianic Vision of Philip II of Spain." *Transactions of the Royal Historical Society* 12 (2002): 167–221.

———. *Success Is Never Final: Empire, War, and Faith in Early Modern Europe.* New York: Basic Books, 2002.

———. *The World Is Not Enough: The Imperial Vision of Philip II of Spain.* Waco, Tex.: Markham Press Fund, 2000.

Parmelee, Lisa Ferraro. *"Good Newes from Fraunce": French Anti-League Propaganda in Late-Elizabethan England.* Rochester: University of Rochester Press, 1996.

Penzi, Marco. "Loys Dorléans and the 'Catholiques Anglois': A Common Catholic History Between Violence, Martyrdom and Cultural Networks." *Culture and History Digital Journal* 6, no. 1 (2017): e004. doi: http://dx.doi.org/10.3989/chdj.2017.004.

Pettegree, Andrew. *Brand Luther: 1517, Printing, and the Making of the Reformation.* New York: Penguin, 2016.

Pettegree, Andrew, and Malcolm Walsby. *Netherlandish Books: K–Z.* Leiden: Brill, 2011.

Pirillo, Diego. *The Refugee-Diplomat: Venice, England, and the Reformation.* Ithaca: Cornell University Press, 2018.

Pissurno, Fernanda Paixão. "O Casamento do Cardeal: Notas sobre a trajetória e um possível matrimônio de D. Henrique, Rei de Portugal." *Cadernos de História* 9, no. 2 (December 2014): 107–22.

Pollen, J. H. "Dr. Nicholas Sander." *English Historical Review* 6, no. 21 (January 1891): 36–47.

———. *The English Catholics in the Reign of Queen Elizabeth.* New York: Longmans, Green and Co., 1920.

Popper, Nicholas. *Walter Ralegh's "History of the World" and the Historical Culture of the Late Renaissance*. Chicago: University of Chicago Press, 2012.

Pritchard, Arnold. *Catholic Loyalism in Elizabethan England*. London: Scolar Press, 1979.

Questier, Michael. *Dynastic Politics and the British Reformations, 1558–1630*. Oxford: Oxford University Press, 2019.

Rankin, Mark, Christopher Highley, and John N. King, eds. *Henry VIII and His Afterlives*. Cambridge: Cambridge University Press, 2009.

Read, Conyers. *Lord Burghley and Queen Elizabeth*. New York: Knopf, 1960.

Redworth, Glyn. *The She-Apostle: The Extraordinary Life and Death of Luisa de Carvajal*. Oxford: Oxford University Press, 2008.

Reinhardt, Nicole. *Voices of Conscience: Royal Confessors and Political Counsel in Seventeenth-Century Spain and France*. Oxford: Oxford University Press, 2016.

Rodríguez-Salgado, M. J. "The Anglo-Spanish War: The Final Episode in the 'Wars of the Roses'?" In *England, Spain and the Gran Armada, 1585–1604*, edited by M. J. Rodríguez-Salgado and Simon Adams, 1–44. Edinburgh: John Donald, 1991.

———. *Felipe II: El "Paladín de la Cristiandad" y la Paz con el Turco*. Valladolid: Universidad de Valladolid, 2004.

———. "Paz ruidosa, guerra sorda: Las relaciones de Felipe II e Inglaterra." In *La monarquía de Felipe II a debate*, edited by Luis Antonio Ribot García, 63–120. Madrid: Sociedad Estatal para la Conmemoración de los Centenarios de Felipe II y Carlos V, 2000.

Rombauts, Edward. *Richard Verstegen: Een polemist der contra-reformatie*. Brussels: Algemeee Drukinrichtig, 1933.

Rowe, Erin Kathleen. *Saint and Nation: Santiago and Teresa of Avila, and Plural Identities in Early Modern Spain*. Pittsburgh: Penn State University Press, 2011.

Ruiz, José M. "Robert Persons, S.J. (1546–1610) y su obra más polémica: *A Conference About the Next Succession to the Crowne of Ingland*." *ES: Revista de filologia inglesa* 7 (1977): 117–217.

Ruiz, Teofilo. *A King Travels: Festive Traditions in Late Medieval and Early Modern Spain*. Princeton: Princeton University Press, 2012.

Rurale, Flavio. *I religiosi a corte: Teologia, politica, e diplomazia in antico regime*. Roma: Bulzoni, 1998.

Said, Edward. "Reflections on Exile." In *Reflections on Exile and Other Literary and Cultural Essays*. Cambridge: Harvard University Press, 2002.

Salmon, J. H. M. "Catholic Resistance Theory, Ultramontism, and the Royalist Response, 1580–1620." In *The Cambridge History of Political Thought, 1450–1700*, edited by J. H. Burns with Mark Goldie, 219–53. Cambridge: Cambridge University Press, 1991.

Sánchez-Molero, José Luis Gonzalo. *Felipe II: La mirada de un rey*. Madrid: Polifemo, 2014.

Scarisbrick, J. J. "Robert Persons's Plans for the 'True' Reformation of England." In *Historical Perspectives: Studies in English Thought and Society*, edited by Neil McKendrick, 19–42. London: Europe Publications, 1974.

Sharpe, Kevin. *Selling the Tudor Monarchy: Authority and Image in Sixteenth-Century England*. New Haven: Yale University Press, 2009.

Siebert, Ferdinand. "Zwischen Kaiser und Papst: Kardinal Truchseß von Waldburg und die Anfänge der Gegenreformation in Deutschland." Ph.D. diss., University of Berlin, 1951.

Simpson, Richard. *Edmund Campion: A Biography*. London: John Hodges, 1896.

Smith, Charles. *The Ancient and Present State of the County of Kerry*. Dublin, 1756.

Spohnholz, Jesse, and Gary K. Waite, eds. *Exile and Religious Identity, 1500–1800*. New York: Routledge, 2014.

Starn, Randolph. *Contrary Commonwealth: The Theme of Exile in Medieval and Renaissance Italy*. Berkeley: University of California Press, 1982.

Stroud, Theodore A. "Ben Jonson and Father Thomas Wright." *English Literary History* 14, no. 4 (December 1947): 274–82.

———. "Father Thomas Wright: A Test Case for Toleration." *Biographical Studies* 1 (1951–52): 189–219.

Strype, John. *Annals of the Reformation and Establishment of Religion*. Oxford: Clarendon Press, 1824.

Terpstra, Nicholas. *Religious Refugees in the Early Modern World: An Alternative History of the Reformation*. Cambridge: Cambridge University Press, 2015.

Tierney, M.A., ed. *Dodd's Church History of England*. London: Charles Dolman, 1840.

Trevor-Roper, Hugh. *Europe's Physician: The Various Lives of Theodore de Mayerne*. Edited by Blair Worden. New Haven: Yale University Press, 2006.

Truman, Ronald. "Felipe de la Torre and His *Institución de un rey Christiano* (Antwerp 1556): The Protestant Connexions of a Spanish Royal Chaplain." *Bibliothèque d'humanisme et renaissance* 46, no. 1 (1984): 83–93.

———. *Spanish Treatises on Government, Society and Religion in the Time of Philip II*. Leiden: Brill, 1999.

Tutino, Stefania. *Empire of Souls: Robert Bellarmine and the Christian Commonwealth*. Oxford: Oxford University Press, 2010.

———. "The Political Thought of Robert Persons's *Conference* in Continental Context." *Historical Journal* 52, no. 1 (2009): 43–62.

Tyacke, Nicholas. "Puritan Politicians and King James VI and I." In *Politics, Religion, and Popularity: Early Stuart Essays in Honor of Conrad Russell*, edited by Thomas Cogswell, Richard Cust, and Peter Lake, 21–44. Cambridge: Cambridge University Press, 2002.

Valérian, François. *Un prête anglais contre Henri IV, archéologie d'une haine religieuse*. Paris: L'Harmattan, 2011.

Valladares, Rafael. *La conquista de Lisboa: Violencia military y comunidad politica en Portugal, 1578–1583*. Madrid: Marcial Pons, 2008.

Vázquez de Prada, Valentín. *Felipe II y Francia: Política, religión y razón de estado (1559–1598)*. Pamplona, Spain: EUNSA, 2004.

Veech, Thomas McNevin. *Dr. Nicholas Sanders and the English Reformation, 1531–1581*. Louvain, Belgium: Bibliothèque de l'Université, 1935.

Wainwright, John B, ed. "Some Letters and Papers of Nicholas Sander." In *Miscellanea XIII*. London: Whitehead & Son, 1926.

Walsham, Alexandra. *Church Papists*. London: Boydell, 1993.

Ward, Leslie J. "The Law of Treason in the Reign of Elizabeth." Ph.D. diss., Cambridge University, 1985.

Wernham, R. B. *The Making of Elizabethan Foreign Policy, 1588–1603*. Berkeley: University of California Press, 1980.

Williams, Michael. *St. Alban's College Valladolid: Four Centuries of English Catholic Presence in Spain*. New York: St. Martin's Press, 1986.

———. "William Allen: The Sixteenth Century Spanish Connection." *Recusant History* 22, no. 3 (1994): 123–40.

Zamora, José María Jover, and María Victoria López-Cordón Cortezo. "La imágen de Europa y el pensamiento político internacional." In *Historia de la cultura Española "Ramón Menéndez Pidal": El siglo del Quijote*, edited by José María Jover Zamora, 494–502. Madrid: Espasa, 1996.

Zerner, Catherine. *Juan de Herrera: Architect to Philip II of Spain*. New Haven: Yale University Press, 1993.

Index

De iustitia Britanica, sive Anglica (On British or English justice), 32

Dell'unione del regno di Portogallo alla corona di Castiglia (On the union of the Kingdom of Portugal with the Crown of Castile; Conestaggio), 138

De origine ac progressu schismatis Anglicani (On the origin and progress of the English schism; Sander). See De schismate Anglicano

De rege et regis institutione (On kingship and the education of the king; Mariana), 194–97, 203

De regiae successionis apud Anglos iure (On the English law of royal succession; Persons), 174, 175–76

De Romano Pontifice (On the Roman pontiff; Bellarmine), 174

De schismate Anglicano (Sander), 19–21, 34, 37–47, 79, 190–91
ambiguity of, 62–63
1585 edition, 30–31, 52, 53, 54, 55, 57, 58, 62
1586 edition, 30–31, 50, 53, 58, 60, 73, 88
goals of, 90
influence of, 92, 121–22
legitimacy of, 62
Pollini edition, 147
Ribadeneyra's use of, 82–83, 84
Spanish translation of, 25, 66

De signis ecclesiae dei (Bozzio), 147

De unitate ecclesiastica (On ecclesiastical unity; Pole), 56

Devereux, Robert, earl of Essex, 6, 148–49, 170–71, 182, 183–84

De visibili monarchia libri octo (Eight books on the visible monarchy; Sander), 24, 25

Diez libros de la razón de estado (The ten books on reason of state; Botero), 139

Dorléans, Louis, 112, 113, 115

Dormer, Jane, 68

Dractan, Charles, 156

Drake, Francis, 66

Dudley, Robert, earl of Leicester, 26, 51

Dutch Revolt, 3, 16–17, 51, 71, 110, 128

ecclesiastical history of the English schism, The (Ribadeneyra). See Historia ecclesiastica del scisma de Inglaterra

Education of a Christian prince (Torres). See Institución de un rey Christiano

Edward VI, 19, 57, 59–60

Eight books on the visible monarchy (Sander). See De visibili monarchia libri octo

Eleanor of Aquitaine, 158

Elizabeth I, 3, 5–7, 19, 28–30, 40–42, 46, 51–52, 60, 65, 80, 113–14, 122–27, 131–33
excommunication of, 6, 24–25, 39–40
as illegitimate, 38–42, 74
sex of, as limitation, 6, 29, 40–41

Elizabeth of York, 160

England, 3, 5, 43–46, 44, 114, 175–76
Dutch alliance, 49, 50
invasion of Cádiz, 152, 181–82
Jesuit mission to, 4, 7, 9, 24, 36, 40, 55, 74
provocations by, 42, 71

Englefield, Francis, 7–8, 9–10, 121, 157, 165

English Catholics, 4, 6, 8–13, 24, 88–89, 114, 207
De schismate Anglicano and, 25, 61
radicalizing of, 36
reliance on Spain, 101
Spanish mistrust of, 98–99, 100
in Spanish political culture, 208–9
as unsupported, 35, 46

English succession, 6, 15, 27, 65, 153, 157–58, 161, 172, 174

Escalante, Bernardino, 3

Escobedo, Juan de, 107

Essex, earl of. See Devereux, Robert

Example of letters [. . .] to William Cecil (Creswell). See Exemplar literarum [. . .] ad D Guilelmum Cecilium

Excercise of a Christian Life, The (Loarte), 88–89

excommunication, 32
of Elizabeth I, 6, 24–25, 39–40

Execution of Justice in England (Cecil), 28

Exemplar literarum [. . .] ad D Guilelmum Cecilium (Example of letters [. . .] to William Cecil; Creswell), 140–41

Idiáquez, Juan de, 5, 50, 98, 121
Ignatius of Loyola, 76, 78
Illescas, Juan de, 25
Imperial history (Mexia). See *Historia imperial y cesárea*
Innocent IV, 169
Inquisition, 98, 100, 101, 107, 113
Institución de un rey Christiano (*Education of a Christian prince*; Torres), 81
Ireland, 6, 20, 123
    exiles in, 23, 24
Irish rebellion, 6–7, 24, 51
Isabel Clara Eugenia, infanta of Spain, 102–3, 143, 155, 170
    claim to England, 158, 159–60, 176–78
Italy, 163

James VI, 4, 123, 152, 154, 161, 171
Jesuits. *See* Society of Jesus
João I, 158
John, king of England, 158, 175
John of Gaunt, 155, 156, 160

Lancasters, 155, 160
Leicester, earl of. *See* Dudley, Robert
Leicester's Commonwealth, 26, 27–28, 29, 37, 38, 87
León, Lucrecia de, 67–68
Leslie, John, bishop of Ross, 153–54, 155, 161
Lewis, David, 20
Liefrinck, Hans, 110
Lisbon, Portugal, 98
Loarte, Gaspar de, 88–89, 90
Loaysa, García de, 194
López Mançano, Juan, 102
Louis VIII, 158
Low Countries, 71, 163
Luther, Martin, 14
Lutheranism, 32, 125

Machiavellianism, 87
Mariana, Juan de, 92, 194–97, 203, 206
martyrs, 30, 72, 99, 102–4, 106–7, 145, 147
Mary Stuart, 4, 6, 25, 79–81, 88, 123, 132, 138, 153–54

Mary Tudor, 7, 8, 39, 56, 65, 79, 122
    Catholic reforms, 19, 57–59, 191
Memorial for the Reformation of England, A (Persons), 152, 182–83, 185–90, 191–92, 197–201, 204, 205–6
memoriall of a Christian Life, A (Granada), 88–89
Mendoza, Bernardino de, 51, 99
Mexia, Pedro, 81
missionaries, 24, 28, 35, 36, 40, 97, 130
Montoya, Pedro López de, 76
More, Thomas, 55, 56
Moura, Cristóbal de, 1–2, 112
Muslims, 128–29, 135, 136

Nadal, Jerónimo, 73
Netherlands, 3, 16–17, 34, 42, 52, 164
Newes from Spayne and Holland (Persons), 128
Norfolk, duke of. *See* Howard, Thomas
Norman Conquest, 161
Northern Rebellion, 6, 25, 126
Northumberland, earl of. *See* Percy, Thomas
nuns of Syon Abbey, 103, 156–57

O'Donnell, Hugh, 152
Olivares, count of. *See* Guzmán, Enrique de
On British or English justice. See De iustitia Britanica, sive Anglica
On ecclesiastical unity (Pole). See *De unitate ecclesiastica*
O'Neill, Hugh, 152
On kingship and the education of the king (Mariana). See *De rege et regis institutione*
On the English law of royal succession (Persons). See *De regiae successionis apud Anglos iure*
On the just authority of Christian republics over impious and heretical kings (Gifford). See *De iusta reipublicae christiana in reges impios et hereticos authoritate*
On the justification against the Altenburg colloquy (Sander). See *De iustificatione contra colloquium Altenburgense*